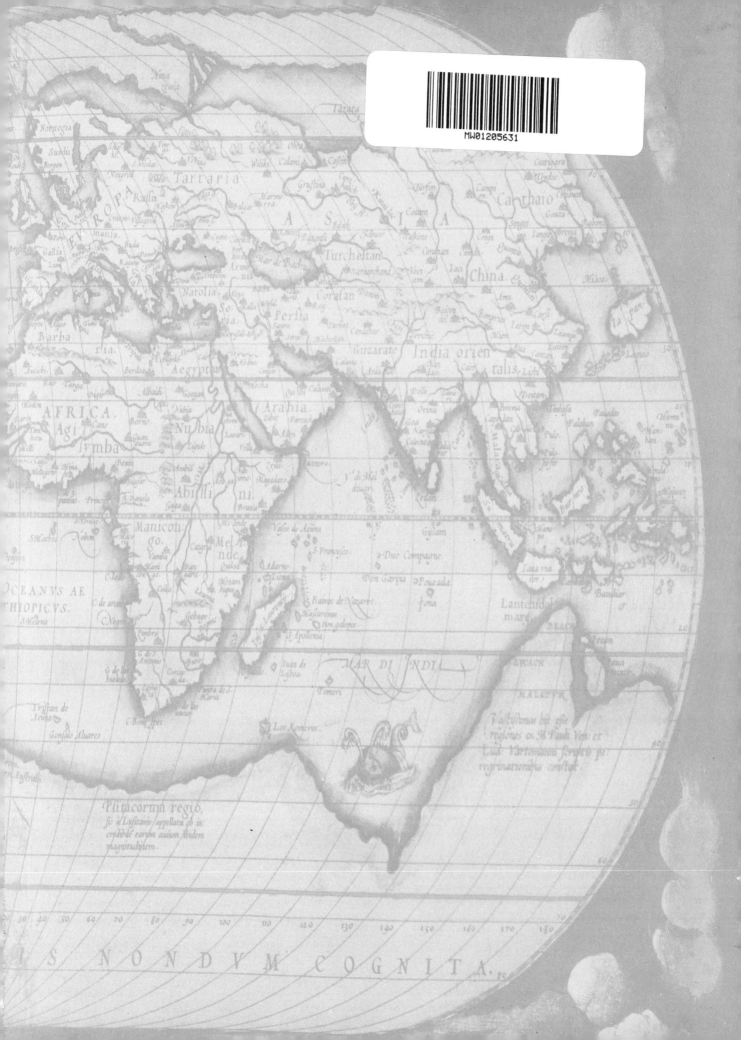

Handbook for Reading Social Studies

One important thing you will do this year is to read this textbook. In order to understand important facts and ideas it is necessary to read in a certain way. This Reading Handbook will show you some helpful ways to read social studies.

Main Idea and Supporting Details

As you read, look for the **main idea** and **supporting details**. The main idea is what a paragraph or section is mostly about. The details support or expand the main idea. Keeping track of the main idea and supporting details will help you remember what you read.

- The first sentence or two of a paragraph often—but not always—contains the main idea.

- Use the titles and subheads in your book as a guide in identifying the main idea.

- Make an outline of the main ideas and supporting details of a lesson to help you review.

To Find the Main Idea
Ask yourself:

- What is this paragraph or section mostly about?

To Find the Supporting Details
Ask yourself:

- What words give more information about the main idea?

In your book you will read about our country's people, who they are and what they do. Read this paragraph to find the main idea and supporting details.

People are the key resource that makes our country work. Farmers plan how and when to plant their crops. Miners and oil workers produce the fuels we need. Factory workers make cars, furniture, clothing, and a thousand other products, including the book you are reading. Without human resources, natural resources would be worthless to us.

from page 28

Main Idea:
People make our country work.

Supporting Details:
People hold important jobs such as farmers, miners, oil workers, and factory workers.

TRY IT!

Read this paragraph about the environment of different regions in the United States. Copy and complete the main idea and supporting details chart below.

Each of the five regions also has its own special environment. The West is a region of high mountains. The Northeast has mountains that are lower and rounded. The Middle Western states have rich soil.

from page 53

Main Idea	Each region has its own environment.		
Details	West: high mountains	Northeast: lower and rounded mountains	

- How did you find the main idea and details?

Keep in Mind...

For more help in reading social studies, try these strategies:

☑ **Reread**
Review each sentence carefully. Make sure you understand what each sentence means before you read further.

☑ **Look up unknown words**
Use a dictionary or the glossary in your book to find the meaning of any words or terms you do not know.

☑ **Form a mental picture**
As you read, think about what your reading would look like.

Practice Activities

1 **READ** Read the first paragraph under "Down the Colorado" on page 60. Copy the chart above and record the main idea and supporting details.

2 **WRITE** Write a paragraph about the weather in the area where you live. Include a main idea with supporting details.

Context Clues

As you read a sentence or paragraph in your book, you may find a word or term that you do not know. One way to find the meaning of a new word is to look for **context clues**. Context clues are the words and sentences around the unfamiliar term. Using context clues helps you to become a better reader.

To Use Context Clues
Ask yourself:

• What word is new to me?

• What might the word mean?

• What other words, phrases, and sentences help me figure out the meaning of the new word?

• What information do these other words, phrases, and sentences provide?

In your book you will read about the different cultures in our country. Read this paragraph about different tools people use to eat. Use context clues to help identify the meaning of the word *chopsticks*.

■ Have you heard this word before? How was it used?

■ Write down the context clues you used to find the meaning of the new word.

■ Use the new word in a sentence of your own to help you remember it.

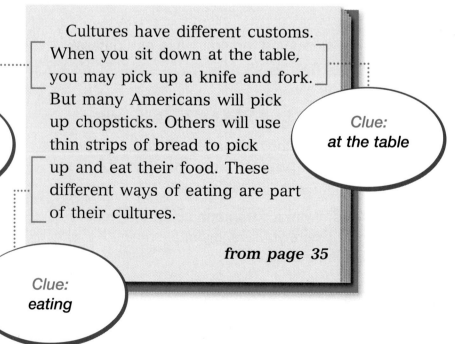

Cultures have different customs. When you sit down at the table, you may pick up a knife and fork. But many Americans will pick up chopsticks. Others will use thin strips of bread to pick up and eat their food. These different ways of eating are part of their cultures.

from page 35

Clue:
knife and fork

Clue:
at the table

Clue:
eating

TRY IT!

Read the paragraph below about American Indians in Oklahoma City. Copy and complete the chart below to find context clues for the term *Red Earth*.

One present-day Indian festival is called Red Earth. It is held every June in Oklahoma City. Red Earth is a celebration of American Indian art, music, and dance. The outdoor art festival is very popular. It shows the works of hundreds of American Indian artists. Singing, flute playing, a parade, pottery and basketmaking, and dancing are all part of the fun.

from page 107

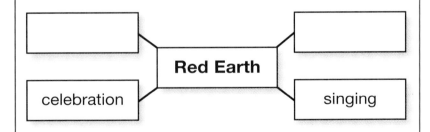

Red Earth

celebration

singing

• How did you find the meaning of *Red Earth*?

Keep in Mind...

For more help in reading social studies, try these strategies:

☑ **Reread**
Review each sentence carefully. Make sure you understand what each sentence means before you read further.

☑ **Form the big picture**
As you read, think about the topic and the most important information in each paragraph or section.

☑ **Make predictions**
As you read, think about what might happen next in your reading.

Practice Activities

1 **READ** Read the first paragraph under the section marked "Technology and the Future" on page 257. Make a chart showing the context clues for *high technology*.

2 **WRITE** Write a paragraph using a new word from the dictionary. Include context clues.

Sequencing

As you read, look for the order in which things happen. **Sequencing** events is listing them in the order in which they happen. Sequencing events helps you understand and remember what you read.

■ Look for dates—years, months, or centuries—that tell when events happened.

■ Look for words like *first, next, then, followed, finally, last, before,* and *later* to identify the order of events.

■ Use chapter time lines to help you remember the sequence of events.

To Use Sequencing
Ask yourself:

• Which event happened first?

• Which event happened next?

• Which order of events makes sense?

Read the following paragraph about early explorers. Pay attention to the sequence of events.

President Jefferson asked Richard Sparks to explore the Red River in 1806. Sparks and his group left from present-day Louisiana. Their plan was to explore an area that is now southeastern Oklahoma. Along the way Sparks and his men were met by a group of Spanish soldiers. Since Sparks' group was small, they immediately turned back. It would be another 50 years before a complete exploration of the Red River would happen.

from page 131

First Event:
Jefferson asked Sparks to explore the Red River.

Second Event:
Sparks and his men left Louisiana.

Third Event:
They met a group of Spanish soldiers.

Fourth Event:
They turned back.

TRY IT!

Read this paragraph about the beginning of hard times. Copy and complete the chart with events in sequence.

> On October 24, 1929, stock prices fell suddenly and sharply. People across the country ran to sell their stocks. The stock market "crashed." This marked the beginning of hard times for the people of our state and our country. A long period of hardships called the Great Depression had begun.
>
> *from page 187*

First Step: Prices fell suddenly and sharply.

⬇

Second Step:

⬇

Third Step:

⬇

Fourth Step:

• How did you find out the sequence of events?

Practice Activities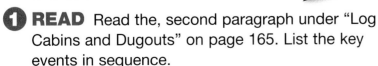

1 **READ** Read the, second paragraph under "Log Cabins and Dugouts" on page 165. List the key events in sequence.

2 **WRITE** Write about the events of your day. Include words such as *first, then, next,* and *finally*.

Keep in Mind...

For more help in reading social studies, try these strategies:

☑ **Look up unknown words**
Use a dictionary or the glossary in your book to find the meanings of any unfamiliar words.

☑ **Reread**
Review each sentence carefully. Make sure you understand what each sentence means before you read further.

☑ **Summarize**
In your own words, briefly describe what your reading is about. Look for topic sentences that contain the main ideas.

Make Predictions

As you read a paragraph or section in your book, think about what might come next. What you think will happen is your **prediction**. A prediction does not have a correct or incorrect answer. Making predictions helps you to carefully consider what you are reading.

To Make a Prediction
Ask yourself:

• What happened in this section?

• What background knowledge do I already have about the events in the text?

• What similar situations do I know of?

• What do I think might happen next?

In this book, you will read about our state's many natural resources. Oil is one of them. Read the following paragraph about oil and follow the steps to make a prediction.

■ Think about other things you know that will help you make an "educated guess."

■ Test your prediction: read further to see if you are correct.

■ Revise your prediction: read further to see if more information changes your prediction.

On April 15, 1897, the first productive oil well in Oklahoma was discovered near Bartlesville. It was named the "Nellie Johnstone," after a Cherokee girl. Her father had helped to drill the well. The oil was called "black gold" because it was valuable, like gold.

from page 181

Text Information:
Oklahoma's first oil well was discovered in 1897.

Background Information:
Oil is an important and valuable natural resource.

Prediction:
Oil will help Oklahoma's economy grow.

TRY IT!

Read the following paragraph about home-steaders. Copy and complete the prediction chart below.

Homesteaders often had to travel long distances to find wood to build fires. Stalks from large plants were sometimes used. But these stalks produced too much smoke inside the settlers' homes.

from page 167

Text Information

Burning stalks can make too much smoke.

Background Information

My Prediction

The home-steaders will find something else to burn.

• On what did you base your prediction?

Keep in Mind...

For more help in reading social studies, try these strategies:

✔ **Sequencing**
As you read, think about the order in which things happened.

✔ **Form the big picture**
As you read, think about the topic and the most important information in the paragraph or section.

✔ **Relate to personal experience**
Think about how what you are reading about relates to your own life.

Practice Activities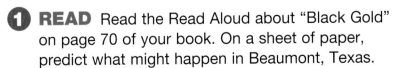

1 **READ** Read the Read Aloud about "Black Gold" on page 70 of your book. On a sheet of paper, predict what might happen in Beaumont, Texas.

2 **WRITE** On television, the weather person tells you what the weather in your region will be tomorrow. Write a paragraph about a weather prediction you heard recently. How can you test this prediction?

Compare and Contrast

This book often **compares** and **contrasts** people or events. To compare things is to see how they are alike. To contrast things is to see how they are different. Comparing and contrasting helps you understand the relationships between things.

■ To compare, look for clue words such as *like, similar, in common, same,* and *resemble.*

■ To contrast, look for clue words such as *before, after, different from, unlike,* and *by contrast.*

To Compare
Ask yourself:

• What are the things being compared?

• How are they alike?

To Contrast
Ask yourself:

• What are the things being contrasted?

• How are they different?

In your book you will read about how groups of people celebrate. Read this paragraph to compare and contrast these celebrations.

People remember their heritage in celebrations and festivals. Fiestas help Southwesterners remember their Mexican heritage. Many Middle West towns hold Oktoberfests. These harvest festivals were brought by immigrants from Germany. A Northeastern clambake is a cookout that features seafood. It shows how important the sea is in the Northeast.

from page 52

Contrast:
People in the Southwest celebrate fiestas.

Compare:
All of these groups celebrate to remember their heritage.

Contrast:
People from Germany celebrate Oktoberfest.

Contrast:
People in the Northeast celebrate with clambakes.

TRY IT!

Read this paragraph about two crops grown in Oklahoma. Copy and complete the diagram comparing and contrasting wheat and cotton.

> Some crops grow well in the cooler climate in the northern parts of our state. There, wheat is an important crop. The type of wheat grown by farmers in the north can be planted in the fall and harvested in the spring. Cotton, on the other hand, needs warm temperatures most of the year. It is grown in Southwest Oklahoma.
>
> *from page 219*

Wheat   **Cotton**

Found in the north; grows in a cool climate

Grown in our state

Grown in the southwest

• What steps did you take to compare and contrast?

Keep in Mind...

For more help in reading social studies, try these strategies:

☑ **Look up unknown words**
Use a dictionary or the glossary in your book to find the meaning of any unfamiliar words.

☑ **Form the big picture**
As you read, think about the most important information of the paragraph or section.

☑ **Summarize**
In your own words, briefly describe what your reading is about.

Practice Activities

1 **READ** Read the second paragraph under "Climate" on page 88. Compare and contrast the weather in two different parts of our state.

2 **WRITE** Write a paragraph that compares and contrasts the weather in your community for the months of July and December.

Summarize

After you read a paragraph or section of this book, you can **summarize** what you have read. In a **summary**, you briefly tell in your own words about the most important information in the section. Summarizing is a way to help you understand what you read.

■ Look for titles, headings, and key words that identify important information.

■ Keep your summary brief, and organize the information in a clear way.

■ Don't include information and facts that are not the most important.

To Summarize

Ask yourself:

• What is this paragraph or section about?

• What information is most important?

• How can I say this in my own words?

In your book you will read about different kinds of jobs people have. Read this paragraph and sample summary about a water quality expert.

Alva Richardson is a <u>water quality expert in Oregon</u>. His job is to <u>make sure that his county's rivers and streams are clean</u>. He travels around the area collecting water in bottles. "Then we bring the bottled samples back to the lab to study them. <u>If the water contains any pollution, we try to figure out where it is coming from</u>," Alva says. <u>Alva's skills and knowledge help protect one of Oregon's natural resources</u>.

from page 28

Sample Summary:
Alva Richardson works to protect his county's water supply from pollution.

Important information is underlined.

TRY IT!

Read this section about life in Oklahoma in the 1800s. Copy and complete the summary diagram.

Many areas did not have enough water to use for washing, cooking, or drinking. Many families were far from a river or stream. To get water, they left barrels outdoors to catch rainwater. Sometimes they used windmills to gather water. Windmills used wind power to pump underground water up from wells to the surface.

from page 167

Important Ideas

Many families lived far from the river.

They used barrels to catch rainwater.

Summary

Families in areas with little water used different methods to gather it.

• How did you choose what to include in the summary?

Keep in Mind...

For more help in reading social studies, try these strategies:

☑ **Reread**
Review each sentence. Make sure you understand what each sentence means before you read further.

☑ **Form the big picture**
As you read, think about the topic and the main ideas of the paragraph or section.

☑ **Make an outline**
As you read, write an outline of the topic and the main ideas of the reading.

Practice Activities

1 **READ** Read the Many Voices feature on page 257. Summarize the feature in your own words.

2 **WRITE** Write a paragraph to summarize a movie.

Use Visuals

One way to learn is to use **visuals.** Visuals are charts, pictures, and maps in your book. They give information in an easy-to-study form.

■ Read the caption and labels for information they give.

■ Be sure to find the meanings of special symbols.

To Use Visuals

Look closely at the visual. Ask yourself:

• What does the graph, chart, picture, or map show?

• How does it help me to understand what I have read?

• How does it add to the information I have read?

• What information do the visual's labels and captions provide?

In your book you will read about recycling. Study this diagram showing how lunch trays are recycled.

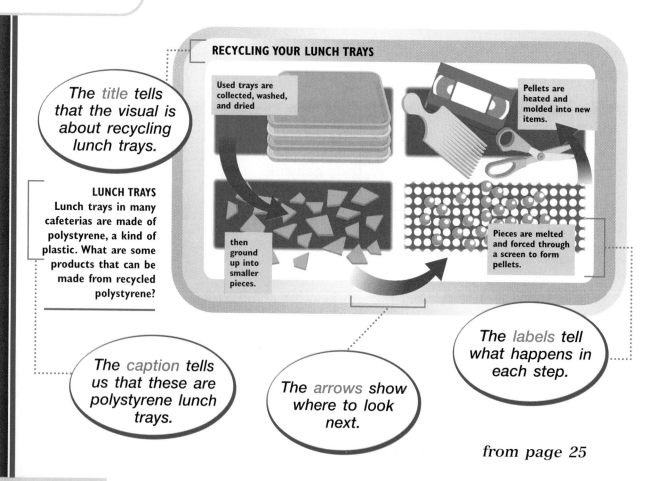

RECYCLING YOUR LUNCH TRAYS

Used trays are collected, washed, and dried

then ground up into smaller pieces.

Pieces are melted and forced through a screen to form pellets.

Pellets are heated and molded into new items.

The title tells that the visual is about recycling lunch trays.

LUNCH TRAYS Lunch trays in many cafeterias are made of polystyrene, a kind of plastic. What are some products that can be made from recycled polystyrene?

The caption tells us that these are polystyrene lunch trays.

The arrows show where to look next.

The labels tell what happens in each step.

from page 25

TRY IT!

Study these pictures of different types of transportation. Copy the chart. Think about the information shown in the pictures and complete the chart.

Transportation means moving goods or people from one place to another. What are some jobs people have in transportation?

from page 48

Visual: Cars travel on a highway with many lanes.	**Visual:** A train with boxcars rolls down a track.

Visual:

Caption: Transportation means moving goods and people.

Keep in Mind...

For more help in reading social studies, try these strategies:

☑ **Use Visuals**
Review captions and labels carefully. Make sure you understand what each sentence means before you read further.

☑ **Study the charts and graphs**
Charts and graphs provide information in an easy-to-understand form.

☑ **Study the unit and chapter openers**
The first page of a unit or chapter often summarizes what you will read about. It also may contain useful maps and pictures.

Practice Activities

1 READ Study the photos and caption on page 22. What information do the pictures give you?

2 WRITE Find a photograph that interests you. Write a story based on information in the photo.

Oklahoma

ADVENTURES IN TIME AND PLACE

James A. Banks

Barry K. Beyer

Gloria Contreras

Jean Craven

Gloria Ladson-Billings

Mary A. McFarland

Walter C. Parker

NATIONAL
GEOGRAPHIC
SOCIETY

THIS MISTLETOE IS MADE OF
STAINED GLASS AND THE SCISSOR-
TAILED FLYCATCHER IS CARVED
FROM WOOD. MISTLETOE IS
OUR STATE FLOWER. OUR STATE
BIRD IS THE SCISSOR-TAILED
FLYCATCHER.

McGraw-Hill
School Division

New York   Farmington

PROGRAM AUTHORS

Dr. James A. Banks
Professor of Education and Director of the Center for Multicultural Education
University of Washington
Seattle, Washington

Dr. Barry K. Beyer
Professor Emeritus, Graduate School of Education
George Mason University
Fairfax, Virginia

Dr. Gloria Contreras
Professor of Education
University of North Texas
Denton, Texas

Jean Craven
District Coordinator of Curriculum Development
Albuquerque Public Schools
Albuquerque, New Mexico

Dr. Gloria Ladson-Billings
Professor of Education
University of Wisconsin
Madison, Wisconsin

Dr. Mary A. McFarland
Instructional Coordinator of Social Studies, K–12, and Director of Staff Development
Parkway School District
Chesterfield, Missouri

Dr. Walter C. Parker
Professor and Program Chair
Social Studies Education
University of Washington
Seattle, Washington

NATIONAL
GEOGRAPHIC
SOCIETY
Washington, D.C.

OKLAHOMA SENIOR CONSULTANTS

Geneva Hudson
Retired Teacher
Edmond School System
Edmond, Oklahoma

Whit Edwards
Director of Education
Oklahoma State Historical Society
Oklahoma City, Oklahoma

Dr. Charles Ziehr
Professor of Geography
Northeastern State University
Tahlequah, Oklahoma

Mary Jane Warde
Oklahoma State Historical Society
American Indian Affairs
Stillwater, Oklahoma

Dr. Ronald Foore
Former Member Board of Directors
Oklahoma Council on Economic Education
Chairman, Social Studies Department
Booker T. Washington School
Tulsa, Oklahoma

GRADE-LEVEL CONSULTANTS

Marie Harris
Fourth Grade Teacher
Ralph Downs Elementary School
Oklahoma City, Oklahoma

Jan Johnson
Certified Reading Specialist
Westside Elementary School
Claremore, Oklahoma

Charlotte Mann
Fourth Grade Teacher
Traub Elementary School
Midwest City, Oklahoma

Richard Powell
Fourth Grade Teacher
Chickasha Public Schools
Chickasha, Oklahoma

Neil Womack
Principal
Western Oaks Elementary School
Bethany, Oklahoma

CONTRIBUTING WRITERS

Ken Elish
New York, New York

Linda Scher
Raleigh, North Carolina

CONSULTANTS FOR TEST PREPARATION

THE PRINCETON REVIEW

The Princeton Review is not affiliated with Princeton University or ETS.

Acknowledgments

The publisher gratefully acknowledges permission to reprint the following copyrighted material:

p. 16 excerpt from **The Everglades: River of Grass** by Marjory Stoneman Douglas. Copyright © 1989 by Marjory Stoneman Douglas. Used by permission of Pineapple Press, Inc.
p. 17 quote by Ansel Adams from **Ansel Adams: The American Wilderness**. Copyright © 1990 by Little Brown and Company.
p. 39 excerpt from **"Let America Be America Again"** by Langston Hughes from *A New Song*. Copyright © 1936 by Langston Hughes. Used by permission of Random House.
p. 58 excerpt from **Down the Colorado** by Jim Carrier. Copyright © 1989 by Roberts Rinehart, Inc.

(continued on page R36)

McGraw-Hill School Division

A Division of The McGraw-Hill Companies

McGraw-Hill School Division
Two Penn Plaza
New York, New York 10121

Printed in the United States of America

ISBN 0-02-149174-7

2 3 4 5 6 7 8 9 071 03 02 01

Teacher's Multimedia Edition

ISBN 0-02-149175-5

2 3 4 5 6 7 8 9 071 03 02 01

CONTENTS

FEATURES

CHARTS, GRAPHS, & DIAGRAMS

TIME LINES

MAPS

YOUR TEXTBOOK
at a glance

Your book is called *Oklahoma: Adventures in Time and Place*. It has eleven chapters. Each chapter has two or more lessons. There are also many special features for you to study and enjoy.

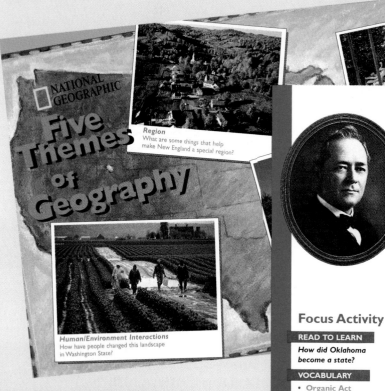

NATIONAL GEOGRAPHIC

Five Themes of Geography

Region
What are some things that help make New England a special region?

Human/Environment Interactions
How have people changed this landscape in Washington State?

▲ Special pages bring you ideas and **Adventures** in geography from **National Geographic**.

RED CARPET COUNTRY

Red Carpet Country is the northwestern part of our state. Its name comes from the red clay soil that covers the region. Not many people live here. Those who do are proud of how friendly people are here. They "roll out the red carpet" to welcome visitors.

Red Carpet Country is a land of plains and prairies (PRAIR ees). Grasslands on the plains are called prairies. The plains and prairies of this region have one of the most important natural resources of Red Carpet Country: farmland. Wheat grown in Red Carpet Country helps feed the United States and other countries in the world.

The Red Carpet country is also used for raising cattle. The region has many huge ranches. On them cattle graze on the short grasses of the flat, treeless plains. Farm animals like sheep are also raised on ranches in Red Country.

Mesquite (mes KEET) trees can be seen in this region. These small, thorny trees have long roots that grow deep to find water. Mesquites can be found in places that are too dry for other trees. Farmers sometimes make flour from mesquite trees and use it as food to help feed their animals.

Besides farming and grazing land, Red Carpet country has another important natural resource is natural g natural gas for cooki heating homes and The deepest gas wel are found here.

WHY IT MATTERS

After the Mound Builders disappeared, groups of other American Indians came to live in the area we now call Oklahoma. For many years they were the only people to live here. In the next lesson you will see how the lives of the American Indians were forever changed.

MAIN IDEAS
- The first people in Oklahoma came here over 20,000 years ago.
- The early American Indians of Oklahoma were both hunters and gatherers and farmers.
- The Spiro Mound people lived in years ago. Scientists do not know why the Mound Builders disappeared from Oklahoma.

THINK ABOUT IT
1. How did scientists learn about the lives of the Spiro people?
2. What did the first Oklahomans eat?
3. **FOCUS** Who were the first people to live in the area that is now Oklahoma?
4. **THINKING SKILL** Compare and contrast the Mound Builders?
5. **GEOGRAPHY** Give two examples of natural resources in Oklahoma that were important to the American Indians of long ago.

DO YOU KNOW?
What are mesquite trees used for? Have you ever eaten raw peas right from the pod? Mesquite trees have similar pods. A long time ago, Native Americans used to grind the seeds inside into flour. Today every people use mesquite wood to make their barbecues taste better...

Tools, weapons, and pieces of pottery were among the artifacts buried at Spiro Mounds.

the items in the mound came from faraway places. Shells and pearls came from the Gulf of Mexico. Copper came from areas in what is now the Great Lakes area of our country. A powerful group, the Spiro people controlled trade between the plains to the west and the woodlands to the east.

What Happened?
No one knows for sure what happened to the Spiro people and other Mound Builders. Some scientists believe other American Indians attacked their villages and forced them to leave. Others think that a long time without enough rain to grow crops forced the Mound Builders to move. By the time the owners... Europeans came to Oklahoma in the...

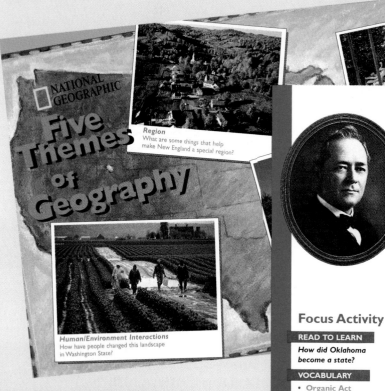

LESSON 2

1880   1889   1907 1910   1920

Oklahoma Becomes a State

Read Aloud
"When the brilliant rays of this morning's sun spread over our land, it lighted forty-five strong states between the two oceans. The sun will set tonight and its last rays will light a grander nation now grown to forty-six states."

These words were spoken by Charles Haskell, as he took office on the day that Oklahoma became a state. He was Oklahoma's first governor.

Focus Activity

READ TO LEARN
How did Oklahoma become a state?

VOCABULARY
- Organic Act
- Curtis Act
- Enabling Act

PEOPLE
- Charles Haskell

PLACES
- Oklahoma Territory
- Twin Territories
- Guthrie

Oklahomans heading to southwest Oklahoma to build new lives in 1901.

THE BIG PICTURE
Despite many hardships, homesteaders slowly built successful communities in the western part of what is now Oklahoma. The American Indians continued to live in eastern Oklahoma, with a smaller number in the western area. As the number of homesteaders increased, many of the newcomers wanted to form a new state. But the American Indians wanted to govern themselves in their own state. They wanted their own laws and ways of life.

174

◄ Some lessons have features called **Links** and **Did You Know?**— activities to try and interesting information to share.

Look for a variety of lessons and features. **Infographics** inform you with pictures and maps. You will build **Skills**, learn about **Legacies** that connect us to the past, and meet people who show what **Citizenship** is.

CITIZENSHIP
VIEWPOINTS

Three DIFFERENT Viewpoints

CHARLES B. AMES
Attorney
Excerpt from the resolutions of the Oklahoma City Commercial Club in 1903

The resources of the two territories cry aloud for union. Oklahoma is almost [entirely] agricultural. The great wealth of the Indian Territory is in her mines and forests. With the...

Legacy
LINKING PAST AND PRESENT
Wildcatters

When they struck "black gold"...

If they did not find oil, wild-catters often ended up without...

Geography Skills

Reading Road Maps

Helping Yourself box to guide you in reading the road maps.

USING THE SKILL

Look at the road map of Oklahoma on...

TRYING THE SKILL

Suppose you wanted to plan a trip from Tulsa to Oklahoma City. Along the way you want to visit...

Helping yourself

- A road map helps to guide travelers from one place to another.

REVIEWING THE SKILL

1. What kind of information does a road map show?
2. On the map, which inter...

WHY IT MATTERS

Maria made some good decisions and created a local Oklahoma business. Like Maria, you may one day start a business and play an important part in our state's economy. By buying or selling products, you too are helping Oklahoma's free enterprise system work.

Reviewing Facts and Ideas

MAIN IDEAS

- In a free enterprise system, people are free to choose the products they make and consume. Geography is important to a community's economy.
- Investors provide money in order to help start businesses.
- Labor, raw materials, and transportation are among the costs of businesses. The price of goods and services depend on supply and demand.

THINK ABOUT IT

1. What is labor?
2. How does a business make a profit?
3. FOCUS How does the free enterprise system work in Oklahoma?
4. THINKING SKILL What *decisions* would you have to make before going into business?
5. GEOGRAPHY In what ways can the geography of Oklahoma affect its economy?

Infographic

interNET CONNECTION Visit our website: www.mhschool.com

Local Businesses

The local economy of any area can include many different businesses. These pages show different local businesses that are common in Oklahoma. What business or businesses are in your community?

Whether constructing large buildings (left) or making boots in a shop (below), Oklahomans work hard to provide the things we need.

Many small businesses support the high tech industry in Oklahoma. A computer technician repairs a computer (above). Some Oklahomans enjoy working outdoors, like this rancher (below).

Local businesses sell the food you will eat today. This baker is selling today's fresh bread.

208

209

OKLAHOMA T...

In the last chapter... the land runs of 188... up the Unassigned... ment. However, as... homesteaders want...

In 1887 the Unite... ment began making... with the American... homa's western are... given a small plot... of land. Each child... The rest of the Ind... west was opened...

As homesteaders began... their communities, they formed local governments. Still, many people made their own laws. They often protected each other by forming peacekeeping groups.

Oklahoma was... territories in 1900. They were Indian Territory and Oklahoma Territory. They became known as the Twin Territories.

The end of your book has a **Reference Section** with many types of information. Use it to look up words, people, and places.

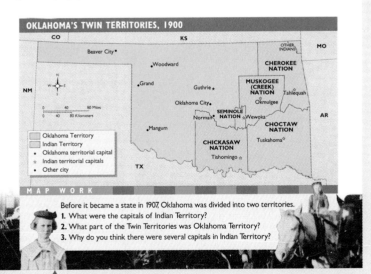

OKLAHOMA'S TWIN TERRITORIES, 1900

CO
KS
Beaver City
OTHER INDIANS
MO
NM
Woodward
CHEROKEE NATION
Grand
Guthrie ★
MUSKOGEE (CREEK) NATION
Tahlequah
Oklahoma City ●
Okmulgee
SEMINOLE NATION
Norman
Wewoka ☆
CHOCTAW NATION
Mangum
CHICKASAW NATION
Tuskahoma ☆
AR
TX
Tishomingo ☆

0 40 80 Miles
0 40 80 Kilometers

Oklahoma Territory
Indian Territory
● Oklahoma territorial capital
☆ Indian territorial capitals
● Other city

MAP WORK

Before it became a state in 1907, Oklahoma was divided into two territories.
1. What were the capitals of Indian Territory?
2. What part of the Twin Territories was Oklahoma Territory?
3. Why do you think there were several capitals in Indian Territory?

Lessons begin with a **Read Aloud** selection and **The Big Picture**. Study with the **Read to Learn** question and a list of words, people, and places. Enjoy **Many Voices**—writings from many different sources.

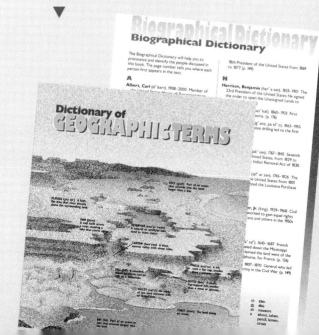

Biographical Dictionary

The Biographical Dictionary will help you to pronounce and identify the people discussed in this book. The page number tells you where each person first appears in the text.

A

Albert, Carl (al' bart), 1908–2000 Member of the United States House of Representatives...

18th President of the United States from 1869 to 1877 (p. 149)

H

Harrison, Benjamin (har' a san), 1833–1901 The 23rd President of the United States He signed the order to open the Unassigned Lands to...

Dictionary of
GEOGRAPHIC TERMS

National Geographic

Five Themes of Geography

Region
What are some things that help make New England a special region?

Human/Environment Interactions
How have people changed this landscape in Washington State?

Place
What makes Rockefeller Center different from other places in New York?

Location
How does mail get to exactly the right place?

Movement
How do people get from their homes to their jobs?

A Look at Oklahoma

A scientist uses computers and other high-tech equipment to monitor research in agriculture — one of Oklahoma's most important industries.

Evalu Ware Russell is an American Indian storyteller. She travels the world sharing the traditional songs, stories, and dances of the Kiowa people. More than 60 American Indian groups live in Oklahoma.

Oklahoma City celebrates the Arts Festival every April with concerts on Pond Stage.

A Navajo boy shows off his prize lamb at a livestock show in Oklahoma.

In the high plains region of Oklahoma's Panhandle, Black Mesa—at 4,973 feet—is the state's highest point. The landscape of northwestern Oklahoma contrasts sharply with the forests and lakes of the Ozark Plateau in the eastern part of the state.

GEOGRAPHY SKILLS

PART 1
Using Globes

VOCABULARY

ocean   hemisphere
continent   equator

What does a globe show?

- A globe is a small copy of Earth. Like Earth, a globe is a round object, or sphere.

- Globes show the parts of Earth that are land and the parts that are water. Earth's largest bodies of water are called oceans. There are four oceans—the Atlantic, Arctic, Indian, and Pacific oceans. Look at the globe shown here. What color is used to show oceans?

- Globes also show the seven large bodies of land called continents. The continents are Africa, Antarctica, Asia, Australia, Europe, North America, and South America. Find North America and South America on the globe below. Which oceans are shown bordering these continents?

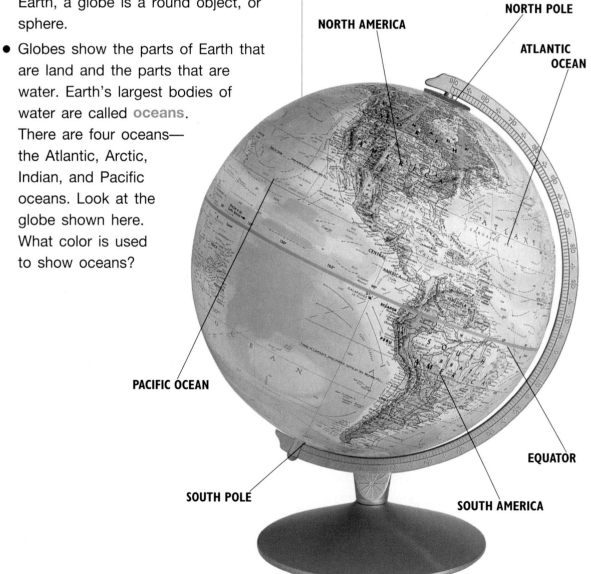

NORTH AMERICA

NORTH POLE

ATLANTIC OCEAN

PACIFIC OCEAN

SOUTH POLE

SOUTH AMERICA

EQUATOR

What are the four hemispheres?

- Look again at the globe on the previous page. Can you see the whole globe? You can see only half of a globe or sphere at any one time. A word for half a sphere is hemisphere. The word *hemi* means "half."

- Earth is divided into the Northern Hemisphere and Southern Hemisphere by the equator. The equator is an imaginary line that lies halfway between the North Pole and the South Pole. Look at these maps. What continents are located on the equator?

- Earth can also be divided into two other hemispheres. What are the names of these hemispheres? In which hemispheres do you live?

More Practice

There are other maps in this book that show the equator. For examples, see pages 170–171.

THE HEMISPHERES

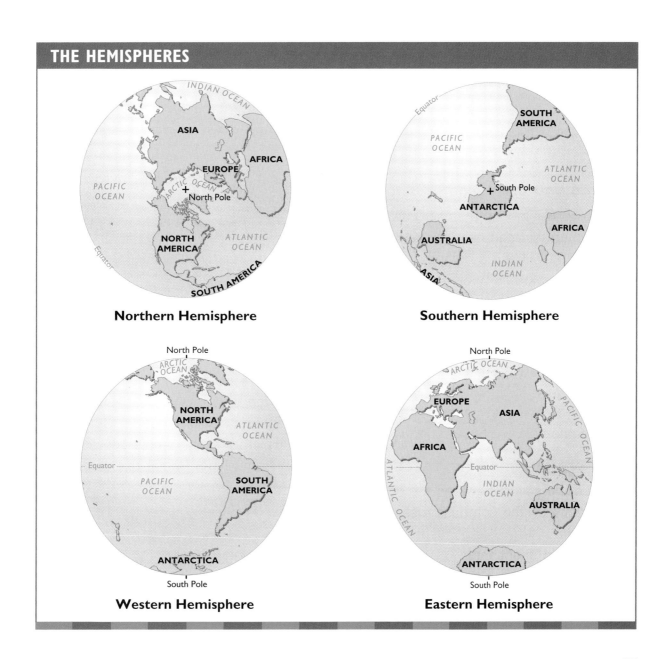

Northern Hemisphere

Southern Hemisphere

Western Hemisphere

Eastern Hemisphere

PART 2
Using Maps

VOCABULARY
cardinal directions
compass rose
intermediate directions
symbol
map key
scale
locator

What are cardinal directions?

- North, south, east, and west are the main directions, or cardinal directions.

- If you face the North Pole, you are facing north. When you face north, south is directly behind you. West is to your left. What direction is to your right?

How do you use a compass rose?

- A compass rose is a small drawing on a map that can help you find directions. You will see a compass rose on most maps in this book.

- The cardinal directions are sometimes written as **N**, **S**, **E**, and **W**. Find the compass rose on the map of South Carolina. In which direction is Camden from Newberry? In which direction would you travel to get from Lancaster to Beaufort?

What are intermediate directions?

- Notice the spikes between the cardinal directions on the compass rose. These show the intermediate directions, or in-between directions.

- The intermediate directions are northeast, southeast, southwest, and northwest. The direction northeast is often

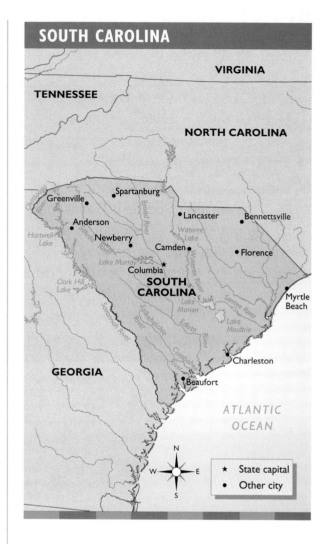

SOUTH CAROLINA

written as **NE**. What letters are used for the other intermediate directions? Which intermediate direction lies between south and east? Which one is between north and west?

- Use the compass rose again. Which direction is Columbia from Charleston? In which direction would you travel to get from Myrtle Beach to Beaufort?

More Practice

You can practice finding directions with a compass rose on most maps in this book. For examples, see maps on pages 125 and 211.

G8

Why do maps have titles?

- When using a map, first look at the map title. The title names the area the map shows. It may also tell you the kind of information shown on the map. Look at the maps below. What is the title of each?

Why do maps include symbols?

- A symbol is something that stands for something else.

- On a map common symbols include dots, lines, triangles, and colors. Many maps use the color blue to stand for water, for example. What do dots sometimes stand for?

- Maps often use symbols that are small drawings of the things they stand for. A drawing of a tree, for example, might stand for a forest. What could an airplane stand for?

How can you find out what map symbols stand for?

- Often the same symbol stands for different things on different maps. For this reason many maps include a map key. A map key gives the meaning of each symbol used on the map.

- When you look at a map, you should always study the map key. Look at the maps on this page. What does the cow stand for on the Louisiana map? What symbol marks places of interest on the map of Washington, D.C.? What does the square stand for on the Washington, D.C. map?

More Practice

There are many maps with symbols and map keys in this book. For examples, see pages 93, 125, and 211.

LOUISIANA: PRODUCTS

ARKANSAS

Shreveport Monroe

MISSISSIPPI

TEXAS

Alexandria

LOUISIANA

Baton Rouge   Lake Pontchartrain

Lake Charles   Lafayette   Kenner   New Orleans

Mississippi River

Sabine River

Calcasieu River

Gulf of Mexico

★ State capital   🐄 Animal products
• Other city   Cotton
Oil   Soybeans
Natural gas   Forest products

N
W   E
S

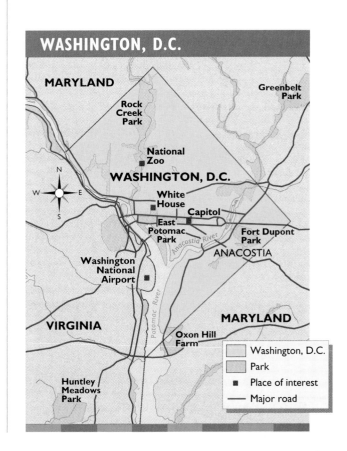

WASHINGTON, D.C.

MARYLAND

Greenbelt Park

Rock Creek Park

National Zoo

WASHINGTON, D.C.

White House

Capitol

N
W   E
S

East Potomac Park

Fort Dupont Park

ANACOSTIA

Washington National Airport

Anacostia River

Potomac River

VIRGINIA

MARYLAND

Oxon Hill Farm

Huntley Meadows Park

Washington, D.C.
Park
■ Place of interest
— Major road

CALIFORNIA

State capital
Other city
Mountain peak
National Park

What is a map scale?

- All maps are smaller than the real area that they show. So how can you figure out the real distance between places? Most maps include a scale. The scale shows the relationship between distances shown on a map and the real distances.

- The scales in this book are drawn with two lines. The top line shows distance in miles. What unit of measurement does the bottom line use?

How do you use a map scale?

- You can use a ruler to measure distances on a map.

- You can also make a scale strip like the one shown below. Place the edge of a strip of paper under the scale lines on the map of California. Mark the distances in miles. Slide your strip over and continue to mark miles until your strip is long enough to measure the whole map.

- Use your scale strip to measure the distance between Eureka and Sacramento. Place the edge of the strip under the two places. Line the zero up under Eureka. What is the distance between Eureka and Sacramento in miles?

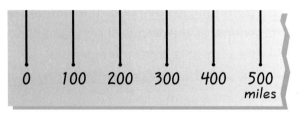

What do locators show?

- A locator is a small map set onto the main map. It shows where the area of the main map is located. Where is the locator on the map of California?

- Most of the locators in this book show either the United States or the world. The area shown by the main map is highlighted in red on the locator. Look at the map of California. What area does the locator show?

More Practice

You can find scales and locators on maps in this book. For examples of scales, see pages 211 and 231. For examples of locators, see maps on pages 60 and 125.

PART 3

Different Kinds of Maps

VOCABULARY
political map
physical map
landform map
transportation map
historical map

What is a political map?

- A political map shows information such as cities, capital cities, states, and countries. What symbol is used to show state capitals on the map below?

- Political maps use lines to show borders. The states or countries are also often shown in different colors. Look at the map below. What color is used to show Indiana?

More Practice

There are more political maps in this book. For examples, see pages 231 and R4–R5.

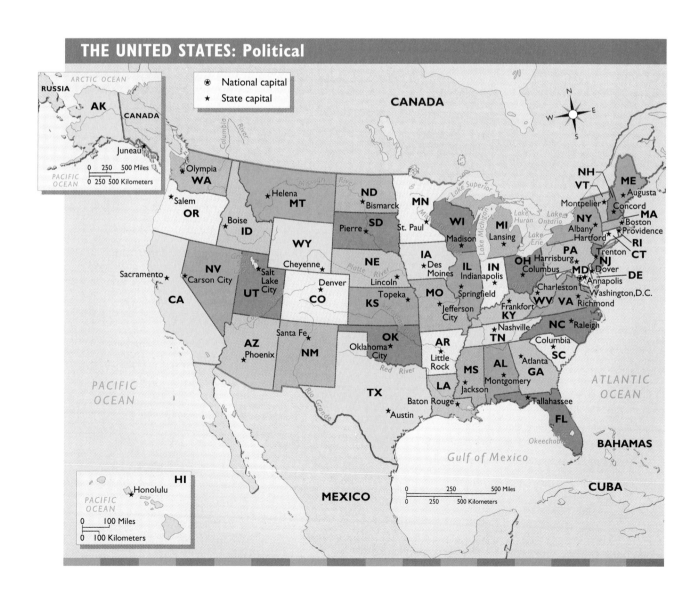

THE UNITED STATES: Political

What are physical maps?

- Maps that show the natural features of Earth are called physical maps. There are different kinds of physical maps in this book.

- One kind of physical map shows landforms, or the shapes that make up Earth's surface. These maps are called landform maps. Mountains, hills, and plains are all examples of landforms. Landform maps also show bodies of water such as lakes, rivers, and oceans.

- Look at the map of the United States. What kinds of landforms are found in the United States? What large bodies of water are shown?

What is a transportation map?

- A transportation map is a kind of map that shows how you can travel from one place to another.

- Some transportation maps show roads for traveling by car, by bike, or on foot. Others may show bus, train, ship, or airplane routes. What kinds of routes are shown on the map of Oklahoma at right? Which cities have airports?

More Practice

For other physical maps, see pages 12–13 and R6–7.

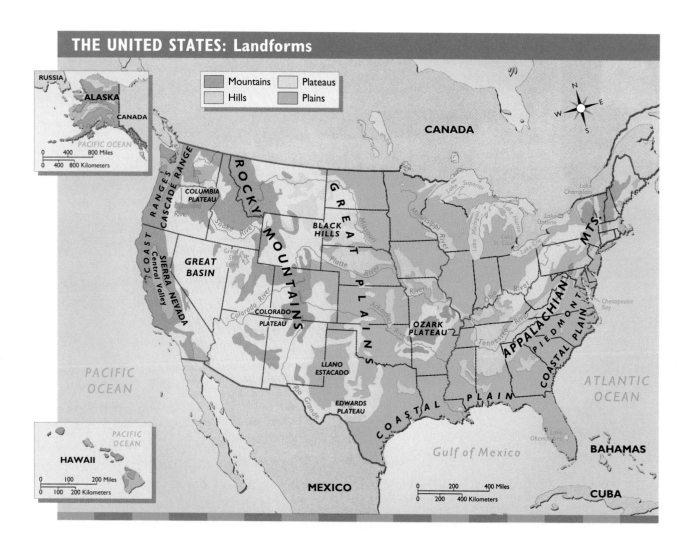

THE UNITED STATES: Landforms

Mountains   Plateaus
Hills   Plains

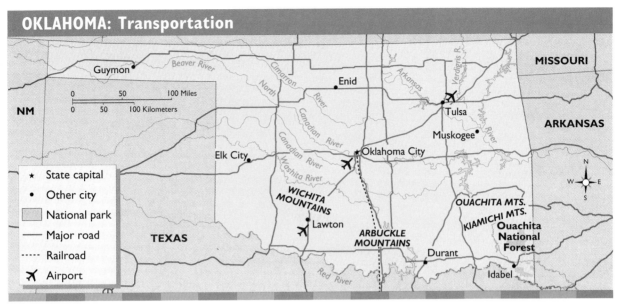

OKLAHOMA: Transportation

Legend:
* State capital
* Other city
National park
— Major road
----- Railroad
✈ Airport

What is an historical map?

- An historical map is a map that shows information about past events and where they occurred. Historical maps often show places and political boundaries that differ from those that exist today.

- When you look at an historical map, first study the map title. What does the title tell you about the historical map to the right?

- Historical maps often show dates in the title or on the map. Study the map at right. What time period does it show?

- Next look at the map key. The map key tells you what kinds of events are shown on the map. Which battle took place in Virginia? Which side won that battle? How many of the battles shown were fought in 1775?

More Practice

There are other historical maps in this book. For examples, see pages 125 and 154.

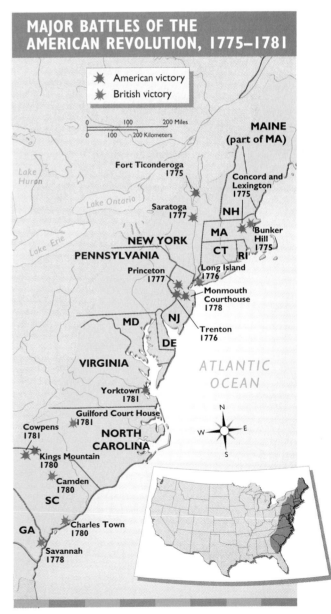

MAJOR BATTLES OF THE AMERICAN REVOLUTION, 1775–1781

American victory
British victory

INTERSTATE 35
IN OKLAHOMA'S
ARBUCKLE
MOUNTAINS.

STATUE OF
ABRAHAM LINCOLN
IN THE LINCOLN
MEMORIAL IN
WASHINGTON, D.C.

United States, Land and People

"... as far as the eye could see."

from James Marcus's journal
See page 11.

Why Does It Matter?

The United States is one of the world's richest countries, both in land and in resources. It has mountains that seem to touch the sky. It has plains that seem never to end. Great variety can be found within its borders. Parts of it are freezing cold all year. Parts of it have perfect swimming weather almost every day.

People from all over the world have made the United States their home. In different parts of our country, people have different ways of life. What makes Americans different from one another? What do we have in common? Read on. Unit 1 introduces the geography and people that make the United States the special country that it is.

FIND OUT MORE!
Visit our website:
www.mhschool.com

*inter*NET
CONNECTION

Adventures
with
NATIONAL GEOGRAPHIC

Speaking of the Weather

One thing about weather: We get a lot of it, and it often packs a punch! The United States suffers more severe storms and floods than any other nation—violent thunderstorms (background), floods along the California coast spawned by El Niño. Across the country, snow and ice can bring us to our knees —though sometimes for fun. Scientists use Doppler radar to follow hurricanes in Florida and portable radar to track tornadoes on the wide open Plains. Many of us keep track of weather at home and at school. Rain or shine, windy or calm—it pays to pay attention to the weather.

GEO JOURNAL

Keep a record of the weather in your region. How does it change from season to season, week to week, day to day, hour to hour?

Our Country's Environment

THINKING ABOUT
GEOGRAPHY AND CITIZENSHIP

The United States is a huge country. It has many different types of land, bodies of water, weather, and resources. Look at the photographs on the next page. Using the colored squares, match each photograph to its location on the map. What could you learn on a trip across the country?

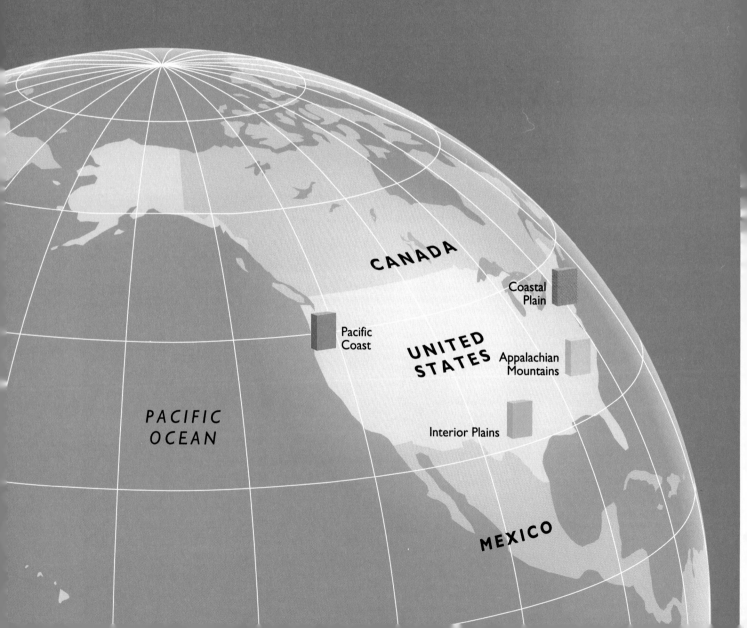

CANADA

Coastal Plain

Pacific Coast

UNITED STATES

Appalachian Mountains

PACIFIC OCEAN

Interior Plains

MEXICO

Coastal Plain in CONNECTICUT

Winter brings snow and ice to most northern parts of our country. Get out your skates!

Interior Plains in OKLAHOMA

The wide Interior Plains seem to stretch forever across the middle of our country. The soil is good for growing crops like these fields of wheat.

Appalachian Mountains in NORTH CAROLINA

Forests cover the slopes of these mountains, which run through the eastern part of our country. Stop and enjoy the view!

Pacific Coast in OREGON

The United States lies between two oceans. A beautiful sunset by the Pacific Ocean reminds these families how important it is to keep our environment clean.

Our Country's Geography

Read Aloud

Suppose that you had to write a description of your neighborhood. To prepare, you might step outside and make some notes. But what if your assignment were to write a description of the United States? How would you even begin?

Focus Activity

READ TO LEARN

What would you see on a trip across the country?

VOCABULARY

- geography
- landform
- plain
- plateau
- basin
- coast
- desert
- environment

PLACES

- Coastal Plain
- Appalachian Mountains
- Interior Plains
- Mississippi River
- Rocky Mountains

THE BIG PICTURE

Geography (jee AHG ruh fee) is the study of Earth and all the different kinds of things on it. Land and water, plant and animal life, and human activities are part of what geographers study.

One way to learn about our country's geography would be to drive across it. In 1998, that's exactly what one family did. The Marcus family includes James, Iris, and one-year-old Nathaniel. They left Water Mill, New York, on September 3 and began their drive west. Their goal: a new home in Oregon. You can share their adventure by reading the journal James kept.

LANDFORMS

Before you begin sharing the Marcus family's journey, you should know what a landform is. Landforms are the shapes that make up Earth's surface.

Hills, for example, are one kind of landform. Mountains are another. So is a plain, a large area of nearly flat land. What plains can you find on the Infographic on pages 12–13?*

Two other landforms you will come across are a plateau and a basin. A plateau is a high, flat area that rises steeply above the surrounding land. A basin is just the opposite: a low, bowl-shaped landform surrounded by higher land.

Now you are ready to head west with the Marcuses. As you read, follow their route on the Infographic on pages 12–13. Let's go!

The Coastal Plain

James and his family began their trip near the East Coast. A coast is the land along an ocean. Water Mill, New York, is located on the Coastal Plain. This landform is a narrow, flat strip along the Atlantic Ocean. To the south, it is much wider. All of Florida is on the Coastal Plain. Use the Infographic to see what other states are located on this plain.

Only a few hours after leaving Water Mill, the Marcuses passed through New York City. They took a last look at the Atlantic Ocean. James had grown up near this ocean. "We waved goodbye," Iris recalls. "We knew we wouldn't see the Atlantic again for a long time."

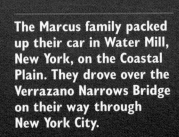

The Marcus family packed up their car in Water Mill, New York, on the Coastal Plain. They drove over the Verrazano Narrows Bridge on their way through New York City.

FROM THE COAST TO THE PLAINS

Let's begin sharing James's journal. We are now moving westward from the Atlantic Ocean. James wrote:

Leaving New York behind, we headed southwest into Pennsylvania. The flat land of the Coastal Plain soon gave way to rolling hills. We reached Front Royal, Virginia, and drove up into the Appalachian (ap uh LAY chee un) Mountains.

These rounded mountains stretch all the way from Maine to Alabama. The road wound along the mountaintops. James wrote:

The Appalachian Mountains are at their most beautiful here in the Blue Ridge. Looking west, we could see miles into the Shenandoah (shen un DOH uh) River valley. Everywhere there were wildflowers,

trees, and the bluish haze that gives the Blue Ridge its name.

The Marcuses spent two days in the Appalachian Mountains. They hiked up and down the steep mountain trails. Nathaniel rode in a backpack the whole way.

The Interior Plains

After their hike, the Marcuses continued their drive. They traveled southwest into the hills of eastern Tennessee. James wrote:

We took two days crossing Tennessee. As we drove west, the hills were growing gentler. It looked like somebody had flattened them with a rolling pin.

On their way south, the Marcuses looked over the Shenandoah River valley. Iris took this picture of James and Nathaniel as they hiked in the Appalachian Mountains.

The Marcuses drove through the Interior Plains in Oklahoma. This is good country for raising cattle.

The Marcuses were entering the Interior Plains. These wide plains stretch for hundreds of miles between two of our great mountain ranges.

A week after leaving New York, they crossed the Mississippi River. This river is one of the longest in North America. Find this river on the Infographic. In what state does it begin? Across what landforms does it flow?*

Flat Lands, Big Sky

The land of the Interior Plains is known for its rich soil. The Marcus family was now traveling across the plains of eastern Arkansas. They passed enormous fields of rice, soybeans, and other crops. James wrote:

The fields west of the Mississippi stretched from the edge of the road as far as the eye could see.

But as the Marcuses drove into Oklahoma and Texas, the landscape began to change.

Grass or scrub brush covered the ground, with an occasional tree or windmill poking its nose in the air. Cattle watched us pass and then went back to grazing. Not just the land had changed. The sky seemed bigger and bluer than before. I never knew there could be so much sky. When it was windy, we would watch the enormous shadow of a cloud racing over the land far in the distance.

Our Country's Land and Water

In this lesson you are following the Marcus family's journey across the United States. What landforms did they cross? What changes in geography did they see? This map shows you the places James and Iris saw, and more.

ALASKA
Mt. McKinley
20,320 ft. (6,194 m)
ALASKA RANGE
RANGE
PACIFIC OCEAN

0   500   1,000 Miles
0   500   1,000 Kilometers

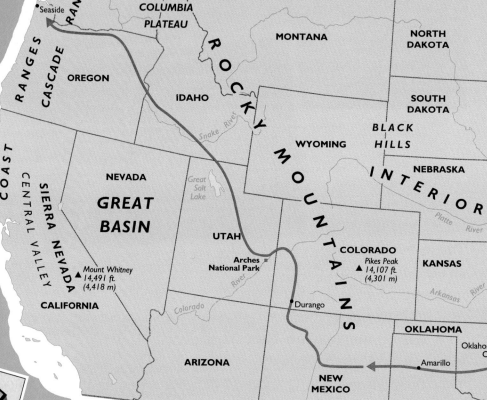

WASHINGTON
COLUMBIA PLATEAU
Seaside
RANGES
CASCADE RANGES
OREGON
COAST RANGES
SIERRA NEVADA
CENTRAL VALLEY
NEVADA
GREAT BASIN
Mount Whitney
14,491 ft.
(4,418 m)
CALIFORNIA
Snake River
IDAHO
MONTANA
ROCKY MOUNTAINS
WYOMING
Great Salt Lake
UTAH
Arches National Park
River
Colorado
Durango
NORTH DAKOTA
SOUTH DAKOTA
BLACK HILLS
NEBRASKA
INTERIOR
Platte River
COLORADO
Pikes Peak
14,107 ft.
(4,301 m)
KANSAS
Arkansas River
OKLAHOMA
Oklahoma City
Amarillo
NEW MEXICO
ARIZONA
TEXAS
Rio Grande

CAPE FOULWEATHER
OREGON COAST

GREETINGS from the
ROCKY MTS.

HAWAII
PACIFIC OCEAN
Mauna Kea
13,796 ft.
(4,205 m)

0   100 Miles
0   100 Kilometers

UNITED STATES: Physical

✳ National capital
• Other city
▲ Highest peak
▲ Other peak
← Route of Marcus family

Old National Trail
U.S. 40

Find These Places

Coastal Plain
Appalachian Mountains
Interior Plains
Lake Huron
Mississippi River

Ozark Plateau
Rocky Mountains
Great Basin
Coast Ranges
Alaska Range

Extra Credit
Find the highest mountain in the United States.

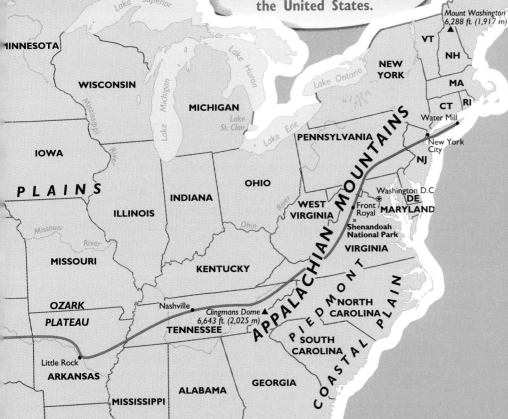

MAINE

Mount Washington
6,288 ft. (1,917 m)

VT
NH
MA
RI
CT

NEW YORK

Lake Ontario

MINNESOTA

Lake Superior

WISCONSIN

Lake Huron

Lake Michigan

MICHIGAN

Lake St. Clair

Lake Erie

PENNSYLVANIA

Water Mill

New York City

NJ

IOWA

Mississippi River

P L A I N S

OHIO

INDIANA

WEST VIRGINIA

Washington D.C.

Front Royal

MARYLAND

DE

ILLINOIS

Missouri River

Ohio River

Shenandoah National Park

VIRGINIA

MISSOURI

KENTUCKY

APPALACHIAN MOUNTAINS

OZARK PLATEAU

Nashville

Clingmans Dome
6,643 ft. (2,025 m)

TENNESSEE

P I E D M O N T

NORTH CAROLINA

C O A S T A L   P L A I N

Little Rock

ARKANSAS

SOUTH CAROLINA

MISSISSIPPI

ALABAMA

GEORGIA

LOUISIANA

C O A S T A L   P L A I N

FLORIDA

LIBERTY BELL

Philadelphia
PENN.

ROADRUNNER

STATE BIRD OF
NEW MEXICO

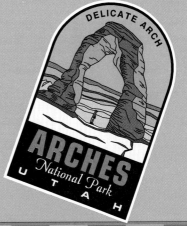

DELICATE ARCH

ARCHES
National Park
U T A H

MOUNTAINS AND A BASIN

The Marcuses had now crossed Texas into New Mexico. The road began to climb once more. They were now at the foot of the Rocky Mountains. These mountains stretch through the western United States.

As their name suggests, the Rocky Mountains are high and jagged. The Appalachian Mountains had seemed pretty high when we were coaxing the car over their peaks. But the Rockies truly seem to touch the sky.

James, Iris, and Nathaniel stopped for several days in Durango, Colorado. This old mining town is more than a mile above sea level.

We were surrounded on every side by steep slopes covered in green forest. Some were so tall that their tops were hidden by clouds. Others were capped by snow, even though it was still September. It was hard to believe that we were only a day's drive from the open, flat plains.

The Great Basin

Leaving Durango, the Marcus family continued northwest into Utah. Here they entered a desert called the Great Basin. A desert is a place where very little rain falls. Again they saw the landscape change before their eyes. James wrote in his journal:

Instead of mountains and pine trees, we were looking at miles of reddish rock. We stopped to explore Moab (MOH ab), Utah, including Arches National Park. We had the feeling we were on another planet. Wind and water and time had carved the rocks into unbelievable shapes.

The End of the Journey

From Utah the Marcuses drove northwest through Idaho. Finally they reached Oregon and headed

Arches National Park in Utah is famous for its natural arches of sandstone. James took this picture of Iris there.

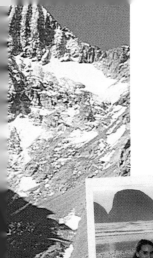

The Marcuses crossed the Rocky Mountains in Colorado. At the end of the journey, Iris's family came to meet them at the Pacific coast.

west for the Pacific. They crossed the Cascade Mountains and then the Coast Ranges, which stand along the Pacific Ocean.

It was a wonderful feeling. On September 26 we came down from the mountains and suddenly, as we rounded a bend, we saw the Pacific Ocean below. Iris and I let out a cheer, which made Nathaniel laugh. Those choppy, blue-gray waters meant that our journey was over.

Studying the Environment

You have shared the Marcus family's journey. You have learned about our environment (en VĪ run munt). Environment is the surroundings in which people, plants, or animals live.

Different environments are home to different kinds of plants and animals. Take a warm, rainy area such as the Blue Ridge, in the Appalachian Mountains. There the Marcuses saw deer, turkeys, and raccoons in the forest. But these animals could

not survive in the Great Basin. There they saw jackrabbits and lizards. These animals know how to survive in a desert.

WHY IT MATTERS

Our country is one of the largest in the world. And it has a great variety of landforms and environments. It has mountains that seem to touch the sky. It has plains that never seem to end. It has hot, barren basins and soggy swamps. In studying its geography, we realize how special our country is.

✓ Reviewing Facts and Ideas

MAIN IDEAS

- Geography is the study of Earth and everything on it.
- The shapes that Earth's surface takes are called landforms.
- Landforms and environments can differ from one place to another.

THINK ABOUT IT

1. Which oceans border the two coasts of the United States?

2. What is a landform?

3. **FOCUS** Name one plain, one river, and one mountain range that can be found in the United States.

4. **THINKING SKILL** *Compare* and *contrast* the Interior Plains and the Coastal Plain.

5. **GEOGRAPHY** Locate Oklahoma on the Infographic. On what landforms is it located? On what kind of landform do we live?

National Parks

Have you ever visited a national park? Then maybe you've seen first-hand some of the scenery shown on these pages. National parks are lands our government has set aside to protect. They are a legacy for all Americans to enjoy. A legacy is something we have received from the past that we want to pass on to the future.

National parks are a source of wonder. Some artists and writers have left us their thoughts about how important nature is to our lives. As you read the words and look at the pictures, think about what nature means to you. Thanks to our national parks, you may have the chance to visit some of these places yourself!

Everglades National Park is a huge swamp in Florida where many rare plants and animals live. Marjory Stoneman Douglas wrote this description in *The Everglades: River of Grass.*

" The miracle of the light pours over the green and brown expanse of sawgrass and of water, shining and slow-moving below, the grass and water that is the meaning and the central fact of the Everglades of Florida. It is a river of grass. "

Ansel Adams took this photograph at Yosemite National Park in California in 1960. This is what he said about the legacy of national parks in a speech:

❝ You must be able to touch the living rock, drink the pure water, scan the great vistas [views], sleep under the stars, and awaken to the cool dawn wind. Such experiences are the heritage of all people. ❞

Thomas Cole painted this picture of Mount Desert Island in Maine in 1844. Today Acadia National Park is on this island. He described the scene in a letter he wrote in 1844:

❝ The whole coast along here is iron bound—threatening crags [cliffs], and dark caverns in which the sea thunders. The view . . . is truly fine. ❞

Reading Elevation Maps

VOCABULARY
elevation

WHY THE SKILL MATTERS

On their trip the Marcus family crossed several mountain ranges. How could they have found a good place to go hiking? The Infographic on pages 12–13 would have shown them some things. For example, the Appalachian Mountains and the Sierra Nevada are both mountain ranges. But it would not have shown them other things. For example, the Sierra Nevada peaks are two to three times higher than the Appalachian peaks!

For this kind of information, they would need an elevation map. Elevation (el uh VAY shun) is the height of the land above the level of the sea. Elevation at sea level is 0 feet.

An elevation map uses different colors to show different elevations. You can see the map key on this page. All the places shown on the map in yellow are between 3,000 feet and 7,000 feet above sea level.

USING THE SKILL

Of course, elevation maps tell us about many things besides mountains. For

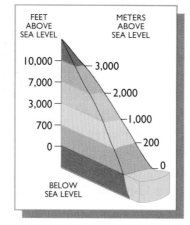

example, they also give us important information about rivers.

Have you ever wondered why the water in a river moves? The answer is simple: because water runs downhill. Every river begins at a higher elevation than where it ends. Gravity pulls the water downward toward a lower elevation. Let's say the land slopes down toward the east. Then the river will flow from west to east. If it slopes downward toward the south, the river will flow south. That's why an elevation map can help you to understand a river's course.

Let's try using an elevation map to trace the path of a river. Locate the Rio Grande on the map. As you can see, the Rio Grande begins in western Colorado. This is high in the Rocky Mountains. What color is the area where the river begins? Check the map key to find out what elevation this color represents. You can see that the river begins at an elevation of 10,000 feet above sea level or higher.

Follow the river's path. You will see that the Rio Grande first flows through parts of Colorado and New Mexico. It moves in a southeast direction. Then it flows downward through areas of lower and lower elevation. At last the river reaches the border of Texas. At this point it has dropped more than 3,000 feet! For several hundred miles the Rio Grande forms the border between the state of Texas and the country of

Mexico. Then it empties into the Gulf of Mexico. It has now reached sea level, or 0 feet in elevation.

TRYING THE SKILL

You have traced the path of the Rio Grande. Now use the elevation map to trace the path of the Ohio River.

Does the Ohio River start at a higher or lower elevation than the Rio Grande? In which direction does it flow? What does that show you about the elevation in that direction? Into what other river does the Ohio River flow?

Which mountains are higher, those in Virginia or in Wyoming?

Helping yourself

- **Elevation maps show you how high the land is above the sea.**
- **Study the map key to see which colors stand for different elevations on the map.**

REVIEWING THE SKILL

Now use the elevation map to answer the following questions. Use the Helping Yourself box for hints.

1. What is elevation?

2. Why does an elevation map tell us which way a river flows?

3. What is the elevation of the highest peaks in Oregon? What is the elevation of North Dakota?

4. In what color would this map show a plateau that is 6,000 feet above sea level?

5. How does an elevation map help us learn about geography?

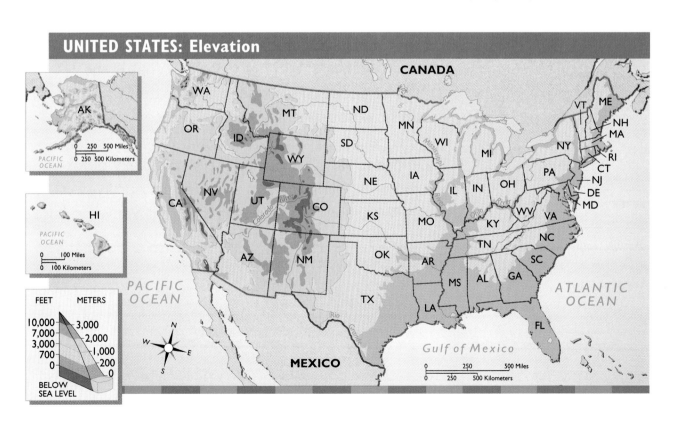

UNITED STATES: Elevation

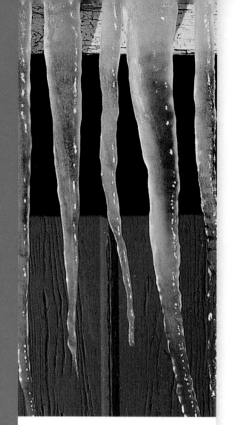

Our Country's Climate

Read Aloud

On a day in May, Point Lay, Alaska, was frozen solid at 8°F. The same day, people in Lake Havasu City, Arizona, watched the thermometer climb to 102°F. Can these places really be in the same country?

Focus Activity

READ TO LEARN

Why is the climate different in different parts of our country?

VOCABULARY

- climate
- temperature
- precipitation

THE BIG PICTURE

These differences are part of weather. Weather describes the air at a certain time and place. It may be hot or cold, rainy or dry, windy or calm. The weather may change very quickly.

Every place has a pattern of weather over many years. This is its climate (KLĪ mit). What is the difference between weather and climate? Weather affects how you live day to day. Climate affects long-range plans.

Different parts of our country have very different climates. Climate plays a big role in our lives. It affects where we live and what clothing we wear. It affects what foods we eat, how we enjoy ourselves, and the type of work we do.

TWO PARTS OF CLIMATE

What questions would you ask to find out about the climate of a certain place in the United States? You might start by asking, "How hot is the summer? How cold is the winter?" These questions ask about temperature (TEM pur uh chur). Temperature is a measure of how hot or cold the air is. Temperature may change quickly. The map below tells you what temperatures to expect in January in the United States.

Another question you would want to ask is "How much precipitation (prih sihp ih TAY shun) falls?" Precipitation is the moisture that falls to the ground. It may be in the form of rain, snow, sleet, or hail. Suppose you lived in Nevada. You might see rain fall only a couple of times a year. Some parts of Hawaii may have rain nearly every day.

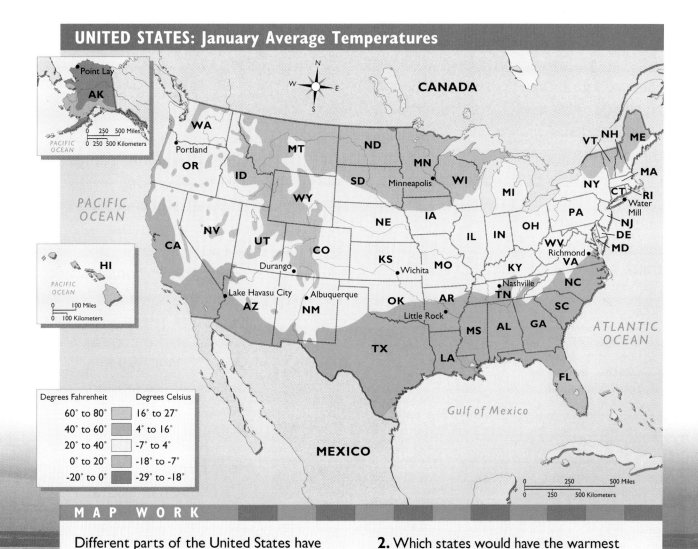

UNITED STATES: January Average Temperatures

Degrees Fahrenheit	Degrees Celsius
60° to 80°	16° to 27°
40° to 60°	4° to 16°
20° to 40°	-7° to 4°
0° to 20°	-18° to -7°
-20° to 0°	-29° to -18°

M A P   W O R K

Different parts of the United States have different temperatures in January.

1. What are the average temperatures in Water Mill, New York?

2. Which states would have the warmest temperatures in January?

3. What is the average temperature in Oklahoma?

INVESTIGATING CLIMATE

You have read about the Marcus family's trip across the United States. As they drove they felt the climate change. Let's find out why.

How Far from the Equator?

The Marcuses left New York in September. Summer was ending, and James had put on a heavy shirt. They reached Nashville, Tennessee, a few days later. The temperature was around 85°F. Even in their T-shirts, they got hot carrying little Nathaniel.

Why was the weather in New York and Nashville different? One reason is that New York is north of Nashville. This means that New York is farther from the equator. The farther from the equator you go, the colder the temperature is.

Find Little Rock, Arkansas, on the map on page 21. Then find Minneapolis, Minnesota. Which city do you think has a cooler climate? Why?

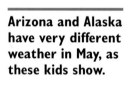

Arizona and Alaska have very different weather in May, as these kids show.

How Far from the Ocean?

Did you ever go swimming on a hot summer day and find your teeth chattering? Water heats up more slowly than air. This means oceans stay cool all through summer. Breezes from the ocean cool the land. Oceans also get cold more slowly than land. In winter, breezes from the ocean bring warmer air to the land.

Places far from the ocean, however, do not feel these breezes. They tend to get hotter in the summer. They also get colder in the winter. "Eastern Oregon was almost as hot as Oklahoma," Iris Marcus said. "The temperature was about 90°F and dry. But as soon as we crossed over the Cascade Mountains, James had to dig out a blanket for Nathaniel." Portland is located near the Pacific Ocean. The summer is not too warm, and the winter not too cold. "We left some of our heaviest winter clothes in New York," she added.

Look at the map on page 21. Will Wichita, Kansas, or Richmond, Virginia, be colder in January?

How High?

The day James and Iris left Albuquerque (AL buh kur kee), New Mexico, they wore shorts and T-shirts. The road climbed steadily into the San Juan Mountains. When they reached Durango, Colorado, they pulled out their sweaters. It did not feel like summer there!

In the last lesson you learned about elevation. Did you realize that it also plays a role in climate? The higher a place is above sea level, the colder its climate usually will be. That's why the Marcuses felt chilly in Durango.

WHY IT MATTERS

People who live in warm climates may not own a single sweater. In cooler climates people have heavy coats, boots, and wool hats.

Our country is very large. This means that the three factors of climate affect different parts of the country in very different ways. As you read about our country, think about how people learn to live in their environment.

Freeze or Fry?

On a day in August in 1996, you would have been shivering in Truckee, California, at 37°F. On the same day in Death Valley, California, the heat really could have been deadly at 118°F! Yet they are only 280 miles apart. Truckee is 5,818 feet above sea level. At its lowest point, Death Valley is 282 feet below sea level!

If you could climb from Death Valley to Truckee, how many feet in elevation would you climb? How many degrees would the temperature have decreased if you had climbed that day in August?

Reviewing Facts and Ideas

MAIN IDEAS

- Climate is the pattern of weather a place has over a long period of time.
- The United States has many different climates.
- Temperature and precipitation are two key parts of climate.
- Three factors that affect climate are distance from the equator, distance from oceans, and elevation.

THINK ABOUT IT

1. What is the difference between climate and weather?

2. As you move away from the equator, what happens to the climate?

3. **FOCUS** Why do different parts of our country have different climates?

4. **THINKING SKILL** _Predict_ whether Maine will usually have a very hot summer. Explain your prediction.

5. **GEOGRAPHY** Describe the climate of your area. How do the three factors of climate affect it?

Our Country's Resources

Read Aloud

The poet Walt Whitman described the Interior Plains as "the inexhaustible land of wheat . . . coal, [and] iron." By "inexhaustible," or unlimited, he meant that our natural riches would last forever. But our country's environment is not unlimited. How do Americans make sure we will have enough of what we need for the future?

Focus Activity

READ TO LEARN

In what ways are resources important?

VOCABULARY

- natural resource
- conservation
- recycle
- renewable resources
- pollution
- nonrenewable resources
- mineral
- fuel

THE BIG PICTURE

As you have read, people's lives are shaped by their environment in many ways. But people also use and shape their environment. For example, people cut down forests for wood. They also build dams to create lakes and reservoirs to hold water. Something in the environment that people can use is called a natural resource (REE sors).

We depend on our environment for clean air, water, food, and other things. The United States is rich in natural resources but they will not last forever. Natural resources can be used up or damaged, and our country's future depends on using them wisely. In this lesson you will learn about natural resources and why is it important to respect and care for them.

CONSERVATION

A few years ago, students in Yuba City, California, noticed a problem. The trays and utensils in their cafeteria were plastic. The plastic was polystyrene (pahl ee STĪ reen). After each meal the trays and utensils were thrown away. This meant tons of garbage piling up somewhere else. It also meant that more natural resources were being used to make new plastic.

The students talked about the problem with their teachers. To show their concern, some students decided not to eat in the cafeteria. They showed their support for conservation (kahn sur VAY shun). Conservation is the careful use of our natural resources.

Recycling

The principal agreed that the students were right. Today the used trays and utensils are rinsed and bagged. Then they are brought to a factory, where they are recycled (ree SĪ kuld). To recycle something is to use it again. Look at the flowchart on this page to see how the lunch trays might be recycled.

Sometimes products are recycled in surprising ways. A factory in Ronkonkoma, New York, makes park benches and picnic tables from recycled plastic bottles. Recycling is one way to practice conservation. What recycled products do you use?

Lunch trays in many cafeterias are made of polystyrene, a kind of plastic. What are some products that can be made from recycled polystyrene?

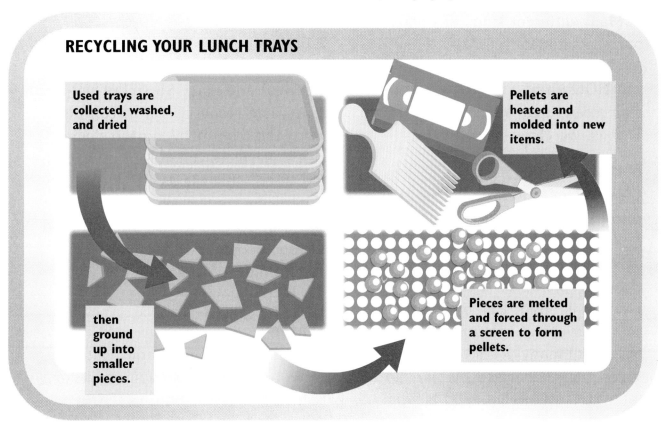

RECYCLING YOUR LUNCH TRAYS

Used trays are collected, washed, and dried

then ground up into smaller pieces.

Pieces are melted and forced through a screen to form pellets.

Pellets are heated and molded into new items.

The farmer tilling his field, the girl drinking water, and the logger hauling trees are all making use of renewable resources.

RENEWING RESOURCES

Many different kinds of things in our environment are natural resources. Some are renewable (rih NOO uh bul) resources. *Renewable* means that we can renew them. That is, we can replace them.

Forests

Trees, for example, are renewable resources because they can be replanted. When a lumber company cuts down an area of forest, workers often plant new trees.

Yet it is important for us to conserve our forest resources. Some trees take many years to grow. Trees may be harmed by pollution (puh LOO shun). Pollution is what makes our air, water, or soil dirty. It is harmful to many plants and animals. Car exhausts and other forms of pollution are damaging trees in many areas.

Soil

Farmers plant crops in the same soil over and over. So soil is also a renewable resource. But it can be worn out from growing too many crops. Farmers renew soil by adding the "food" that plants use up as they grow. Our country has rich soil. It can produce more than enough food for our people. Farmers must be careful that soil does not get worn out or polluted.

Water

No one can live without water. How many things do you use it for? Drinking and washing, watering crops, and making electricity are all necessary to our lives. Every time it rains, water is returned to our land and rivers. This means that water is also a renewable resource.

One problem is that water does get dirty. Pollution may kill fish. It may make water unsafe to drink. Many communities have treatment plants to remove waste from their water supply. There may always be plenty of water in the ocean or in clouds. Still, dry places may run dangerously low on fresh water.

Nonrenewable Resources

Other kinds of resources are nonrenewable. This means that there is a limited supply of the resource. When we have used it up, it will be gone forever.

Minerals are nonrenewable resources. A mineral is a natural substance that is found in the earth. Iron, silver, and copper are all minerals. They are used to make such things as steel, coins, and jewelry.

Fuels (FYOO ulz) such as oil, natural gas, and coal are also non-renewable resources.

We use fuels to make heat or energy. With fuels we heat our homes, plow fields, and cook meals. They power cars, buses, and airplanes.

Fuels for the Future

You can see how much we depend on fuels. But they are non-renewable resources. Someday they will be gone.

We must start preparing for the future now. That's why scientists are trying to develop new sources of energy. Solar power is one possibility. Wind power is another.

Nuclear power is a widely used source of electricity. In 1995 there were 109 nuclear power plants in the United States, about one-third of the world's total nuclear plants. Some people have raised ques- tions about the safety of nuclear power. Because of this, fewer nuclear power plants are being built today.

Gasoline is a fuel you see all the time. Coins and bicycle wheels are made from minerals. These resources are nonrenewable.

27

PEOPLE ARE A RESOURCE

The natural resources you have just read about are found in the earth or water. But there is another important resource you should not overlook: people.

People are the key resource that makes our country work. Farmers plan how and when to plant their crops. Miners and oil workers produce the fuels we need. Factory workers make cars, furniture, clothing, and a thousand other products, including the book you are reading. Without human resources, natural resources would be worthless to us.

Let's look at two examples of human resources. Pam Stills-Dent is a computer programmer in Avon, Connecticut. "Computer programming skills are pretty complex," she says. "You have to learn a whole new language that computers understand." That's why many people study programming for years. Their skills may be used in running machines. They may solve complicated math problems. Or they may create computer games.

Alva Richardson is a water quality expert in Oregon. His job is to make sure that his county's rivers and streams are clean. He travels around the area collecting water in bottles. "Then we bring the bottled samples back to the lab to study them. If the water contains any pollution, we try to figure out where it is coming from," Alva says. Alva's skills and knowledge help protect one of Oregon's natural resources.

The skills people need to use a computer or test water are examples of the importance of human resources. Human resources let us make use of natural resources.

28

Tomorrow's Human Resources

Natural resources need to be developed. So do human resources. In our case, education is the best form of development.

When we are young, education helps us to read and write and do mathematics. Most importantly, it teaches us to ask questions about the world around us. Later on, we may go to school to learn a job skill. Education prepares us for the challenges and adventures of the future.

WHY IT MATTERS

In this lesson you read about resources. They are part of what makes our country strong. So we must make wise choices about using them. We could easily run low on minerals, fuels, or forests. Then we would have to buy them from other countries. That is expensive. If we do not develop our human resources, we cannot make the best use of what we have.

Humans could not survive without natural resources. As you read this book you will study different parts of our country and the world. Think about how people in these different environments have made use of the resources they have. You may find out that your environment has more to do with your life than you thought.

✓ Reviewing Facts and Ideas

MAIN IDEAS

- Natural resources are things in the environment that are useful to people.
- Conservation helps to protect our renewable and nonrenewable resources.
- People are our most important resource.
- The wise use of resources is important to our future.

THINK ABOUT IT

1. Give three examples of natural resources. Are they renewable or nonrenewable?

2. In what ways are people a resource?

3. **FOCUS** Predict what might happen if we fail to protect a key resource such as water?

4. **THINKING SKILL** *Classify* solar power as a resource. Is it renewable or nonrenewable? Why?

5. **GEOGRAPHY** Name one natural resource that is important to the area in which you live. What do people use this resource for?

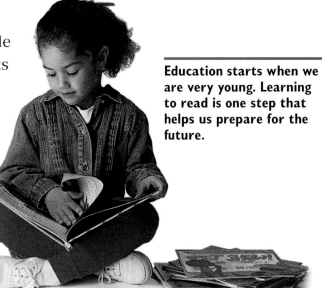

Education starts when we are very young. Learning to read is one step that helps us prepare for the future.

CHAPTER 1 REVIEW

THINKING ABOUT VOCABULARY

Number a sheet of paper from 1 to 5. Next to each number write the letter of the definition that best matches the word.

1. geography
   a. The study of the people who live on Earth
   b. The study of transportation
   c. The study of the way people live on Earth
   d. The study of Earth and the things on it

2. environment
   a. An area where plants grow freely
   b. The surroundings in which people, plants, or animals live
   c. A warm, rainy area
   d. An area where weather and climate have no effect on living things

3. climate
   a. The day-to-day weather of an area
   b. The changes in temperature over a period of a month or more
   c. Distance from the equator
   d. The pattern of weather of an area over a long period of time

4. conservation
   a. The dirt that gets into air or water
   b. The misuse of our environment
   c. The careful use of natural resources
   d. Anything in the environment that people use

5. fuel
   a. Any renewable resource
   b. Any nonrenewable resource
   c. Anything that pollutes the air
   d. Anything that creates heat or energy

THINKING ABOUT FACTS

1. Name three different landforms that are found in the United States.
2. What mountain range stretches from Maine to Alabama?
3. What mountains cover much of the western United States?
4. Across what landforms does the Mississippi River flow?
5. What three factors affect climate?
6. What is the difference between climate and weather?
7. What is pollution?
8. Name a renewable resource.
9. How can people help to protect natural resources?
10. Why are people an important resource?

THINK AND WRITE

WRITING A DESCRIPTION
Write a paragraph that describes the area of Oklahoma in which you live. Include landforms and information about climate in your description.

WRITING AN ADVERTISEMENT
Suppose you want to start a conservation project in your school. Design and write an advertisement about conserving water or some other resource.

WRITING AN EXPLANATION
You have read how climate is affected by three factors. Write an explanation of how the climate in different parts of the country is affected by distance from the ocean, distance from the equator, and elevation.

APPLYING GEOGRAPHY SKILLS

ELEVATION MAPS

Answer the following questions about the map of West Virginia on this page to practice your skill at reading elevation maps.

1. How do you know this is an elevation map?

2. What landform in West Virginia has the highest elevation?

3. In what color would this map show a mountain that is 2,000 feet above sea level?

4. What is the approximate elevation of the city of Wheeling?

5. Why was it useful for the Marcus family to have elevation maps with them on their trip?

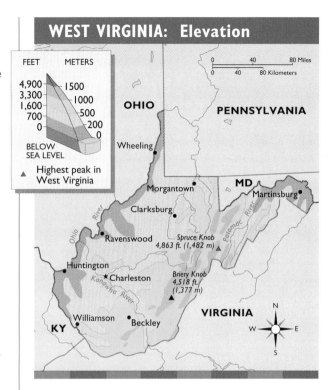

WEST VIRGINIA: Elevation

Summing Up the Chapter

Use the following word map to organize information from the chapter. Copy the word map on a sheet of paper. Then write at least one piece of information in each blank circle. When you have filled in the map, use it to help you write a paragraph that answers the question "How does your environment affect how you live?"

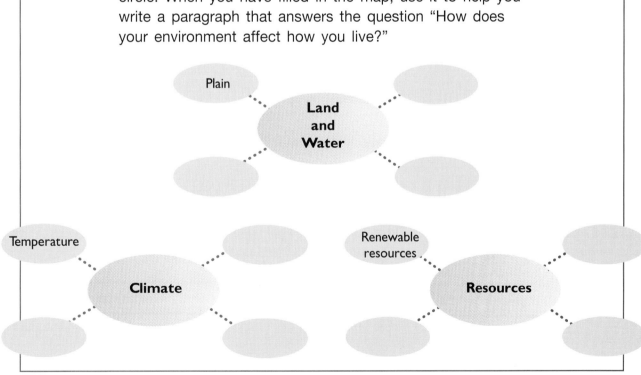

CHAPTER 2

Our Country's People

THINKING ABOUT GEOGRAPHY AND CULTURE

Americans are different in many ways. However, we have many things in common. We obey the same laws. We respect the ideas on which the United States is based.

All Americans also have special customs and ways of living that make us proud of our country. We also work hard to earn a living and keep the United States strong.

CANADA

UNITED STATES

Washington, D.C.

ATLANTIC OCEAN

PACIFIC OCEAN

MEXICO

WASHINGTON, D.C.

We celebrate our country's independence with fireworks on the Fourth of July. The capital is a special place to be on this day.

Our Country's People

Read Aloud

The poet Walt Whitman admired the variety of people who lived in the United States. He wrote: "Here is not merely a nation but a teeming nation of nations." People in America come from all over the world. Yet we share beliefs that make us all Americans.

Focus Activity

READ TO LEARN

What do Americans share?

VOCABULARY

- culture
- custom
- ancestor
- immigrant
- slavery
- heritage
- ethnic group

THE BIG PICTURE

As you read, in the last chapter, our country includes an amazing variety of natural resources. However, countries are made up of more than land and water. Even more important are people.

In order to really understand our country, we must study its people. We must also study their **culture**, or way of life. Culture includes many things people share. People speak languages. They observe holidays. They hold beliefs. They practice religions. They make music. All these things are part of culture. Culture even includes the jobs people do. People in the United States have many different cultures. These cultures have all contributed to the American way of life. Our country has a rich and fascinating culture because so many people have added to it.

PEOPLE AND CULTURE

"Can I have a drumstick?" "Please pass the gravy!" On Thanksgiving, many Americans eat a turkey dinner with all the trimmings.

Customs

Celebrating Thanksgiving is an example of an American custom. A custom is the special way a group of people does something. Customs are an important part of culture. Giving birthday gifts, for example, is a custom in many cultures of the world. What other customs are common in your culture?

Cultures have different customs. When you sit down at the table, you may pick up a knife and fork. But many Americans will pick up chopsticks. Others will use thin strips of bread to pick up and eat their food. These different ways of eating are part of their cultures.

At a Street Fair

Many American towns and cities hold street fairs. Imagine being at the Grand Avenue fair in St. Paul, Minnesota. People in booths are selling crafts they have made. There are games of skill where you can win prizes. But your nose leads you away to the booths where you can try many different foods.

You might have *lefse* (LEF suh), a Swedish potato bread. You could eat some Native American fry bread. A German *bratwurst* on a roll smells good! Or maybe you will try *shish kebab,* an Armenian dish of roasted meat or vegetables. People from Vietnam are cooking egg rolls. The chef of an Ethiopian restaurant is offering a spicy chicken and peanut stew in another booth.

These foods come from different cultures. But they are all served at American tables. A variety of cultures helps to make America an exciting place.

Trying foods from different cultures makes this street fair fun as well as tasty.

OUR ANCESTORS

Why do the American people have so many different customs and cultures? The answer has to do with our ancestors (AN ses turz). Beginning with your parents and grandparents, your ancestors are all those in your family who were born before you. Our ancestors came to this country from many lands.

The First Americans

Some Americans can trace their roots in this country far into the past. These are American Indians, who are also called Indians. Their ancestors were the first people to live on this continent.

American Indians live in all parts of the United States. In addition to English, many American Indians also speak the languages their ancestors spoke.

New Americans

For thousands of years, American Indians were the only people in North America. Today, people from almost every country of the world live here. What happened? In the 1600s, immigrants (IHM ih gruntz) began to arrive. An immigrant is a person who comes to a new land from another place to live.

Most immigrants came here to find a better life. However, around 600,000 Africans were brought here against their will in slavery. Slavery is the practice of making one person the property of another. Enslaved people were forced to work without pay and had no freedom. Slavery ended in the United States in 1865.

Do you have pictures of your ancestors at home? In which countries were they born? Ask members of your family about your ancestors.

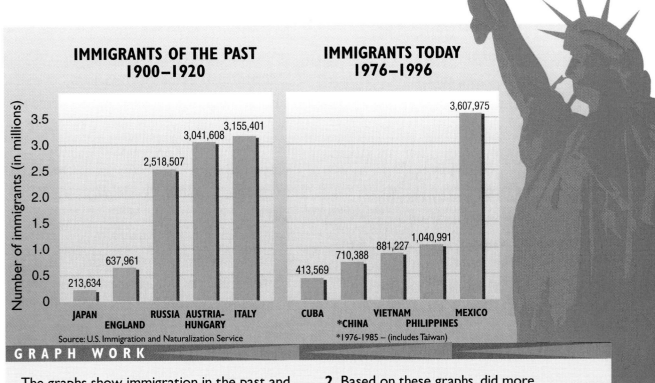

IMMIGRANTS OF THE PAST 1900–1920

Number of immigrants (in millions)

- JAPAN — 213,634
- ENGLAND — 637,961
- RUSSIA — 2,518,507
- AUSTRIA-HUNGARY — 3,041,608
- ITALY — 3,155,401

Source: U.S. Immigration and Naturalization Service

IMMIGRANTS TODAY 1976–1996

- CUBA — 413,569
- *CHINA — 710,388
- VIETNAM — 881,227
- PHILIPPINES — 1,040,991
- MEXICO — 3,607,975

*1976-1985 – (includes Taiwan)

GRAPH WORK

The graphs show immigration in the past and recently.

1. How many immigrants arrived from Italy between 1900 and 1920?

2. Based on these graphs, did more immigrants arrive in the United States between 1900 and 1920 or between 1976 and 1996?

Heritage

In 1996 more than 900,000 immigrants arrived in the United States. Look at the graphs above to compare the immigrants of today with those who came in the past.

One person who came to this country is 12-year-old Earle Carrion. "I came to San Francisco, California, in April," Earle explains. "Before that I lived in Manila, in the Philippines." Find the Philippines on the world map on page R10. Although they now live in the United States, Earle and his family value their Philippine heritage (HER ih tihj). Heritage is the history and traditions a group of people share. At school Earle speaks English. At home, however, the Carrion family speaks both English and Tagalog (tah GAH lug). Tagalog is a language spoken in the Philippines. Earle's mother also continues to prepare foods that are part of Philippine tradition. "One dish that we eat is called *lumpia,*" Earle says. "It's ground meat wrapped in a dough as thin as paper."

A Common Heritage

People with a common heritage form an ethnic group. An ethnic group is a group of people whose ancestors are from the same country or area. Ethnic groups keep customs that started in other places alive here in the United States. Honoring our ethnic heritage as well as our American heritage is part of what it means to be an American.

WHAT AMERICANS SHARE

Many Americans keep alive the heritage of their ethnic groups. Yet we all share many things as Americans. For example, most of us go to school for at least 12 years.

When you step onto the baseball diamond or the basketball court, you are enjoying yourself. But you are also sharing an American custom.

Americans also share important ideas. We obey the same laws. And we respect the freedoms of other people. Respect for others is part of our country's heritage.

Sharing a Dream

As you have read, many people leave their homes in other countries to come to the United States. They hope to find jobs or land.

Immigrants have also looked to the United States as a land of freedom. Here they can practice their religions. They can express their views freely. They can own their own businesses. These rights are ours as Americans.

Not all people who came to the United States found freedom and a better life. Yet all Americans share in the same dream. They dream of a country where all people are treated equally. Read the words of the poet Langston Hughes on the next page. How did he describe coming to the United States?

Parades and sports are two examples of things that bring us together as Americans. They are part of our American culture.

The Granger Collection

MANY VOICES
LITERATURE

**Excerpt from
"Let America Be America Again,"
written by
Langston Hughes in 1936.**

*O, I'm the man who sailed
those early seas
In search of what I meant to be
my home—
For I'm the one who left dark
Ireland's shore,
And Poland's plain, and Eng-
land's grassy lea,
And torn from Black Africa's
strand I came
To build a "homeland of the
free."*

*The free?
A dream—
Still beckoning to me!*

_____
lea: pasture
strand: shore
beckoning: reaching out

WHY IT MATTERS

The search for freedom has drawn many people to the United States. We enjoy many rights as Americans. One of the most important is the right to express our views on how our country is run. The United States was one of the first countries in the world whose people had this right. We'll learn about another right in the next lesson—the right to own and run our businesses.

✓✓ **Reviewing Facts and Ideas**

MAIN IDEAS

- All people have a culture, or way of life.

- Americans came to this country in different ways.

- An ethnic group is made up of people with a common heritage.

- All Americans share our country's heritage.

THINK ABOUT IT

1. What is an ancestor?

2. What can we learn about a group by studying its culture?

3. FOCUS What heritage do all Americans share?

4. THINKING SKILL *Predict* some of the ways in which our country might be different if immigrants had not come here. Explain why your prediction would be accurate.

5. WRITE Suppose you are arriving in the United States for the first time. Write a letter to a friend describing your new home.

GATEWAYS
TO THE United States

During most of our country's history, immigrants have arrived by sea. Most of the immigrants crossing the Atlantic Ocean entered New York Harbor. On the Pacific Coast, San Francisco was the place where most immigrants arrived.

In New York City new arrivals have been greeted by the sight of the Statue of Liberty, built in 1886. Since 1937, immigrants to San Francisco have sailed under the Golden Gate Bridge. Both of these "gateways" are symbols that have become important American legacies. They stand for our country's welcoming of people from all parts of the world.

Today many immigrants to our country arrive by airplane. Airports throughout the United States are "gateways" to thousands of immigrants each year.

The beautiful Golden Gate Bridge was named for the waterway that connects San Francisco and the Pacific Ocean. Ships pass under the bridge as they enter San Francisco Bay.

Over one million people from all over the world visit the Statue of Liberty each year. For newcomers and visitors alike, the statue is a symbol of freedom and opportunity.

The poem below was written by Emma Lazarus in 1883 for the Statue of Liberty. It was then placed on a plaque near the entrance to the statue.

THE NEW COLOSSUS.

NOT LIKE THE BRAZEN GIANT OF GREEK FAME,
WITH CONQUERING LIMBS ASTRIDE FROM LAND TO LAND;
HERE AT OUR SEA-WASHED, SUNSET GATES SHALL STAND
A MIGHTY WOMAN WITH A TORCH, WHOSE FLAME
IS THE IMPRISONED LIGHTNING, AND HER NAME
MOTHER OF EXILES. FROM HER BEACON-HAND
GLOWS WORLD-WIDE WELCOME; HER MILD EYES COMMAND
THE AIR-BRIDGED HARBOR THAT TWIN CITIES FRAME.
"KEEP ANCIENT LANDS, YOUR STORIED POMP!"
        CRIES SHE
WITH SILENT LIPS. "GIVE ME YOUR TIRED, YOUR
        POOR,
YOUR HUDDLED MASSES YEARNING TO BREATHE FREE,
THE WRETCHED REFUSE OF YOUR TEEMING SHORE.
SEND THESE, THE HOMELESS, TEMPEST-TOST TO ME,
I LIFT MY LAMP BESIDE THE GOLDEN DOOR!"

THIS TABLET, WITH HER SONNET TO THE BARTHOLDI STATUE
OF LIBERTY ENGRAVED UPON IT, IS PLACED UPON THESE WALLS
IN LOVING MEMORY OF
EMMA LAZARUS
BORN IN NEW YORK CITY, JULY 22ª 1849
DIED NOVEMBER 19ª 1887.

Thinking Skills

Decision Making

VOCABULARY
decision

WHY THE SKILL MATTERS

Decision making is a skill people use every day. Making a decision is the same as making a choice. You have to make up your mind what to do. Decisions may be simple, like deciding what clothes to wear, or more difficult, like deciding where to live. To make a good decision, you have to know what your goal is.

When immigrants came to this country they made many decisions. First they made the important decision to leave their homeland. Their goal was to find a

better life. When they arrived in this country they had to decide where they wanted to live.

Many early immigrants to Oklahoma decided to work in the coal mines in the southeastern part of our state. They came from countries such as Mexico and Italy. The miners' new lives were very difficult. Coal mining was a hard and dangerous job. The miners were also far away from home. The climate in Oklahoma was much different from what they were used to.

USING THE SKILL

Today, newcomers to Oklahoma have more choices. They can decide to live in one of our state's urban or rural areas. Of course, most people live where they can find work. Let's read about a newcomer to our state who is deciding where to live.

Miguel Rodriguez has just arrived in Oklahoma from Mexico. He is staying with relatives in Oklahoma City while he makes his plans. His relatives want Miguel to stay with them, but he doesn't like big cities. Miguel is thinking of taking a job on a horse ranch outside Ponca City. But this means he would be far away from his family, who are the only people he knows in his new country.

Here are some of the possible results of each choice:

- Miguel may find it difficult to live in a new location where he has no family.
- Miguel may learn to like living in Oklahoma City.
- Miguel may not be able to find a job that uses his skills in Oklahoma City.

If your goal were to find a good place to live, what decision would you make?

TRYING THE SKILL

Suppose your family is planning to take a summer vacation. Your family must choose a place to go camping. Your two choices are in different regions of our state.

Helping yourself

- **A decision** is a choice about what to do.
- **Identify the choices you can make, and predict the results of each choice.**
- **Make the choice that helps you reach your goal.**

The first choice is Chickasaw National Recreation Area in the Arbuckle Mountains. Here, your parents can relax in the cool mountain air. You could swim and fish in the beautiful natural lakes. You and your brother might also enjoy watching birds and other wildlife.

The other choice is Robbers Cave State Park near Wilburton, in the southeastern part of our state. There, you can rent a horse for a guided trail ride. Your parents may like to bicycle and pedal along the miles of bike trails. Your family could also take a hike to visit Robbers Cave. This cave was once a hideout for the famous cowboy Jesse James.

Each member of your family has one vote. You will have to decide which location to choose. Use the Helping Yourself box for hints. What is your goal for the vacation? What do you think the results of either choice might be?

REVIEWING THE SKILL

1. What is a decision?

2. Look at the section called Trying The Skill. If your goal were to learn how to fish, how would you have voted?

3. How will predicting the results of choices help you make a good decision?

4. Why is making a decision an important skill?

Our Country's Economy

Read Aloud

In 1993 over 50,000 Americans were asked this question: What do you think is the most important issue facing the country? More than four out of five gave the same answer: the economy.

Focus Activity

READ TO LEARN

What goes into running a business?

VOCABULARY

- economy
- services
- free enterprise
- profit
- investor
- manufacturing
- transportation
- interdependent

THE BIG PICTURE

As you read, Americans are united in many ways. For example, we work to make our **economy** strong. An economy is the way a country uses or produces natural resources, goods, and **services**. Services are jobs people do to help others.

One of the strengths of our economy is the **free enterprise** system. This system lets people own and run their own businesses. People in business decide what to make or buy and how much to charge for their products. People shopping in stores can choose between different products. The free enterprise system allows Americans to make their own economic decisions.

THE SEEDS OF A BUSINESS

Every year people start thousands of new businesses in our country. Here is how a food business called "Food From the 'Hood" got its start.

Crops to College

In the fall of 1992, 39 students at Crenshaw High School in Los Angeles, California, had an idea. They planted a garden in a weedy area next to the football field. They raised squash, tomatoes, and other vegetables and herbs.

The students wanted to sell their crop. The profit would help pay for them to go to college. Profit is the money a business earns after it pays for tools, salaries, and other costs. In a free enterprise system, people who own businesses can use their profits however they wish. These owners wanted to pay for college.

One student, Jaynell Grayson, said, "We realized the best thing we could do for our community is to get an education."

Salad to Dressing

Selling the vegetables made less profit than the students had hoped. After the first year, sales had earned only $600. The garden had inspired a new product, though. They were already growing vegetables for salad. Why not make a salad dressing?

Recently a new salad dressing appeared in stores. It was called "Straight Out 'the Garden." Soon, over 2,000 stores were selling "Straight Out 'the Garden."

Soon "Food From the 'Hood" had provided nearly $27,000 in college scholarships to its student-owners. One student sums it up in this way: "Together we are making a difference. And it feels great."

The owners of "Food From the 'Hood" proudly show the salad dressing they created.

45

HOW A BUSINESS WORKS

The students at Crenshaw High made their salad dressing into a success. But starting a business and running it means a lot of work. Let's take a closer look at how "Straight Out 'the Garden" dressing got on the shelves in stores.

Investors

Starting up a business costs a lot. Most businesses need to borrow money to get started. An investor is someone who puts money into a business. The investor usually wants to get some of the profit in return. Some community groups gave Food From the 'Hood money to start their company. They did not ask to be paid back because they liked the students' plan to earn their own college money.

The students spent six months trying out recipes in their science class. "We're big into basil and parsley," said Mark Sarria. Then the editor of a food magazine tasted the dressing and liked it. The owners of Food From the 'Hood knew they had a hit on their hands.

Now the students had their recipe. Next they needed to begin manufacturing. Manufacturing means making large amounts of a product in a factory. A manufacturer named Paula Savett explained the process to the students. She showed

them how "Straight Out 'the Garden" could be mixed in huge tubs and put in bottles. Food From the 'Hood uses only natural, healthful ingredients.

An Eyecatcher

Even the most tasty dressing might just sit on the store shelves. To sell, it must be noticed among many other brands. This is why the bottle is important. A student named Ben Osborne created the label. He designed a blossoming garden. "If you look closely," Ben says, "you see pink, purple, green, and red people in the middle of the garden. Everyone is welcome here." Ben hoped that shoppers would notice the bottle and want to try their product.

STATEMENT OF PURPOSE
1. CREATE JOBS.
2. GIVE BACK TO THE COMMUNITY.
3. PROTECT THE ENVIRONMENT.
4. LEARN FROM OUR EXPERIENCE.
5. SHOW WHAT WE CAN ACCOMPLISH.
6. BE PROFITABLE.

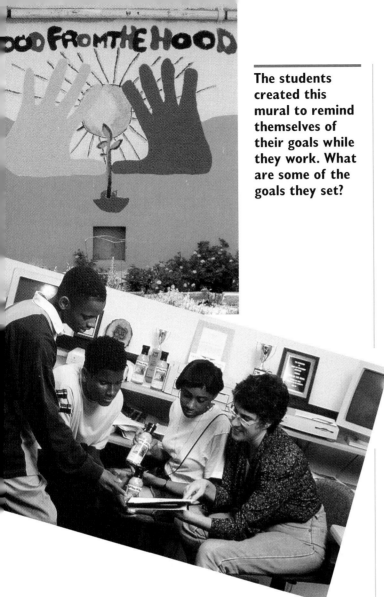

FOOD FROM THE HOOD

The students created this mural to remind themselves of their goals while they work. What are some of the goals they set?

Onto the Shelves

Next the students needed to get the dressing into stores. The students had to convince grocery stores to carry their product. They told them that selling "Straight Out 'the Garden" would make money.

Jaynell Grayson got a group of stores called Lucky Stores to carry "Straight Out 'the Garden." The buyer for Lucky Stores said, "If I was served [this dressing] in a restaurant, I'd be very happy." Soon nearly every large supermarket in Los Angeles was carrying the dressing.

Also, lots of people were pouring it on salads at home.

The dressing started to sell. Now the students had to keep track of their money. How much money had they spent? How much had they made? This was hard work. Some students took extra math courses. An accountant also helped the students. They learned to run a computer program to keep track of the money.

Services

As you can see, the Food From the 'Hood company does much more than just mix dressing.

The students had to sell their product. Selling is an example of a service. Creating a label and keeping track of money are other services. These services are very important to a successful business. In fact, many companies offer services to other companies. They don't make their own products. An advertising company, for example, may help hundreds of other companies. Advertising is a service that helps to sell a product.

Services are a key part of our economy. Teachers provide services. So do doctors, police officers, and government workers. In fact, about 7 out of 10 Americans work in services. About 2 out of 10 Americans work in manufacturing. How would you classify the jobs people in your family do? Would you call them manufacturing or service jobs?

TRANSPORTATION

You have read that "Straight Out 'the Garden" dressing is mixed in huge tubs in a factory. How do the bottles of dressing get to the stores?

Their arrival depends on an important service: transportation. Transportation means moving goods or people from one place to another. Cars, trucks, buses, trains, airplanes, and ships are all used for transportation in our country.

What would happen to our economy without transportation? Farmers would not get their crops to stores. People in cold areas might not have fuel to heat their houses. You could not send a package to a friend. You would only be able to buy products made in your community. For example, you might not be able to buy a pair of sneakers, a can of juice, or a bottle of dressing.

Interdependence

Transportation is very important. Without transportation, no part of the country could meet all the needs and wants of its people. The 50 United States are interdependent. This means that each state needs other states to meet the needs and wants of its people.

Look at the picture on the next page. This basket has food for a picnic. Where does all this food come from? The salad dressing was made in California. Some of the fruit and vegetables were also grown in that state. The bread, however, was

Transportation means moving goods or people from one place to another. What are some jobs people have in transportation?

Every day you eat food that comes from far away. This is one reason why transportation is such an important service.

made from wheat grown in Kansas or Oklahoma. The chicken comes from Arkansas.

Notice that this meal comes from many places. Kansas grows more wheat than any other state. People all over the country eat its wheat. But the climate of Kansas is too cold to grow much lettuce or tomatoes. So it gets them from California or other, warmer states. Kansas and California are interdependent.

WHY IT MATTERS

In a free enterprise system, people make their own economic decisions. Food From the 'Hood made some good decisions that made it a successful business. Our economy depends on people and businesses that are willing to take risks.

Different parts of our country have different resources and make different products. Interdependence allows each part of the country to sell the things it has and buy the things it does not have. In the next lesson you will learn more about what makes each part of our country special.

✔ Reviewing Facts and Ideas

MAIN IDEAS

- An economy is the way a country uses resources to meet its people's needs and wants.
- Manufacturing could not take place without services, which are a growing part of our economy.
- All areas of the United States are interdependent.

THINK ABOUT IT

1. What is the free enterprise system?

2. Why is transportation such an important service?

3. **FOCUS** What activities go into running a business?

4. **THINKING SKILL** *Decide* what kind of business you would like to run. Would you produce goods or supply services? How did you make this decision?

5. **GEOGRAPHY** Identify three products you use that are made outside of your community. Then find on a map where these products come from.

Our Country's Regions

Read Aloud

Four children wearing blindfolds were led to an elephant and asked to describe it. One said, "It is long and skinny like a snake." Another said, "It is thick like a tree trunk." The next said, "It is soft and floppy." The last said, "It is so big I can't get my arms around it." Who gave the best description?

Focus Activity

READ TO LEARN

How does studying regions help us learn about our country?

VOCABULARY

- region
- history

THE BIG PICTURE

The students all gave good descriptions of the elephant. But they were describing different parts. Yet without all of them the elephant would not be an elephant.

What if you were asked to describe the United States? Would you say it was warm or cold most of the year? Would you say it was a place of huge cities or small towns? Would you say its people have lived here for thousands of years or for only a few?

All of these things are true. They are parts of our country, which like pieces of a puzzle fit together to form a whole.

FIVE REGIONS

The puzzle pieces you just read about have a name. Geographers call each piece a **region** (REE jun). A region is an area with common features that set it apart from other areas. In this lesson we will read about five regions of our country. Look at the map below. Which region do you live in?

Geographers find it useful to divide the country into regions. So do other people. For example, the United States Postal Service has its own set of regions. They use ten regions instead of five! Let's say you are sending a letter from Ohio to Montana. It might be sent first to the Allegheny Area office, which is in Pennsylvania. Then it might be sent by airplane with many other pieces of mail to the Western Area office. This office is in Colorado. Your letter would go from Colorado to Montana. This makes delivery quicker and more efficient.

What other regions are you familiar with? Sports such as basketball have regional divisions. Teams in each region of the country play each other. Then the winning teams from each region compete for a national championship.

Dividing the country into regions helps the Postal Service deliver mail quickly. Using regions helps geographers describe and understand our country.

REGIONS OF THE UNITED STATES

WEST · MIDDLE WEST · NORTHEAST · SOUTHWEST · SOUTHEAST

MAP WORK

In this lesson we will learn about our country by studying five **regions**.

1. Which region has the fewest states?
2. Which region looks smallest in area?
3. Find Oklahoma. What region is it in?
4. Have you ever visited another state? What region was it in? Did you notice any differences from your state?

WHAT MAKES A REGION?

The five regions of the United States are the Southeast, the Northeast, the Middle West, the Southwest, and the West. What kinds of common features define each region?

A Region's History

Each region is shaped by the people who have lived there. Each region has its own environment. Each region also has a **history**, a story of the past.

Let's look at one example. The Southwest has long been the home of the Pueblo and Navajo Native Americans. For many years it was part of the country of Mexico. The history of the Southwest makes it different from other regions.

A Region's Heritage

The settlers of the Southwest also helped form its culture. Many Southwesterners today have Mexican ancestors. Many places such as Mesa, Arizona, have names that come from Spanish, the language of Mexico. Even the foods of the Southwest show the region's Mexican heritage. In the United States, foods like tacos and chili were first eaten in the Southwest. Now you can eat these foods anywhere in our country. If you do, you are sharing the culture of the Southwest.

Regions Celebrate

People remember their heritage in celebrations and festivals. Fiestas help Southwesterners remember their Mexican heritage. Many Middle West towns hold Oktoberfests. These harvest festivals were brought by immigrants from Germany. A Northeastern clambake is a cookout that features seafood. It shows how important the sea is in the Northeast.

DID YOU KNOW?

What do you call it?

If you ask for a can of *pop* in the Northeast, you might get some funny looks. A bubbly soft drink there is a *soda*. You might wash down a *hero* sandwich or a *grinder* with it. In New Orleans, Louisiana, however, you would be washing down a *poor boy*. In Los Angeles, California, the same sandwich would be called a *torpedo*.

Here's a riddle. In Alabama it goes by "dam-buster." In Massachusetts they call it a "tree-bender," while Californians know it as a "mud-sender." What is it?

A clambake and a fiesta are both regional festivals. They celebrate what is special about each region.

A Region's Environment

Each of the five regions also has its own special environment. The West is a region of high mountains. The Northeast has mountains that are lower and rounded. The Middle Western states have rich soil.

Of course, regions share parts of their environment. For example, the Southwest and the Southeast are both warm. Most of the Southwest, however, is very dry, while the Southeast gets plenty of rain. Differences in climate are another way that geographers define a region.

WHY IT MATTERS

In the first part of this unit, we have looked at our country's environment. We have also looked at its people and heritage. You have learned about five regions of the United States. In the rest of the unit, we will look at just one region—the Southwest. You will discover the features that make it unique.

✓/// Reviewing Facts and Ideas

MAIN IDEAS

- A region is an area with common features that set it apart from other areas.
- The United States can be divided into five regions.
- Features of its environment, history, and culture make each region unique.

THINK ABOUT IT

1. What is a region?
2. What are the five regions of the United States?
3. **FOCUS** What kinds of features help us define a region?
4. **THINKING SKILL** _Compare_ the landforms of the Middle West with those of the Southeast. Use the information on pages 12–13.
5. **WRITE** Suppose you are visiting a region far from where you live. Write a story about the common features that set this region apart from others.

CHAPTER 2 REVIEW

THINKING ABOUT VOCABULARY

Number a sheet of paper from 1 to 10. Next to each number write the word or phrase from the list that best completes the sentence.

ancestors   history
custom   interdependent
economy   investor
ethnic group   profit
heritage   region

1. An _____ is the way a country uses or produces resources, goods, and services.

2. The members of an _____ share a common heritage.

3. The people in your family born before you are your _____.

4. A _____ is a special way a group of people have of doing something.

5. To be _____ means to need one another.

6. A _____ is a geographical area with features that set it apart from other areas.

7. The history and traditions shared by a group of people is their _____.

8. The money a business earns after it pays its expenses is its _____.

9. _____ is a story of the past.

10. Someone who puts money into a business is called an _____.

THINKING ABOUT FACTS

1. Which American ethnic group has ancestors who were the first people to live on this continent?

2. Why have people from many parts of the world immigrated to the United States?

3. What are some customs in the United States?

4. What are some of the customs and traditions of your family?

5. What goal leads an investor to put up money to start a business?

6. What are some of the things that might make a person successful at running a business?

7. What are some services provided by people in your community?

8. What are some of the differences between the various regions of this country?

9. Why is it useful to divide the country into regions?

10. In which region do you live?

THINK AND WRITE

WRITING A DESCRIPTION
Write a paragraph about a custom you are familiar with. Describe the clothing, food, dance, or activities that are part of the custom.

WRITING A POEM
Write a poem describing the geography of the Southwest.

WRITING A NEWSPAPER ARTICLE
Write a newspaper article on the students who started the business called "Food From the 'Hood."

APPLYING THINKING SKILLS

DECISION MAKING

Suppose that you and your friends enjoy riding your bikes in your neighborhood. You notice that one of the stop signs on your street has disappeared. What do you do about it? Answer the following questions to apply your skill at making decisions.

1. What is your goal?
2. What are the possible choices you can make to reach your goal?
3. What do you believe the results of each choice might be?
4. Which choice will you make?
5. Do you think you made the best decision? Why?

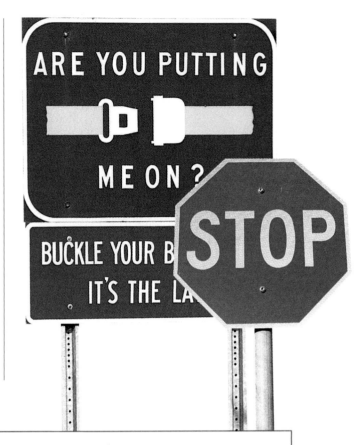

Summing Up the Chapter

Use the horizontal organization chart below to organize information from the chapter. Copy the chart on a sheet of paper. Under each main topic write at least two more words or phrases from the chapter that are related to that topic. When you have completed the chart, use it to write a paragraph titled "What do the people of the United States share?"

ECONOMY	PEOPLE	REGION
investor	custom	history

The Southwestern Environment

THINKING ABOUT GEOGRAPHY AND ECONOMICS

The Southwest region has only four states. Oklahoma, Texas, New Mexico, and Arizona make up this region. Look on the map to find where the photographs were taken. What do these photographs suggest to you about the environment of the Southwest?

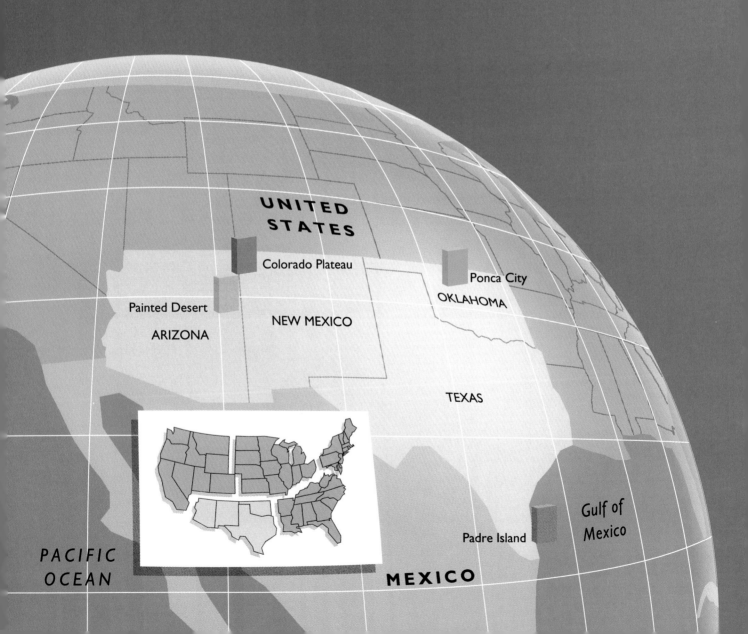

UNITED STATES

Colorado Plateau

Ponca City

OKLAHOMA

Painted Desert

ARIZONA

NEW MEXICO

TEXAS

Gulf of Mexico

Padre Island

PACIFIC OCEAN

MEXICO

Padre Island, TEXAS

The beautiful dunes and beaches of Padre Island National Seashore lie off the coast of Texas, in the Gulf of Mexico.

Ponca City, OKLAHOMA

Oil is one of the Southwest's most important resources. This oil refinery lights up the night.

Painted Desert in ARIZONA

The dry Southwest includes many deserts. Minerals in the rocks give the Painted Desert its amazing red, yellow, and blue colors.

Colorado Plateau in NEW MEXICO

Wild horses roam the rugged Colorado Plateau of Arizona and New Mexico. Much of the region lies on high plateaus such as this.

The Grand Canyon

Read Aloud

"Each morning in the Grand Canyon was a new painting, a creation of rock and rising sun, river and sky." Like most visitors, writer Jim Carrier was amazed by the spectacular beauty of the Grand Canyon.

Focus Activity

READ TO LEARN

What are some of the Southwest's natural features?

VOCABULARY

- mesa
- butte
- canyon
- erosion

PLACES

- Grand Canyon
- Colorado River
- Rio Grande
- Monument Valley

THE BIG PICTURE

The Southwest is made up of only four states: Oklahoma, Texas, New Mexico, and Arizona. It has a variety of landforms. Flat, low land covers the Coastal Plain in Texas. The Rocky Mountains tower above parts of New Mexico and Arizona. It also has mesas (MAY suhz). They look like hills with flat tops. Buttes (BYOOTS) are like mesas, but even smaller. In this lesson you will read about only one natural feature—the Grand Canyon.

A CANYON ERODES

You just read that the Southwest has many high plateaus. One of these is the Colorado Plateau.

Much of the Colorado Plateau is one mile above sea level. It is famous for its canyons. A canyon is a deep, narrow valley with steep sides. Among the deepest is the Grand Canyon.

The Grand Canyon stretches 217 miles through northern Arizona. In some places this gigantic canyon is more than one mile deep! At its widest, the canyon measures 18 miles from one rim, or edge, to the other. If there were a footbridge, it would take about six hours for a person to walk across.

The Power of Erosion

Suppose you were on this footbridge. You would see a ribbon of water at the bottom of the canyon. The ribbon is the Colorado River.

The Colorado River flows southwest out of the Rocky Mountains.

As the river rushes downhill, it causes erosion. This word describes how water, wind, or ice slowly carry away soil and rock.

Over millions of years, the Colorado River cut a path into the plateau. The path gradually grew deeper and deeper. The river also carved the walls of the canyon into fantastic shapes. The mesas and buttes in the Southwest were also formed by erosion.

The Grand Canyon snakes through parts of Arizona. Along the way, park rangers work to keep it clean.

DOWN THE COLORADO

Each year about four million people visit the Grand Canyon. The area is now a national park. In fact it is one of our country's most famous natural features. Many people admire the sights from the rim of the canyon. Others make their way into the canyon itself.

There are several ways to explore the canyon. Visitors can hike along trails to the foot of the canyon. People can also ride mules instead of walking. One of the most exciting ways to explore the Grand Canyon is to go "white water" rafting down the Colorado River.

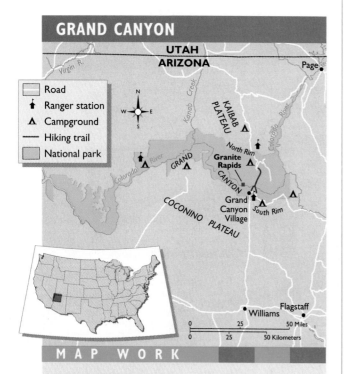

GRAND CANYON

MAP WORK

The Grand Canyon is a deeply eroded canyon of the Colorado Plateau.

1. What tributary of the Colorado River can you find on the map?
2. What plateau lies north of the Grand Canyon?

Into the Canyon

Suppose you wanted to see the canyon by raft. First you must get to the Colorado River. A long hike is ahead of you from the South Rim of the canyon. Find the South Rim on the map on this page.

You begin by going down a steep trail. Far below you can see the Colorado River. From here it looks like a narrow stream. Actually, the river is 300 feet across.

Hours pass as you make your way down the trail. When you stop and look around, you see the beauty of the canyon. The walls drop in terraces, or steps. As you get closer to the river, you see rocks in different shades of blue, gold, purple, and brown in the walls.

Finally you reach the bottom. The river is ice cold. It's much too fast to swim in, but you can dunk your feet to cool off.

Riding the Rapids

Now you climb into a rubber raft. Along with a guide and three other people, you are now ready to "ride the rapids."

What is a rapid? A rapid is where a river flows very swiftly as elevation drops. As the Colorado River flows through the Grand Canyon, it falls over 1,000 feet in elevation. Most of this drop takes place as the river flows over small waterfalls.

"Do you hear that roar?" your guide asks. "We're approaching Granite Rapids." Cold water splashes into the raft as it shoots downward. You feel like you're on a roller coaster. Then, in less than a minute, the water is calm again. There is so much water in the raft that everyone helps to bail it out. Now you know what it is like to be a "river runner"!

Camping and Climbing

Other rapids follow. But then suddenly the river is calm again. You watch the colorful rock walls passing by slowly on either side. A green lizard clings to the underside of a rock. Desert bighorn sheep make their way down a steep slope.

At night your group sets up camp on a sandbar. Moonlight on the rock makes the canyon look black and gray. Far above, stars shine in the night sky.

Your trip down the river takes several more days. Sometimes you stop to hike or climb in the smaller side canyons.

Finally the Grand Canyon's high walls become less steep. The water of the Colorado River is now calm and blue. You have reached the end of the Grand Canyon.

Tourism and the Environment

As you know, millions of visitors enjoy Grand Canyon National Park each year. With such large numbers, visitors must be careful to leave the environment as they found it.

There are strict rules for campers and "river runners." All garbage and waste must be carried out of the canyon. The rules make sure that the park does not become polluted.

A visitor views one of the canyon's many waterfalls (above). Rock climbers work their way up a canyon wall (above right).

Land and Water of the Southwest

The Grand Canyon is probably the best-known natural feature in the Southwest. Of course, the region has many others. What are some of them?

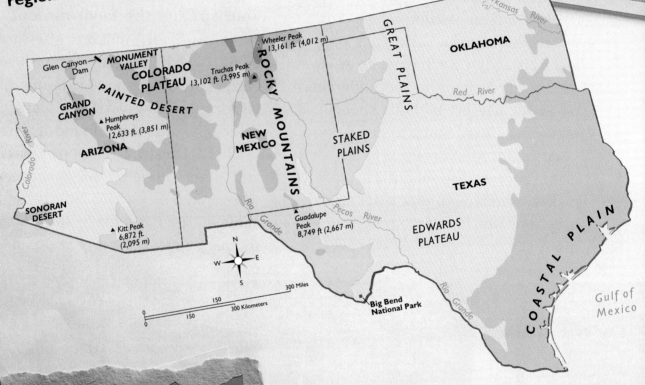

Glen Canyon Dam

MONUMENT VALLEY

COLORADO PLATEAU

Wheeler Peak 13,161 ft. (4,012 m)

Truchas Peak 13,102 ft. (3,995 m)

GRAND CANYON

PAINTED DESERT

Humphreys Peak 12,633 ft. (3,851 m)

NEW MEXICO

ROCKY MOUNTAINS

GREAT PLAINS

OKLAHOMA

Arkansas River

Red River

ARIZONA

STAKED PLAINS

Colorado River

SONORAN DESERT

Kitt Peak 6,872 ft. (2,095 m)

Guadalupe Peak 8,749 ft. (2,667 m)

Rio Grande

Pecos River

TEXAS

EDWARDS PLATEAU

COASTAL PLAIN

Big Bend National Park

Rio Grande

Gulf of Mexico

N W E S

300 Miles

150

0   150   300 Kilometers

THE SOUTHWEST: Elevation

FEET	METERS
10,000	3,000
7,000	2,000
3,000	1,000
700	200
0	0

▲ Highest peak
▲ Mountain peak

BELOW SEA LEVEL

Rocky Mountains

The Rocky Mountains tower over much of New Mexico. The Sangre de Cristo Mountains, shown here, are part of the Rockies.

Great Plains These vast plains, which you read about in Chapter 7, reach into Oklahoma, Texas, and New Mexico.

Colorado Plateau Strange rock formations rise from the floor of Monument Valley, in the Colorado Plateau in Arizona.

Rio Grande The Rio Grande flows out of the Rocky Mountains to form the border between the United States and Mexico. It flows through Big Bend National Park in Texas, shown here.

WHY IT MATTERS

Natural features such as the Grand Canyon are valuable to Americans in many different ways. They amaze us with their beauty and size and the plants and animals living there. They also teach us important lessons about the geography and history of our continent. And as you have read, the Grand Canyon offers many interesting opportunities for recreation. Americans in every region can take pride in their country's natural features.

✓✓ **Reviewing Facts and Ideas**

MAIN IDEAS

- Erosion has carved canyons, mesas, buttes, and other landforms out of Earth's surface.
- Millions of visitors go to Grand Canyon National Park every year.
- The geography of the Grand Canyon provides visitors with many recreational activities.

THINK ABOUT IT

1. What is erosion?

2. Describe how the Grand Canyon was formed.

3. **FOCUS** Why do millions of people from all over the world visit the Grand Canyon every year?

4. **THINKING SKILL** *Predict* what might happen if visitors were not required to carry all trash and waste out of the Grand Canyon.

5. **GEOGRAPHY** Is the elevation of the Colorado River higher at its source or in the Grand Canyon?

The Dry Southwest

Read Aloud

"The waters of the dark clouds drop, drop." This is a line from a song of the Navajo, a Native American people of the Southwest. They sing this song hoping for life-giving rain. In much of this region, however, rain does not fall often.

Focus Activity

READ TO LEARN

How does the Southwest's dry climate affect life in the region?

VOCABULARY

- adaptation
- Dust Bowl
- aquifer
- dry farming

PLACES

- Big Bend National Park
- Sonoran Desert

THE BIG PICTURE

In the last lesson you read about the varied geography of the Southwest. The climate of this region is varied, too. The Coastal Plain in Texas is warm and rainy. High up in the Rocky Mountains, the temperature can drop far below freezing.

Much of the region, however, is hot and dry. Many parts are covered by deserts—dry lands where little rain falls. In this lesson you will learn how this dry climate affects people, animals, and plants of its region.

WHAT IS A DESERT?

People often think of deserts as barren, lifeless places. In fact they are home to many forms of plant and animal life.

Deserts vary in appearance. The Painted Desert in northern Arizona is named for its colorful rocks. The desert in Big Bend National Park in Texas is covered with scrub brush and grass.

Adaptation in the Desert

How have plants and animals been able to live in such a dry climate? They do so by adaptation (ad up TAY shun). Adaptation means that a kind of plant or animal slowly changes over many years allowing it to survive in its environment.

For example, the giant cactus trees called saguaros (suh GWAHR ohs) live in the Sonoran Desert in Arizona. After a rainfall the saguaro stores water in its trunk. One saguaro may store several tons of water. In this way it can survive during the long dry season.

Animals, too, adapt to the hot, dry climate. Most desert animals are light colored. Light colors reflect heat. This helps animals to stay cooler.

The writer Byrd Baylor has written about some animals that have adapted to the desert. How does she describe their environment?

The coyote, shown in this sculpture (right), is a symbol of the Southwest.

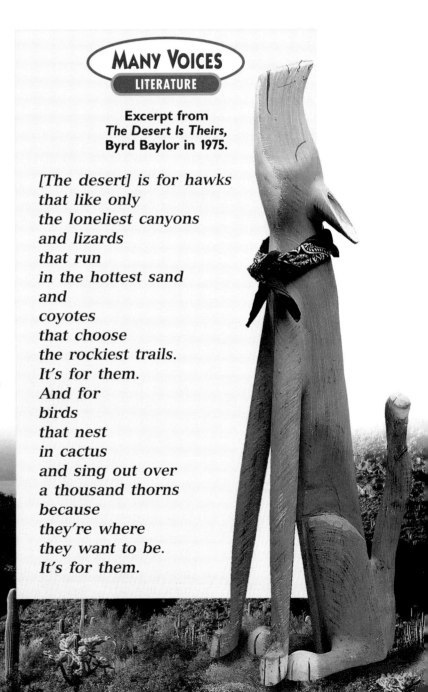

MANY VOICES
LITERATURE

Excerpt from
The Desert Is Theirs,
Byrd Baylor in 1975.

[The desert] is for hawks
that like only
the loneliest canyons
and lizards
that run
in the hottest sand
and
coyotes
that choose
the rockiest trails.
It's for them.
And for
birds
that nest
in cactus
and sing out over
a thousand thorns
because
they're where
they want to be.
It's for them.

LIVING IN A DRY LAND

Not all of the Southwest is desert. Eastern Texas and Oklahoma get more than 40 inches of rain every year. Farmers there grow cotton, peanuts, and other crops.

However, water is still a precious resource throughout the region. A single drought—a period of little or no rain—can ruin crops. A long drought can bring even worse disasters. One such disaster was the Dust Bowl of the 1930s.

The Dust Bowl

The Dust Bowl was an area of the Great Plains that experienced terrible droughts and dust storms. The map on this page shows you where the Dust Bowl occurred.

Until the 1930s, this area had been fertile wheat-growing country. In 1932, however, rainfall dropped to a trickle. The drought continued through most of the 1930s.

At the same time, enormous duststorms blew across the region. Why? Farmers had plowed up the thick prairie grasses to plant wheat. They didn't realize that the wild grasses held the soil in place better than wheat could. Wind eroded the soil right off their wheat fields.

These dust storms brought misery to the people of the Dust Bowl. Thousands of families lost their homes and decided to move away. Many of them migrated to California to get jobs on other people's farms. An Oklahoma farmer named Caroline Henderson described how the dust got everywhere:

It is a daily task to unload the leaves of the geraniums and other house plants. [There is] dust in the beds and in the flour bin, on dishes and walls and windows, in hair and eyes and ears and teeth.

THE DUST BOWL, 1930s

Area of the Dust Bowl

WA, MT, ND, MN, SD, WI, MI, NY, ID, WY, NE, IA, PA, NV, UT, CO, IL, IN, OH, MD, CA, KS, MO, KY, WV, VA, NC, TN, AZ, NM, OK, AR, SC, TX, MS, AL, GA, LA, FL

PACIFIC OCEAN   MEXICO   Gulf of Mexico

0   400   800 Miles
0   400   800 Kilometers

M A P   W O R K

The Dust Bowl was an area of drought and dust storms in the 1930s.

1. What states were in the Dust Bowl?
2. Why do you think dust storms would be worse on plains than in mountains?

Today these lands are green again. Farmers understand better how to work with the soil to resist erosion. But they still search the skies for promising rain clouds.

Finding Water

Where do people in the Southwest get their water? Much of it comes from aquifers (AK wuh furz). These are underground layers of rock or gravel that trap water. People dig wells to bring this water to the surface.

People also get water from the region's rivers. First a dam is built. The dam holds back part of the river to form a reservoir (REHZ ur vwah). A pipe called an aqueduct (AK wuh dukt) carries the water to cities or farms. Aqueducts bring farmers water to irrigate their crops.

Other farmers use dry farming. Dry farming is a way to grow crops with only rain water.

An Oklahoma dust storm in 1936 nearly buried this family's house and fence.

WHY IT MATTERS

For a long time, much of the Southwest was thinly populated. Today, however, more people are moving to the region than ever before. Some newcomers like the warm, sunny climate. Others move there because they like the space and the lack of crowds. Irrigation has made dry land valuable for farmers.

A larger population, however, can be a problem in dry areas. Aquifers may dry up. As the region continues to grow, its most precious natural resource—water—must be protected.

✓// Reviewing Facts and Ideas

MAIN IDEAS

- Plants and animals survive in the desert by adaptation.
- In the 1930s droughts and farming methods caused the Dust Bowl.
- Irrigation and dry farming allow farmers to grow crops in dry areas.

THINK ABOUT IT

1. What is a desert?
2. How has the saguaro cactus adapted to its environment?
3. **FOCUS** How are living things affected by the Southwest climate?
4. **THINKING SKILL** What were two _causes_ of the Dust Bowl? What were some of its _effects_?
5. **WRITE** Suppose your community had a long drought. What effects would there be? Write your ideas down in a paragraph.

CITIZENSHIP
VIEWPOINTS

Water provides recreation for many people. This boy is cooling off in the spray from a sprinkler.

How should the Southwest's water be shared?

Everyone needs water to drink, cook, bathe, and flush toilets. Farmers need water to grow crops. People water their lawns. Factories need water to make their products. Golf courses and swimming pools must have water. Environmental groups concerned with wildlife and people who enjoy fishing also want a say in how water is used.

Much of the water supply in the Southwest is from aquifers. Rain and snow seep back into the aquifers, but this refilling process is slow. Some people, such as Russ Schlittenhart, feel that water for irrigated farming is vital for food production in the United States. Others, like Donald Hutchinson, want to make sure that the water resources are shared among everyone. For Christine Conte, keeping "green" areas for the region's wildlife is very important. Read and consider three viewpoints on this issue. Then answer the questions that follow.

Three DIFFERENT Viewpoints

1 **CHRISTINE CONTE**
Communications Specialist, Tucson, AZ
Excerpt from recent interview

In Arizona our wildlife depends on land along rivers and streams to survive. Migrating birds from Mexico use waterways as stopping places on the "Green Highway" going north and south. We need to protect our natural heritage. Nature preserves along waterways bring millions of tourist dollars into the state.

" . . . protect our natural heritage."

2 **DONALD HUTCHINSON**
Water Engineering Manager, Rio Rancho, NM
Excerpt from recent interview

We must share our water resources among its many users—homeowners, farmers, industry, business people and many more. We must balance the water needs of our factories and businesses that provide jobs, with the water needs of others who provide services, like the farmers who grow our food.

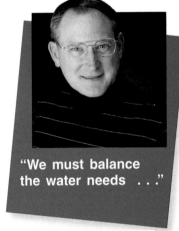

"We must balance the water needs . . ."

3 **RUSS SCHLITTENHART**
Farmer, Eloy, Arizona
Excerpt from recent interview

Setting aside water for irrigated farming should be a top priority. The water that the farmer uses to grow crops produces fresh fruits and vegetables for the consumer. If Americans want to have a constant food supply, water has to be used first to grow food crops. Through irrigation, we can control the conditions under which we produce our crops. We don't have the floods or droughts found in other parts of the country.

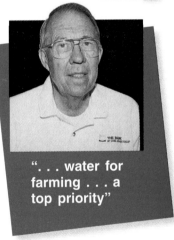

" . . . water for farming . . . a top priority"

BUILDING CITIZENSHIP

1. What is the viewpoint of each person? How does each person support his or her view?

2. In what ways do the viewpoints agree? How do they disagree?

3. What other viewpoints might people have? How could you find out more about this issue in your community?

SHARING VIEWPOINTS

Discuss what you agree with or disagree with about these and other viewpoints. Make a chart showing the various ways water resources are used in the Southwest. Then, as a class, write two statements about using water resources that all of you can agree with.

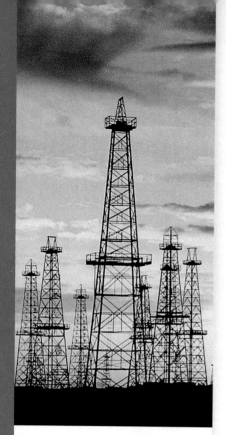

Black Gold

Read Aloud
On January 10, 1901, a newspaper in Beaumont, Texas, reported that a "stream of black petroleum" had shot into the air outside town. The drillers had struck "black gold"!

Focus Activity

READ TO LEARN

Why is petroleum one of the Southwest's most important resources?

VOCABULARY

- petroleum
- crude oil
- refinery
- petrochemical

PEOPLE

- Pattillo Higgins

PLACES

- Beaumont, Texas
- Tulsa, Oklahoma
- Houston, Texas

THE BIG PICTURE

The Southwest has many natural resources. In its east is the rich soil of the Great Plains. Minerals such as copper, silver, and uranium lie beneath the ground. Rivers and aquifers provide water. The Gulf of Mexico is an important resource for fishers.

Sometimes, a single resource can play a big role in shaping a region. In the Southwest, one such resource is oil, a fuel. Oil is a common name for petroleum (puh TROH lee um). Like coal, petroleum formed underground over millions of years from the remains of dead plants. The remains of once-living things are known as fossils, so coal and petroleum are called fossil fuels. In this lesson you will read about how this resource changed the Southwest.

RICHES FROM THE EARTH

As early as the 1600s, European settlers in this country took note of a thick, black oil. It seeped up from the ground in certain spots. Native Americans had been using it as a fuel. Later, other people used it to grease wagon wheels and tools.

In the 1850s a new use was found for this oil. When it was heated, petroleum produced kerosene. Kerosene could be burned in a lamp to give off light.

Petroleum became very valuable. People dug into the ground in hopes of finding it. If they did, they could sell the oil.

The Gusher at Spindletop

Pattillo Higgins was a mechanic who lived in Beaumont, Texas, in the late 1800s. One day he was walking over a nearby hill called Spindletop. He noticed gas bubbles escaping from a stream. Higgins thought this underground gas might lead to an oil deposit. A deposit is a natural pocket of oil in the earth. Throughout the 1890s Higgins tried drilling into Spindletop. He found nothing.

Finally, on January 10, 1901, something amazing happened. A crew was drilling right near the bubbling stream. Suddenly mud exploded from the well. Then a stream of oil shot high into the air!

Nothing like this "gusher" had ever been seen. Oil was shooting up at the rate of 75,000 barrels each day.

Boom Towns

News of the gusher at Spindletop spread quickly. People streamed into Beaumont. Newcomers lived in tents and shacks. Within months the population of this sleepy town climbed from 10,000 to 50,000. It grew so quickly that Beaumont was called a "boom town."

Over the next few years, similar discoveries were made throughout the Southwest. In 1905 a drilling crew hit the giant Glenn Pool near Tulsa, Oklahoma. Wherever oil was discovered, boom towns appeared.

This oil boom changed many industries. Soon ships, locomotives, and factories were powered by this fuel. And a new petroleum product—gasoline—made automobiles run.

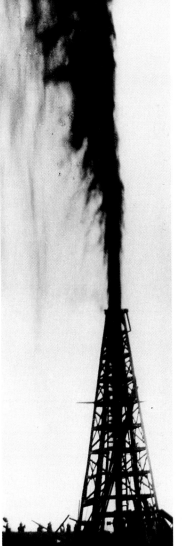

Spindletop (near left) gushed a huge amount of oil before it was brought under control. Pipelines (far left) are used to carry oil to refineries where is it made into gasoline and other products.

FROM CRUDE TO CAR

You have seen people "filling up" at a gas station. How does petroleum travel from deep in the ground to the gas pump? There are many steps in between.

The first step is drilling. Scientists called petroleum geologists predict where oil may be located. A geologist is a scientist who studies Earth. Then workers use an enormous steel bit to drill wells. They sometimes drill a hole a mile down!

If workers strike oil, special pipes are lowered into the hole. These will bring the oil to the surface.

From Well to Refinery

The petroleum that bubbles up from the ground is called crude oil. Crude oil is not very useful. It must be transported to a factory called a refinery (ri FĪ nuh ree). There the crude oil is refined, or separated into parts to be used.

Crude oil is treated at refineries to make different products. In what container is the crude oil separated into fractions?

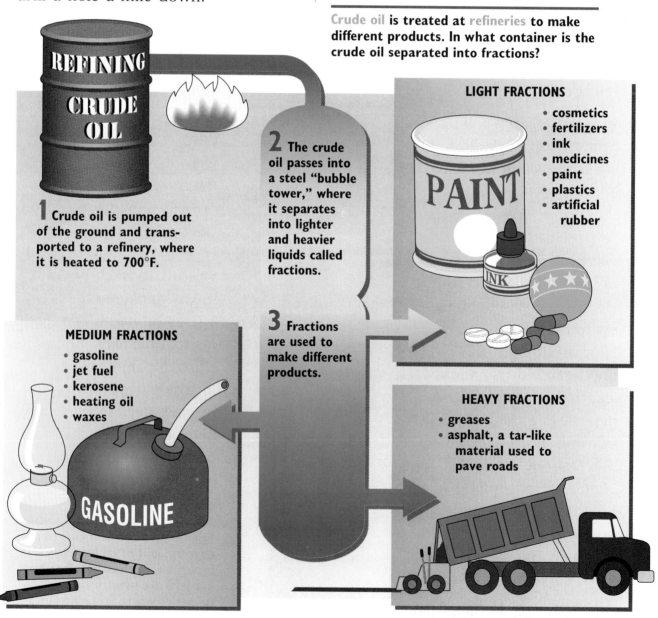

REFINING CRUDE OIL

1 Crude oil is pumped out of the ground and transported to a refinery, where it is heated to 700°F.

2 The crude oil passes into a steel "bubble tower," where it separates into lighter and heavier liquids called fractions.

3 Fractions are used to make different products.

LIGHT FRACTIONS
- cosmetics
- fertilizers
- ink
- medicines
- paint
- plastics
- artificial rubber

PAINT

INK

MEDIUM FRACTIONS
- gasoline
- jet fuel
- kerosene
- heating oil
- waxes

GASOLINE

HEAVY FRACTIONS
- greases
- asphalt, a tar-like material used to pave roads

Some petroleum travels from the well in enormous pipelines. It is also carried in huge boats called tankers. The largest of these tankers can carry up to 500,000 tons of oil.

Houston, Texas, is our country's top oil-refining center. Much of the crude oil in the Southwest ends up in refineries there. Many other countries send their crude oil to refineries in Houston.

At the Refinery

At the refinery, workers heat the crude oil to very high temperatures. The heat allows the crude oil to be separated into different products. Refining also removes unwanted substances from crude oil.

Refineries sometimes vary their products according to the season. For the summer, when more people are on the road, a refinery may produce more gasoline. During the winter months, heating oil becomes a major product.

You can see in the diagram how heat separates the crude oil. Into what products can crude oil be made?

Petrochemicals

At refineries, petrochemicals (pet roh CHEM ih kulz), or chemicals made from petroleum, are produced. An incredible number of useful products can be made from these petrochemicals.

How many? Take a look around your classroom. The paint on the walls is probably made from petro-chemicals. If you are writing with a pen, it may be made from these chemicals too. Even your classmates' clothing or sneakers may be made from petrochemicals!

School bus parts are made from petrochemicals. So are road signs and traffic lights.

On the farm, petrochemicals appear in fertilizers and pesticides. They are also an ingredient in medicines such as aspirin. Petrochemicals are yet another reason why we call petroleum "black gold."

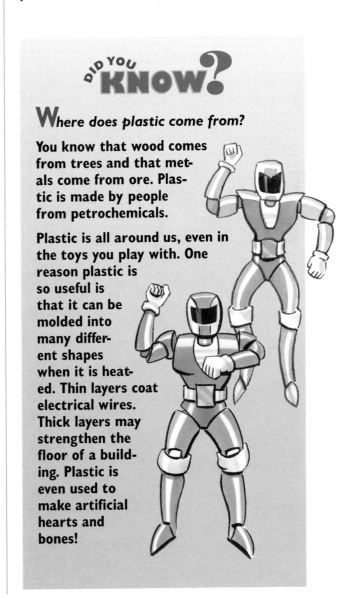

DID YOU KNOW?

Where does plastic come from?

You know that wood comes from trees and that metals come from ore. Plastic is made by people from petrochemicals.

Plastic is all around us, even in the toys you play with. One reason plastic is so useful is that it can be molded into many different shapes when it is heated. Thin layers coat electrical wires. Thick layers may strengthen the floor of a building. Plastic is even used to make artificial hearts and bones!

Infographic

Economy of the Southwest

Oil is one of the Southwest's most valuable resources, and refining is one of its biggest industries. What other goods and services are important to the Southwest's economy?

Black Gold

Every state in the region produces petroleum. In Oklahoma City, there is even an oil well near the governor's offices.

Penny for Your Thoughts!

Arizona produces more than half our country's copper, used for electrical wires and pennies. Uranium, zinc, and silver are also mined in the region.

Nuts and Bolts

Oklahoma and Texas manufacture machinery of all kinds, while Arizona specializes in electrical and communications devices.

Stampede!

Texas leads the country in raising cattle and sheep. Ranching is also an important business in New Mexico and Oklahoma.

Wear It

All four states of the Southwest are cotton growers. In fact, Texas leads the country in cotton production.

At Your Service!

Tourism is one of the Southwest's most important industries. Each year, millions of tourists visit the Grand Canyon, New Mexico's Carlsbad Caverns, the Cherokee Cultural Center in Oklahoma, and the Alamo in Texas.

FUTURE OF OIL

Our country still has large deposits of petroleum. The largest is at Prudhoe (PROO doh) Bay, Alaska.

Oil, however, is a nonrenewable resource. Scientists are not sure how much oil is left in the ground. They all agree, though, that the supply is limited. In the words of a petroleum geologist named Rick Bass: "It disappears. It is here only once."

People are taking several steps to make our oil last longer. Some people are trying to produce oil from a rock called shale. Others are trying to make fuels from such materials as grain, sugar, and animal waste. Still others are building cars that are more fuel-efficient. Such cars would use less gasoline. That would help the petroleum supply last longer.

WHY IT MATTERS

Petroleum made a big contribution to the Southwest. It also helped to build the economy and the way of life in our country. The future of every American depends on finding new ways to conserve and produce this "black gold."

✓ Reviewing Facts and Ideas

MAIN IDEAS

- Petroleum created rapid growth in the Southwest.
- Crude oil must be refined in order to be made into useful products.
- As a nonrenewable resource, petroleum must be carefully conserved.

THINK ABOUT IT

1. What was kerosene used for?
2. What happened at Spindletop in 1901?
3. **FOCUS** Why is petroleum called "black gold"?
4. **THINKING SKILL** *Sort* into groups the different products made from crude oil.
5. **GEOGRAPHY** How could recycling plastic help to conserve our supply of petroleum?

Using electric power for cars may be more fuel-efficient than burning petroleum. One day you might "fill up" a car from pumps like these.

Identifying Fact and Opinion

VOCABULARY
fact
opinion

WHY THE SKILL MATTERS

You have just read about how gasoline is made from crude oil. Suppose somebody told you that most cars run on gasoline. This statement is a **fact**. You can make sure it is true by checking the information in a reference source. A fact is a statement that can be proven true.

Suppose, however, that somebody told you that a car is the best way to travel. This statement cannot be proven. Rather, it is an **opinion**. An opinion expresses one person's belief or feeling. Another person might believe that a train is the best way to travel. Still another might prefer plane travel.

Facts and opinions are very different kinds of statements. The decisions we make should be based on what is true—facts—rather than on opinions. Use the Helping Yourself box to guide you in identifying these two kinds of statements.

USING THE SKILL

Read this passage from a magazine article. Then identify which statements are facts and which are opinions.

The United States is still a major oil supplier. In 1990 we produced over 360 million tons of crude petroleum. To make our oil supplies last, however, we should add a tax to gasoline prices. I think this would lead to fewer cars on the road.

Which statements present facts? Which present opinions? The first two sentences state facts. They could be proven true. You could check the information in a reference source.

Sometimes you can tell opinions by the use of such word clues as *I think, I believe, the best,* or *should.* These words appear in the last two sentences. These sentences could not be proven true. Opinions do not always have word clues like these, however.

- **Facts** are statements that can be proven true. **Opinions** are beliefs or feelings.
- **Opinions** can sometimes be recognized by such word clues as *I think, I believe, the best,* or *should.*

Since oil is a nonrenewable resource, scientists have begun exploring other fuels. Some have experimented with gases such as hydrogen. The best alternative, however, is solar power, or energy that comes from the sun. I believe that in the future, the sun will supply most of the energy that we need.

Which of these statements do you think could be proven true? How? Which statements do you think are opinions? Why? What did you do to identify the facts and the opinions?

TRYING THE SKILL

You have practiced identifying facts and opinions in a passage about oil production. Now read this passage about other kinds of fuels. When you are done, figure out which statements present facts and which express the author's opinions.

REVIEWING THE SKILL

1. In what ways is a fact different from an opinion?

2. Why does a word clue like *the best* often tell you that the speaker is expressing an opinion?

3. How would the reference section of the library help you to decide if certain statements were facts or opinions?

4. Why is it useful to be able to tell a fact from an opinion?

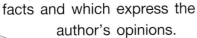

The experimental car (left) and the house in Arizona (far left) are powered by solar energy.

CHAPTER 3 REVIEW

THINKING ABOUT VOCABULARY

A. Write a sentence for each pair of words below. Include details that give clues to the meaning of the first term in each pair.

1. desert, adaptation
2. erosion, canyon
3. crude oil, refinery
4. petroleum, petrochemicals
5. dry farming, aquifer

B. Number a sheet of paper from 1 to 10. Next to each number write the word or term from the list above that best completes the sentence.

1. A _____ gets less than 10 inches of precipitation each year.
2. Many different landforms in the Southwest were formed by _____.
3. Plants and animals are able to survive in the desert because of _____.
4. _____ is refined in order to make it useful.
5. Some Southwestern farmers dig wells to find water in an _____.
6. Mesas, buttes, and _____ are some of the Southwest's interesting landforms.
7. Road signs, traffic lights, and paint are examples of things that are made from _____.
8. Some farmers use _____, which depends on rain to provide enough water for crops.
9. Crude oil from wells in the Southwest often ends up in a _____ in Houston.
10. Petrochemicals such as plastic are made from _____.

THINKING ABOUT FACTS

1. What action caused the Grand Canyon to form?
2. How are plants and animals able to live in desert conditions?
3. Where do people in the Southwest get their water?
4. Why must crude oil be refined?
5. What was the Dust Bowl, and why did it occur?

THINK AND WRITE

WRITING A LIST
Write a list of five vocabulary words from Chapter 3. Then write a paragraph with five sentences using each of the vocabulary words.

WRITING AN ARTICLE
Suppose you took a trip to the Grand Canyon during your summer vacation. Write a travel article about your trip for the school paper.

WRITING A LETTER
Pretend that you are living in the Dust Bowl in the 1930s. Write a letter to a cousin in New York describing what is happening to your family and your farm.

APPLYING THINKING SKILLS

IDENTIFYING FACT AND OPINION

1. What is the difference between a fact and an opinion? Identify items 2, 3, and 4 below as either fact or opinion. Explain your answers.

2. "The Grand Canyon is one of the most beautiful sights in the world."

3. "The Dust Bowl was an area of the Great Plains that was affected by droughts and dust storms during the 1930s."

4. "Life is better in Oklahoma since oil was discovered there."

5. Why is it important to know the difference between a fact and an opinion?

Summing Up the Chapter

Use the following cause-and-effect chart to organize the information in the chapter. Copy the cause-and-effect chart on a sheet of paper. Fill in the blank spaces on the chart. Then use the information to write a paragraph that answers the question "How does the environment of the Southwest affect all living things in it?"

CAUSES	EFFECTS
Wind and water erode parts of the land.	
	Desert plants and animals adapt to the dry environment.
	Boom towns formed.
Geologists predict location of oil.	

UNIT 1 REVIEW

THINKING ABOUT VOCABULARY

Number a sheet of paper from 1 to 10. Beside each number, write **C** if the underlined word is used correctly. If it is not, write the word that would correctly complete the sentence.

1. A <u>basin</u> is a high, flat area that rises above the surrounding land.

2. An <u>environment</u> is an area where very little rain falls.

3. Something in the environment that people can use is a <u>natural resource</u>.

4. Minerals are an example of <u>renewable resources</u>.

5. An <u>erosion</u> is a landform like a plateau, but smaller.

6. The <u>Dust Bowl</u> was a long drought that happened in the 1930s.

7. A <u>refinery</u> is a place where crude oil is separated into parts to be used for different purposes.

8. Making large amounts of goods in a factory is called <u>economy</u>.

9. The way of life that people share is called their <u>ethnic group</u>.

10. A person who comes from another land to live in a new country is an <u>ancestor</u>.

THINK AND WRITE ◄ ═══ ▶

WRITING A LETTER
Suppose you have a pen pal in another country. Your pen pal knows very little about the United States. Write a brief description of your country. In your description include information about environment, people, and heritage.

WRITING A TRAVEL PAMPHLET
You have read about the natural features of the Southwest. Write a travel guide describing the Grand Canyon to a group of students who will be going there on a class trip.

CREATING A POSTER
Make a poster showing how crude oil is made into products we use every day. Refer to page 72 for information. Be sure to include products that are found at home or in school.

BUILDING SKILLS

1. **Elevation maps** Suppose you are planning a bicycle trip in Vermont. Explain why it would be important to have an elevation map with you on your trip.

2. **Elevation maps** Look at the map on page 19. What state has an area that is below sea level?

3. **Elevation maps** Using the map on page 19, find the approximate elevation of the area where you live.

4. **Decision making** What is a good first step when making a decision?

5. **Decision making** Why is it important for you to learn how to make decisions?

YESTERDAY, TODAY & TOMORROW

In Chapter 1 you read about our country's national parks. The National Park System has existed for more than 100 years. Each year millions of people enjoy the natural beauty of these areas. Do you think our country should continue to set aside land for national parks? Why or why not?

READING ON YOUR OWN

Here are some books you might find at the library to help you learn more.

LADY WITH A TORCH
by Eleanor Coerr
The fascinating story behind the building of the Statue of Liberty.

COME BACK, SALMON
by Molly Cone
A group of students adopt a nearby stream and clean it up so that it can once again be a home to fish.

WISH YOU WERE HERE: EMILY'S GUIDE TO THE 50 STATES
by Kathleen Krull
Read about a young girl traveling through the United States with her grandmother.

UNIT 1 REVIEW PROJECT

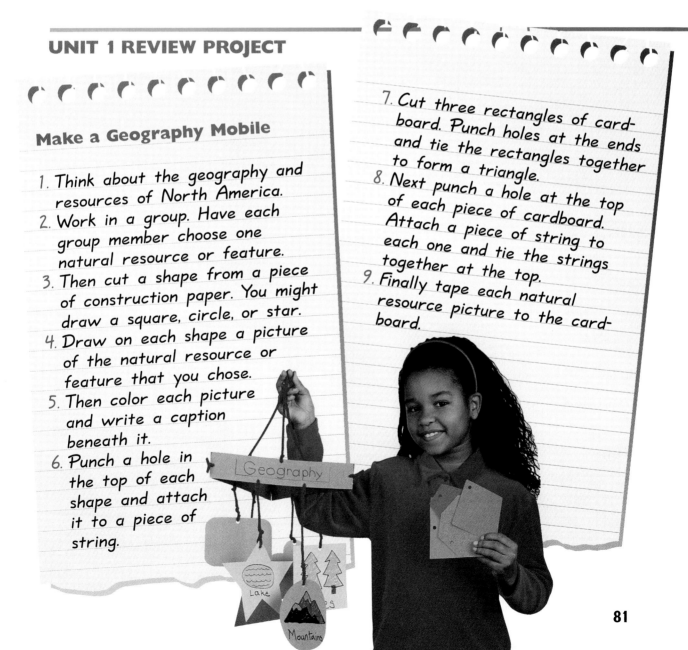

Make a Geography Mobile

1. Think about the geography and resources of North America.
2. Work in a group. Have each group member choose one natural resource or feature.
3. Then cut a shape from a piece of construction paper. You might draw a square, circle, or star.
4. Draw on each shape a picture of the natural resource or feature that you chose.
5. Then color each picture and write a caption beneath it.
6. Punch a hole in the top of each shape and attach it to a piece of string.
7. Cut three rectangles of cardboard. Punch holes at the ends and tie the rectangles together to form a triangle.
8. Next punch a hole at the top of each piece of cardboard. Attach a piece of string to each one and tie the strings together at the top.
9. Finally tape each natural resource picture to the cardboard.

WILL ROGERS STATUE (FAR RIGHT);
TULSA SKYLINE (BELOW);
MARIA TALLCHIEF (LEFT);
OKLAHOMA WHEAT FIELD (RIGHT)

A Place Called Oklahoma

"Oklahoma is . . . where dreams come true."

from a description by Oklahoma Supreme Court Judge Yvonne Kauger
See page 102.

Why Does It Matter?

What does Oklahoma look like? Are all parts of Oklahoma the same? What are its resources? Who lives in Oklahoma? What is their culture like?

Oklahoma offers great riches, both in land and in resources. Oklahoma has sweeping plains and green woodlands. Our state also has tall skyscrapers and rich farmlands.

Oklahoma is also a rich blend of people and cultures. In our state people celebrate their culture in many different ways. In Unit 2 you will learn more about Oklahoma's land and people and what makes our state so special.

FIND OUT MORE!
Visit our website:
www.mhschool.com

*inter*NET
CONNECTION

The Land of Oklahoma

THINKING ABOUT GEOGRAPHY AND CULTURE

Oklahoma has mountains and plains, woodlands and farm-lands. Our state also has many natural resources and miles of rivers. In this chapter you will learn about these landforms and resources. You will also see how Oklahoma's geography affects the way Oklahomans live and play today.

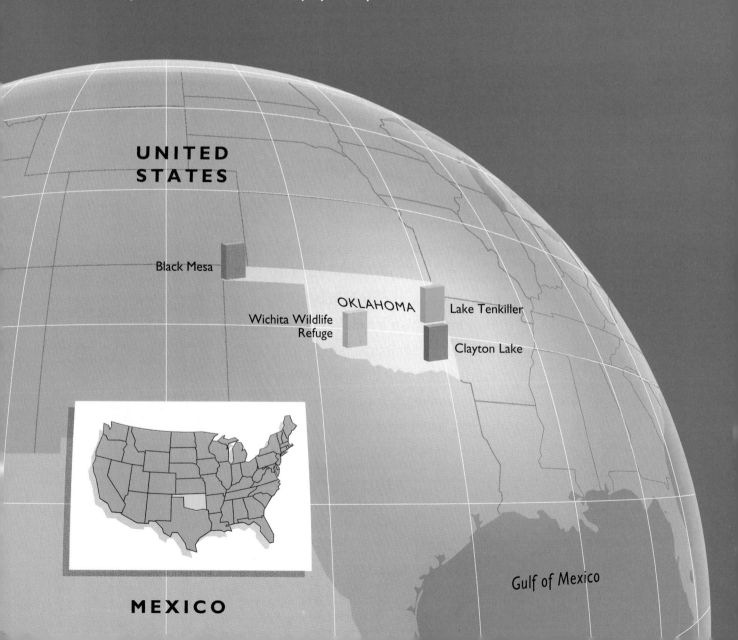

UNITED STATES

Black Mesa

OKLAHOMA

Wichita Wildlife Refuge

Lake Tenkiller

Clayton Lake

Gulf of Mexico

MEXICO

Black Mesa, CIMARRON COUNTY

Black Mesa is our state's highest point. Many people visit here every year to see its natural beauty.

Lake Tenkiller, CHEROKEE COUNTY

Oklahoma has more lakes built by people than any other state. At Lake Tenkiller, Oklahomans often enjoy fishing, boating, and relaxing.

Wichita Wildlife Refuge, COMANCHE COUNTY

Bison are protected today in places like the Wichita Wildlife Refuge. The refuge is also home to coyotes, elk, and wild turkeys.

Clayton Lake, PUSHMATAHA COUNTY

One of many lakes in Oklahoma created by building dams, Clayton Lake provides water for the people in the surrounding area.

A Special Place

Read Aloud

"This area consists of great grassy plains, forests in groves, and clumps of trees. Over these lands still roam the elk, the buffalo, the wild horse, in all their native freedom."

Washington Irving, a famous American writer, wrote these words more than 100 years ago about the land that became the state of Oklahoma.

Focus Activity

READ TO LEARN

What is special about Oklahoma's geography?

VOCABULARY

- plateau
- mesa

PLACES

- Red Rock Canyon
- Idabel
- Black Mesa
- Canadian River
- Lake Eufaula

THE BIG PICTURE

The shape of Oklahoma is different from that of any other state. Many people think Oklahoma is shaped like a pan. The long, thin strip of land in the northwest part is called the Panhandle. In fact, our whole state is sometimes called the Panhandle State. In this lesson you will learn what the land of the Panhandle State is like.

Wheat grows on the rolling prairies of central Oklahoma.

86

THE PANHANDLE STATE

Shape is an important part of geography. As you read in Chapter 1, geography is the study of Earth's land and water and of its plants, animals, and people.

An Uphill Climb

What are some of the features of the geography of our state? To find out, pretend that you and some friends are taking a bus tour across Oklahoma. Of course, you will need a map to prepare for it. Look at the map on this page. It shows some of the landforms of our state. Mountains, hills, plains, and plateaus (pla TOHZ) are some common landforms. A plateau is a high, flat area of land that rises steeply above the surrounding land. In Oklahoma we also have landforms like canyons. On the map locate Red Rock Canyon. Each year many people visit the canyon to go hiking.

Your group is to begin its tour in the town of Idabel (ID u bel), in southeastern Oklahoma. This is one of the lowest areas of our state. Your first goal is to reach Oklahoma City in the center of our state. What kinds of landforms will you see on the way? Will you be biking uphill or downhill?

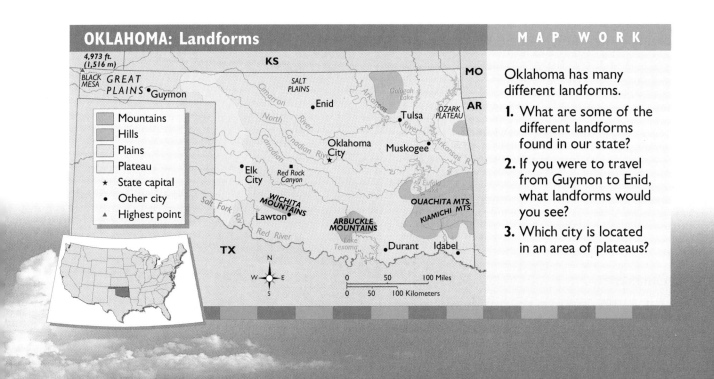

OKLAHOMA: Landforms

4,973 ft. (1,516 m)
BLACK MESA
GREAT PLAINS • Guymon
KS
SALT PLAINS
• Enid
Oologah Lake
MO
OZARK PLATEAU
AR
• Tulsa
Cimarron River
North Canadian River
Canadian River
Arkansas River
Arkansas R.
Oklahoma City ★
Muskogee
Elk City •
Red Rock Canyon ■
Salt Fork River
WICHITA MOUNTAINS
Lawton •
ARBUCKLE MOUNTAINS
Lake Eufaula
OUACHITA MTS.
KIAMICHI MTS.
Red River
TX
Lake Texoma
• Durant
Idabel •

Legend:
- Mountains
- Hills
- Plains
- Plateau
- ★ State capital
- • Other city
- ▲ Highest point

N W E S

0   50   100 Miles
0 50 100 Kilometers

MAP WORK

Oklahoma has many different landforms.

1. What are some of the different landforms found in our state?

2. If you were to travel from Guymon to Enid, what landforms would you see?

3. Which city is located in an area of plateaus?

BLACK MESA

Your final stop is Black Mesa in the Panhandle. From the map on page 87 you can see that it is located in the northwestern part of our state. A mesa is a flat-topped hill. Your muscles surely will be sore when you reach the top, because Black Mesa is almost 5,000 feet high. From Black Mesa you can look out and see for many miles around. Congratulations! You and your friends are at the highest point in our state!

Along your trip, you have gone from a lowland to the top of a high mesa, and you have seen many different landforms. You also may have crossed some bodies of water. Oklahoma has many lakes and rivers. On your trip you may have crossed the Canadian River, which flows through central Oklahoma. If you traveled east on it, you would have run into Lake Eufaula (YOO-fa-la). It is our state's largest lake. In the next lesson you will learn more about the land and water in each part of our state.

Climate

Landforms are an important part of geography. Weather and climate are also part of geography. What the air is like outdoors each day is called weather. The weather may be hot or cold, wet or dry, windy or very calm.

Oklahoma's climate is unusual. On any given day, our weather may be very different from one part of the state to another. For example, on a spring day the Red River Valley in the southeastern part of our state might be very warm. On the same day people in the Panhandle in northwest Oklahoma might feel a winter chill.

Black Mesa (above) is the highest point in Oklahoma. Tornadoes (right) can cause great damage.

Temperature

For most of the year, though, the temperature in our state is pleasant. Cold "spells" in the winter months may drive the temperature below freezing, but these periods usually do not last more than a few days. During heat "waves" in the summer months, the temperature may reach 100°F or higher.

The amount of precipitation our state gets also changes greatly. Precipitation is any form of water that falls to the ground, such as rain, hail, or snow. Oklahoma's average yearly precipitation changes greatly across the state from east to west. The western part of our state gets much less precipitation than the eastern part.

WHY IT MATTERS

In this lesson you have learned about Oklahoma's geography. Our state has an unusual shape and has many different kinds of landforms. Even our weather is very different from one part of the state to another. By studying Oklahoma's geography and climate you can see how special our state is. As you read, this information will help you to understand how Oklahoma's geography affects the way its people live, work, and play.

Reviewing Facts and Ideas

MAIN IDEAS

- The shape of Oklahoma is very different from other states in our country.

- Oklahoma has many different landforms.

- Oklahoma's climate is different from one place to the next.

THINK ABOUT IT

1. What is the highest point in Oklahoma?

2. How would you describe the land and climate of Oklahoma?

3. **FOCUS** How is Oklahoma's geography special?

4. **THINKING SKILL** *Compare* and *contrast* Oklahoma's landforms in the eastern and western parts of the state.

5. **GEOGRAPHY** Locate the area near your community on the map on page 87. Near what landforms do you live?

Reading Road Maps

VOCABULARY

road map
interstate highway

WHY THE SKILL MATTERS

In the last lesson you read about a bus trip through Oklahoma. How do most Oklahomans travel today? Most people in our state use one of our most important transportation systems—our highways.

There are many thousands of miles of highways in our country. People travel to work on the highways. Truckers bring goods from factories to stores. Many tourists drive to our country's national parks or historic sites along them.

The highway system is very large. Nobody knows the whole system by heart. Instead, travelers use a road map, which shows them which roads to use to get from one place to another. Use the Helping Yourself box to guide you in reading the road maps.

USING THE SKILL

Look at the road map of Oklahoma on the next page. It shows several different kinds of roads. Look at the map key. As you can see, a heavy green line shows that the road is an interstate highway. An interstate highway connects two or more states. Usually these roads have at least two lanes in each direction.

Look back at the map key. What kind of road does a red line stand for? A black line?

You probably noticed that most roads on the map have numbers. The number of the road appears inside a symbol. What is the number of the road that connects Guthrie and Norman?

If you follow some roads with your finger, you will see that they have more than one number. That's because more than one route may "share" the same road for a distance.

You may have noticed something else, too. Most roads that run east–west have even numbers. Odd-numbered roads usually run north–south. This fact can help drivers figure out which way they are going.

TRYING THE SKILL

Suppose you wanted to plan a trip from Tulsa to Oklahoma City. Along the way you want to visit Guthrie. Which route would you take? What kind of roads are on the route? How can you tell?

Suppose you wanted to return from Oklahoma City to Tulsa on a different route. Which route would be the most direct? What kind of road is this route?

Road maps also show parks, historic sites, or other features of interest. How can you find a national forest on this map?

Helping yourself

- A **road map** helps to guide travelers from one place to another.

- Road maps show highways and other information needed by road travelers.

- Study the map key to identify the symbols and colors used on the map.

REVIEWING THE SKILL

1. What kind of information does a road map show?

2. On the map, which interstate highway would you take to get from Lawton to Texas? Which one connects east Oklahoma with Arkansas? What did you do to find the answer?

3. Why do road maps usually show more than one kind of road?

4. What kind of road is Highway 35? How can you tell?

5. Why is it important to be able to read a road map?

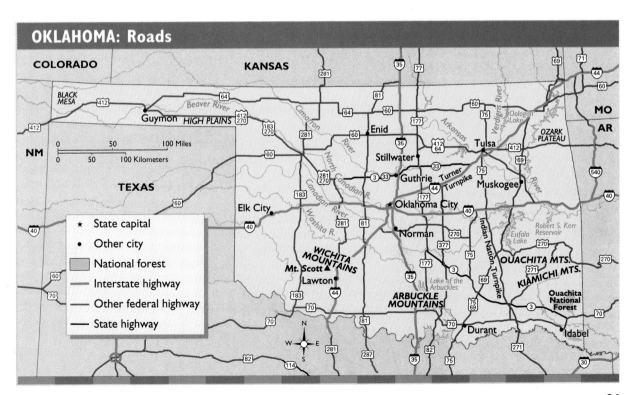

OKLAHOMA: Roads

Key:
- ★ State capital
- • Other city
- National forest
- — Interstate highway
- — Other federal highway
- — State highway

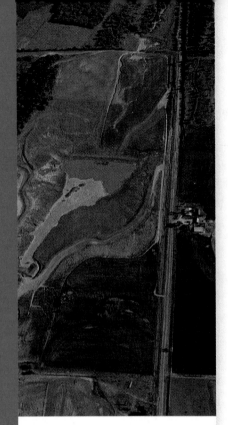

The Six Parts of Oklahoma

Read Aloud

"…glistening like a brilliant field of snow in the summer sun…"

In the early 1800s the explorer George Sibley used the above words to describe the Salt Plains. Many things have changed in Oklahoma over the last 100 years. But our landforms have been the same for thousands of years.

Focus Activity

READ TO LEARN

What important land-forms and natural resources are in the six parts of Oklahoma?

VOCABULARY

- prairie
- mesquite
- frontier

PLACES

- Ozark Plateau
- Arkansas River
- Oklahoma City
- Wichita Mountains
- Red River
- Arbuckle Mountains
- Kiamichi Mountains

THE BIG PICTURE

You learned in Lesson 1 that Oklahoma has many kinds of landforms. These different landforms make it easy to divide our state into six parts. These parts are called the Six Countries of Oklahoma. Of course, they are not really countries in the way that the United States is a country. They are regions with natural features that make each of Oklahoma's countries special in their own way.

The Great Salt Plains National Wildlife Refuge is north of the Salt Fork River, in Red Carpet Country.

GREEN COUNTRY

Anyone who has been to Green Country surely knows how it got its name. Green grasslands are found throughout this part of our state. From the map below you can see this region is located in the northeastern part of our state.

The forested hills and grassy areas of Green Country rise in its east to form the Ozark Plateau. The land of this area has much limestone. This is a kind of rock which makes the soil good for growing things. Fruits and vegetables are widely grown in Green Country.

Green country has many hills, fast running streams, and deep valleys. The Arkansas River is one of Oklahoma's most important rivers. It flows through Green Country. The Verdigris, Cimarron, and Canadian rivers all flow into the Arkansas River. The Arkansas River flows through Oklahoma and Arkansas to the Mississippi River. The Mississippi River is one of the longest rivers in the North American continent.

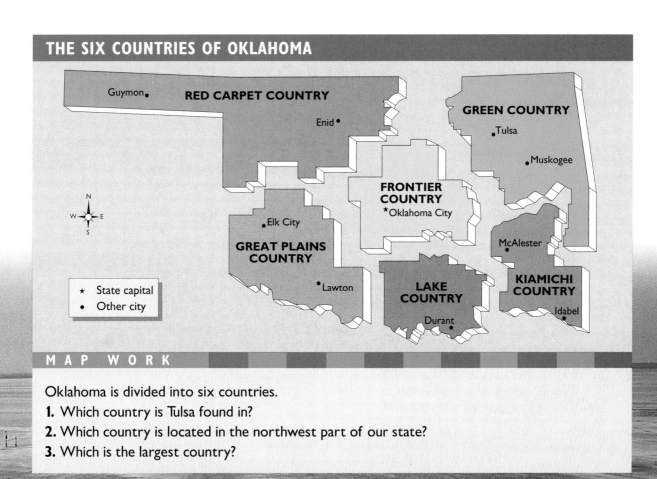

THE SIX COUNTRIES OF OKLAHOMA

- Guymon
- RED CARPET COUNTRY
- Enid
- GREEN COUNTRY
- Tulsa
- Muskogee
- FRONTIER COUNTRY
- ★Oklahoma City
- Elk City
- GREAT PLAINS COUNTRY
- McAlester
- KIAMICHI COUNTRY
- Lawton
- LAKE COUNTRY
- Durant
- Idabel

★ State capital
• Other city

M A P   W O R K

Oklahoma is divided into six countries.
1. Which country is Tulsa found in?
2. Which country is located in the northwest part of our state?
3. Which is the largest country?

93

RED CARPET COUNTRY

Red Carpet Country is the north-western part of our state. Its name comes from the red clay soil that covers the region. Not many people live here. Those who do are proud of how friendly people are here. They "roll out the red carpet" to welcome visitors.

Red Carpet Country is a land of plains and prairies (PRAIR eez). Grasslands on the plains are called prairies. The plains and prairies of this region have one of the most important natural resources of Red Carpet Country: farmland. Wheat grown in Red Carpet Country helps feed the United States and other countries in the world.

The Red Carpet country is also used for raising cattle. The region has many huge ranches. On them cattle graze on the short grasses of the flat, treeless plains. Farm animals like sheep are also raised on ranches in Red Country.

Mesquite (mes KEET) trees can be seen in this region. These small, thorny trees have long roots that grow deep to find water. Mesquites can be found in places that are too dry for other trees. Farmers sometimes make flour from mesquite trees and use it as food to help feed their animals.

Besides farming and grazing land, Red Carpet country has another important natural resource. This resource is natural gas. People use natural gas for cooking food and heating homes and other buildings. The deepest gas wells of Oklahoma are found here.

DID YOU KNOW?

What are mesquite trees used for?

Have you ever eaten raw peas right from the pod? Mesquite trees have similar pods. A long time ago, Native Americans used to grind the seeds inside into flour. Today many people use mesquite wood to make their barbeques taste better. But not everyone likes mesquite trees. Mesquite trees push out grasses that cows and cattle eat. Some farmers and ranch owners sometimes consider the mesquite tree a weed.

FRONTIER COUNTRY

Frontier Country is right in the middle of our state. It was given this name because Oklahoma was once part of the western frontier (frun TIHR) of the United States. A frontier is the land at the edge of an area where people have settled.

The region has gently rolling plains, and once had many trees and prairies. An area of land called the Cross Timbers runs through this region. The Cross Timbers is a thick woodlands area that extends from the northeast part of Oklahoma to the south–central part.

Our state's capital and largest city, Oklahoma City is also located in Frontier Country. Scattered among the skyscrapers of this city, you will find oil wells pumping this important natural resource from the ground.

Red clay prairies sweep towards the Glass Mountains in Red Carpet Country (below). As late as the 1970s, there was an active oil well in front of the Capitol Building in Oklahoma City (above).

MANY MOUNTAINS

You have just read that our state has many rolling, flat plains. If you visit the southwestern and south central parts, you will see that Oklahoma also has many mountains.

Great Plains Country

To the south of Red Carpet Country is Great Plains Country. This area is part of a large area of the United States called the Great Plains. Oklahoma's best farmland is found in this region. Wheat, peanuts, cotton, and corn are grown in Great Plains Country. Cattle are also raised here.

The Wichita Mountains are rugged peaks rising up in the center of Great Plains Country. Its highest point is Mt. Scott, which is about 2,464 feet above sea level.

Lake Country

Lake Country is fun country! There are many natural lakes and lakes built by people here. Swimming, fishing, sailing, hiking, and camping are just some of the exciting things to do here, in south–central Oklahoma.

The Red River plains stretch north of the Red River. It is one of our state's most important rivers. It forms Oklahoma's border with Texas.

The Arbuckle Mountains are in the northern part of Lake Country. Today scientists study the Arbuckles to find out what the land of Oklahoma was like millions of years ago.

Wheat grows high in Great Plains Country's rich soil (below). At Turner Falls (below, left) in the Arbuckle Mountains (above), rafters have fun playing in the water.

Kiamichi Country

Kiamichi (ki u MISH ee) Country is located in the southeastern corner of Oklahoma. This is a mountainous and thickly-forested region. It gets its name from the Kiamichi Mountains, which are a part of the Ouachita Mountains, which cover most of this region. These mountains are covered with trees. Many people who live here make their living from timber and lumber.

Besides trees, Kiamichi Country has large deposits of coal. However, not much coal has been mined here in recent years.

WHY IT MATTERS

As you have learned, Oklahoma's Six Countries have different types of land and resources. These resources are important to people in Oklahoma. In the next chapter you will learn that Oklahoma's people, like its natural resources, are unique.

✔// Reviewing Facts and Ideas

MAIN IDEAS

- Oklahoma is divided into six "countries."
- Each of these countries has different landforms.
- Each country also has different natural resources.

THINK ABOUT IT

1. What are the names of Oklahoma's Six Countries?

2. What are the Cross Timbers?

3. **FOCUS** What are the important landforms and natural resources of the six parts of Oklahoma?

4. **THINKING SKILL** *Classify* each of Oklahoma's countries according to its landforms. Which have plains? Which have mountains? Which have both types of landforms?

5. **WRITE** Suppose you are visiting a part of Oklahoma far from where you live. Write a letter to a friend describing the common features of this region.

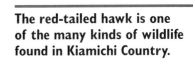

The red-tailed hawk is one of the many kinds of wildlife found in Kiamichi Country.

CHAPTER 4 REVIEW

THINKING ABOUT VOCABULARY

Number a sheet of paper from 1 to 5. Next to each number write the word that best completes the sentences.

frontier
mesa
mesquite
plateau
prairie

1. A _____ is a small, thorny tree.

2. The _____ is land on the edge on an area where people have settled.

3. Grassland on a plain is called a _____.

4. A _____ is a high, flat area of land.

5. A flat-topped hill with steep sides is a _____.

THINKING ABOUT FACTS

1. Name the six "countries" of Oklahoma.

2. What important crop is grown in Red Carpet Country?

3. What is the highest point in Oklahoma?

4. Name the state capital of Oklahoma.

5. Where is Oklahoma's best farmland found?

6. What are three kinds of landforms that are found in Oklahoma?

7. Where in Oklahoma is natural gas found?

8. In what region of Oklahoma is Oklahoma City located?

9. Why are fruits and vegetables widely grown in Green Country?

10. Which river flows through Central Oklahoma?

11. How does the amount of precipitation vary around Oklahoma?

12. What are three rivers in Oklahoma?

13. What part of Oklahoma is on the Great Plains?

14. What different recreational activities can people do in Lake Country?

15. What is an important business in Kiamichi Country?

THINK AND WRITE

WRITING A COMPARISON
Write a paragraph comparing Great Plains Country and Kiamichi Country. Describe what is the same, and what is different in the two regions.

WRITING A DESCRIPTION
Suppose you are taking a trip to Red Carpet Country. Write a paragraph describing what you might see as you travel through the region.

WRITING AN EXPLANATION
Write a paragraph that explains why you think the climate in Oklahoma is unique.

APPLYING GEOGRAPHY SKILLS

USING ROAD MAPS

Refer to the map of Tulsa to help you answer the following questions.

1. What does a road map show?

2. How does the map show which roads are highways?

3. According to the map, which highway goes through Mohawk Park?

4. In which direction does Memorial Drive run?

5. Why is it important to be able to read a road map?

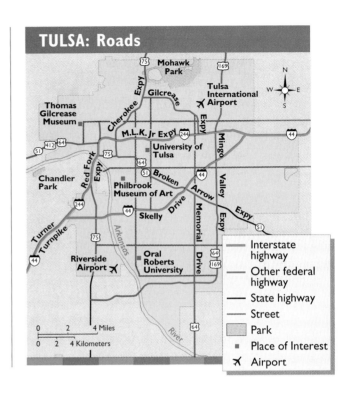

TULSA: Roads

Legend:
- Interstate highway
- Other federal highway
- State highway
- Street
- Park
- ■ Place of Interest
- ✈ Airport

Summing Up the Chapter

Use the following spider map to organize information from the chapter. Copy the map on a sheet of paper. Then write at least one piece of information in each blank circle. When you have filled in the map, use it to write a paragraph that answers the question, "Why are Oklahoma's resources and landforms important to the state?"

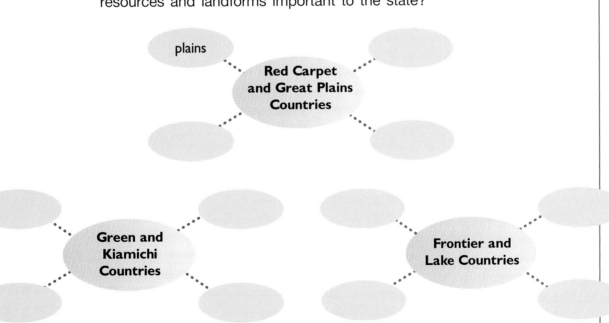

plains

Red Carpet and Great Plains Countries

Green and Kiamichi Countries

Frontier and Lake Countries

CHAPTER 5

The People of Oklahoma

THINKING ABOUT GEOGRAPHY AND CULTURE

Have you ever thought about the many people in our state yesterday and today? In Oklahoma we have people from many different backgrounds and cultures. In Chapter 5 we will learn about some of the ways Oklahomans of yesterday and today celebrate and enjoy our state's rich cultures.

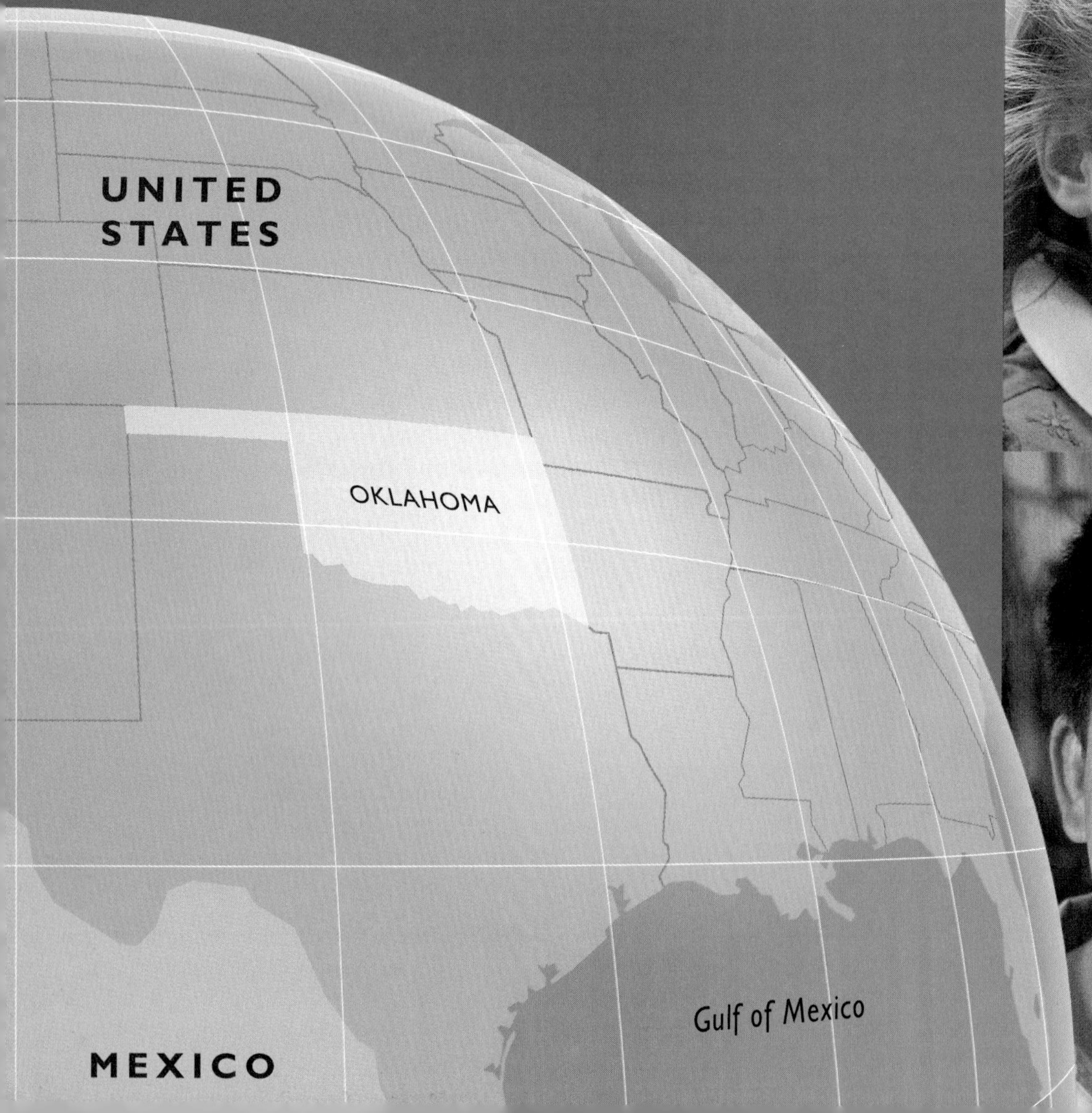
UNITED STATES
OKLAHOMA
Gulf of Mexico
MEXICO

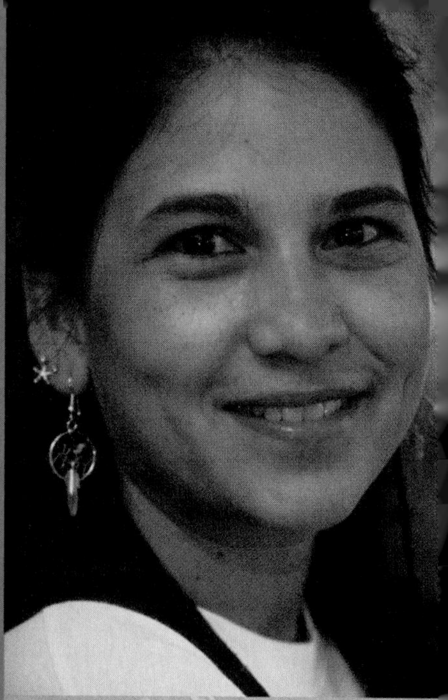

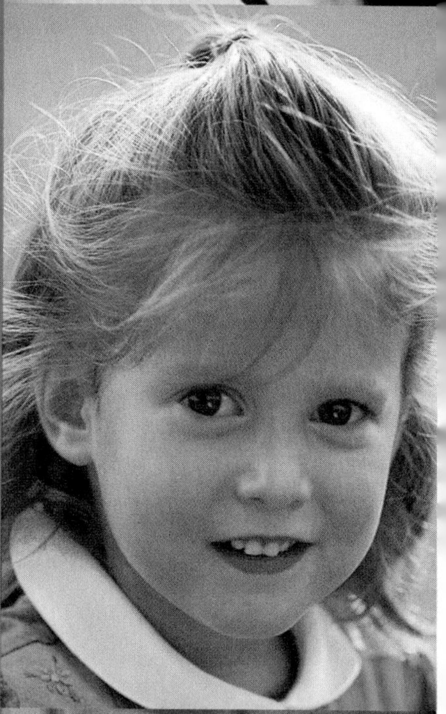

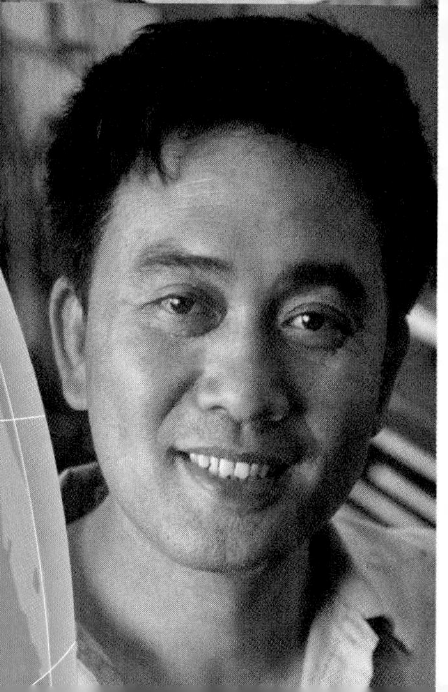

A Frontier People

Focus Activity

READ TO LEARN

What is special about the people of Oklahoma?

VOCABULARY

- population
- labor

PEOPLE

- Jim Thorpe
- Will Rogers

PLACES

- Oologah
- Prague

Read Aloud

"Oklahoma is still the promised land where dreams come true."

These words were spoken by Yvonne Kauger, a judge on the Oklahoma Supreme Court. In this lesson you will read about how people in our state have worked hard to make Oklahoma a place to be proud of.

THE BIG PICTURE

Why do people like Yvonne Kauger think Oklahoma is a special place? One reason is its people. Have you ever wondered where our state got its name? The name Oklahoma is an American Indian word. It means "land of the red people." Indians settled the land of our state thousands of years ago. Later, other settlers came.

OUR PEOPLE

About a third of all American Indians in the United States today live in Oklahoma. More Indians live here than in any other state. Today more than 60 different groups of American Indians are part of Oklahoma's population (pahp yu LAY shun). Population is the number of people living in a place. They include groups such as the Cherokee, Ponca, Chocktaw, Kiowa, Cheyenne, and Chickasaw.

Indians from other areas and European Americans settled here in the 1800s. Both groups brought enslaved African Americans with them. They helped to cut down forests, herd cattle, and build farms. Today Oklahoma's population of three million four hundred thousand includes many different ethnic groups. Look at the circle graph on this page. It shows our state's population. What different groups of people are shown?

Working People

Oklahoma's state seal has the Latin words, "*Labor Omnia Vincit.*" This motto means "Labor Conquers All Things." Labor means work.

The motto also shows the spirit of the early people who settled Oklahoma. American Indians worked hard to build schools and farms. Later, European settlers and others worked hard to build railroads and bridges to cross over our land. They also had to build farms and businesses. This spirit lives on in the Oklahomans of today.

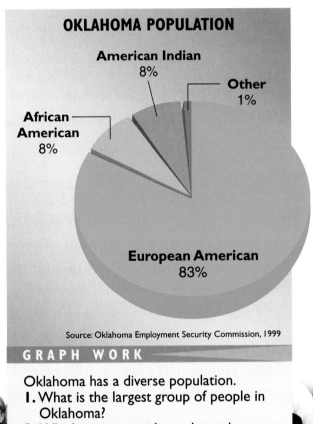

OKLAHOMA POPULATION

American Indian 8%

Other 1%

African American 8%

European American 83%

Source: Oklahoma Employment Security Commission, 1999

GRAPH WORK

Oklahoma has a diverse population.
1. What is the largest group of people in Oklahoma?
2. Which two groups have about the same population?

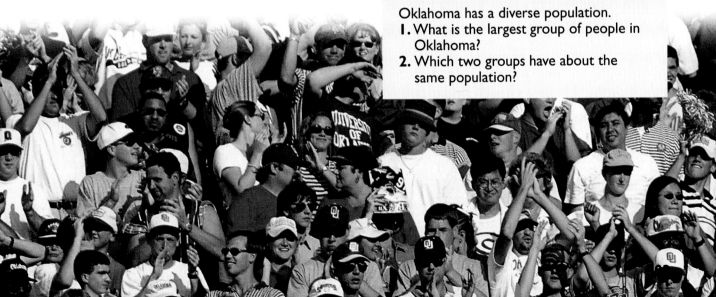

two gold medals and set records that had never been matched.

After the Olympics, Thorpe played professional baseball and football. He was a success in both sports. Jim Thorpe's popularity made football become a well-known sport in our country.

TWO FAMOUS OKLAHOMANS

Two Oklahomans who lived by the spirit of our state's motto were Jim Thorpe and Will Rogers. Their determination and hard work made them successful in almost everything they did.

Jim Thorpe

Jim Thorpe grew up near Prague (PRAH ge). Both of his parents were American Indians, and Thorpe was proud of his Sac and Fox heritage. His Indian name, Wa-tho-Huck, means "Bright Path." The path Jim Thorpe followed through life led to many successes. He became a world-famous athlete.

In 1912 Thorpe competed in track and field in the Olympics. He won

Will Rogers

Will Rogers is another famous Oklahoman. Like Jim Thorpe, Rogers was of American Indian ancestry. He was part Cherokee. Growing up in Oologah (oo LOW gah), Will Rogers loved to ride horses and to do rope tricks. He practiced with the rope every chance he had.

After many years of hard work, Rogers became a good rider and talented roper. In the early 1900s he was a rodeo star. Roger's favorite trick was roping a horse and its rider at the same time with two different ropes!

Will Rogers was also well known as a humorist. A humorist is a person who writes and tells funny stories. Crowds gathered wherever Rogers appeared in the country to hear his stories and to see him do rope tricks.

Will Rogers soon became a radio and movie star. He also wrote books and his own newspaper column.

Like Jim Thorpe, Will Rogers worked hard at many things. Because of his hard work, he became a great success. Since 1937, the airport in Oklahoma City has been named after him. Today he is still remembered as a great Oklahoman.

Will Rogers was a famous cowboy and entertainer. He wore these boots during his days as a rodeo star.

WHY IT MATTERS

Jim Thorpe and Will Rogers are only two Oklahomans who worked hard to make their dreams come true. Many other Oklahomans, from different backgrounds and with other talents, have also worked hard and succeeded. Through the efforts of many Oklahomans, our state continues to grow today.

Reviewing Facts and Ideas

MAIN IDEAS

- Oklahomans come from many different backgrounds.
- Oklahomans work hard at many things and take pride in their labor.
- Will Rogers and Jim Thorpe were two famous Oklahomans who succeeded through hard work.

THINK ABOUT IT

1. Who were the first people to live in Oklahoma?

2. What word on the state seal of Oklahoma shows the spirit of hard work?

3. **FOCUS** What is special about the people of Oklahoma?

4. **THINKING SKILL** *Compare* and *contrast* the lives of Jim Thorpe and Will Rogers.

5. **WRITE** Suppose you could interview Will Rogers or Jim Thorpe. List three questions you could ask to learn more about their lives.

Oklahoma's Culture

Read Aloud

"There is a circle/whose heart is a drum and it pounds/and it pounds/and it pounds and we are the circle."

This is a poem written by an Oklahoman named Charles Red Corn. The different Oklahomans that you read about in the last lesson make up the circle he writes about.

Focus Activity

READ TO LEARN

What are some special features of Oklahoma culture?

VOCABULARY

• Red Earth

PEOPLE

• Jim Shoulders
• Maria Tallchief
• Charles Banks Wilson

THE BIG PICTURE

The way of life of a group of people is called their culture. As you have read, culture includes a group's language, religion, and arts. It also includes sports and celebrations. In the last lesson you learned that many different kinds of people live in Oklahoma. Now let's see how these people make up a special culture for our state.

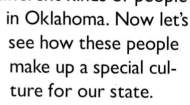

A NATIVE AMERICAN POWWOW

Suppose you are in a place filled with all the colors of the rainbow. Indian American women are dressed in beaded buckskins. They dance to the beat of a drum. If you have ever been to a powwow, it is easy to understand this scene. A pow-wow is a gathering of American Indians. At these events there is often dancing and music. Powwows were held for many reasons. Sometimes they were a social gathering. Other times, they were held for events like harvesting and droughts. Today they are a way for American Indians to celebrate the ways and beliefs that are handed down from one generation to the next.

"As long as the powwows continue, the Indian heritage will be kept alive. They are the Indians' way of life," says Ann Shadlow, an American Indian storyteller. Today, the Indian way of life continues with powwows and traditional dances across our state.

Red Earth Powwow

One present-day Indian festival is called Red Earth. It is held every June in Oklahoma City. Red Earth is a celebration of Indian American art, music, and dance. The outdoor art festival is very popular. It shows the works of hundreds of American Indian artists. Singing, flute playing, a parade, pottery and basketmaking, and dancing are all a part of the fun.

American Indians celebrate their culture at the Anadarko Indian Festival.

SPORTS AND DANCE

The cowboys and cowgirls ride in on horses. They are followed by colorful rodeo clowns. The crowd jumps to its feet and cheers as the announcer shouts, "Let's rodeo!"

This scene is played out over and over across Oklahoma every year. A rodeo, like a powwow, is an event that has been passed down over time. It had its beginning more than 100 years ago in friendly games between cowboys.

Life for the working cowboy on the plains was often boring. To break up the boredom, the cowboys played games. They used their skills of roping, branding cattle, and riding. The games soon became contests. These contests were called "rodeos." *Rodeo* is a Spanish word meaning "round-up."

The names of many Oklahomans can be found on a list of rodeo champions. One that stands above all is Jim Shoulders. He has won 16 world rodeo championships. This is more than anyone else in the history of the sport! This famous rodeo star is in the Cowboy Hall of Fame in Oklahoma City. Other well-known Oklahoma athletes are the baseball player Mickey Mantle and Olympic gymnast Shannon Miller.

Rodeo is only one of the many sports that Oklahomans enjoy. Oklahomans can be found in many different sports arenas at different times of the year cheering for one of our state's popular teams.

Saturday Means Football

The fall season means football in Oklahoma. Throughout our state thousands of people enjoy cheering for teams from the University of Oklahoma and Oklahoma State University. Like the rodeo it is part of our heritage. Each year the excitement rises in anticipation of this football game between these two friendly Oklahoma rivals.

Sports are an important part of Oklahoma's culture. Oklahomans take great pride in their teams' talents. The hard-working spirit that helped Oklahomans settle the frontier can be seen in the exciting sports of our state.

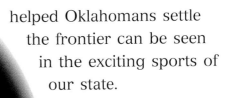

Dance

The year is 1949. All eyes in the house are drawn to the graceful figure on the stage. The audience watches as Maria Tallchief dances the leading role in a well known ballet. The ballet is called "Firebird."

Oklahoma has been home to more famous ballerinas than any other state. Five leading ballerinas have come from our state. They include Yvonne Chouteau, Maria Tallchief, Marjorie Tallchief, Moscelyne Larkin, and Rosella Hightower. All were of American Indian heritage. Maria Tallchief was the best known of these dancers. She was born in Fairfax, Oklahoma. Her father was an Osage Indian. She danced in many ballets all over the world.

Rodeos and football are two sports Oklahomans enjoy. Jim Shoulders (left) is a famous rodeo star. Maria Tallchief (above) is shown in the ballet "Firebird."

OTHER ARTS

Dance is just one of the arts that is important to Oklahoma culture. Painting, writing, music, and many other art forms are also important.

Oklahoma is home to several famous painters. Charles Banks Wilson is one of them. He has been called "America's finest artist historian." Some of his large wall paintings, or murals, are in the State Capitol in Oklahoma City. They show more than 400 years of our state's history.

Wilson has painted such famous Oklahomans as Jim Thorpe and Will Rogers. He also painted Oklahoma's Indians. In addition, Wilson has painted scenes of Oklahoma's beautiful lakes, creeks, and farms.

Charles Banks Wilson at work painting in his studio.

WHY IT MATTERS

Do you remember the poem at the beginning of this lesson? It says, "There is a circle . . . and we are the circle." As you read, the powwow, the rodeo, other sports, and arts such as music, dance and painting are all at the heart of this circle. By joining together and sharing cultures, Oklahomans can make their state special.

✓/ Reviewing Facts and Ideas

MAIN IDEAS

- The many different kinds of people in Oklahoma all contribute to our state's culture.
- Native American powwows are an important part of Oklahoma's heritage.
- Rodeos, other sports, and dance are all cultural activities enjoyed by Oklahomans.
- Painting, writing, and music are other arts important to Oklahomans

THINK ABOUT IT

1. What is a rodeo?

2. What can we learn about Oklahomans by studying their culture?

3. FOCUS In what ways is Oklahoma's culture special?

4. THINKING SKILL How would you *classify* the different cultural events in Oklahoma?

5. WRITE Suppose that you are an Oklahoma newspaper reporter at the Red Earth powwow today. What different events might you write about? How will you describe them?

MAKING A DIFFERENCE

Teaching and Learning Through Art

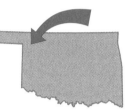

WOODWARD, OKLAHOMA— When you walk into the office at Horace Mann Elementary School, one of the first things you notice are colorful murals hanging on the walls. "They sure add spark to the school," said teacher Patsy McIlvan. Her fourth grade class made them with the help of students from nearby Woodward High School.

The students are part of a program called the "Picasso Art Project." It was started in 1995 by a teacher named Roxy Merklin. She wanted to introduce art to younger students. She asked her high school students to help teach them. Mrs. Merklin thought the teenagers could benefit as well. "If you want someone to learn something," she explained, "have them teach it to someone else."

Every year the high school students help fourth graders paint murals of rain forests, the solar system, wildlife, state history, and other subjects. Each class creates its own mural. The high school students visit the elementary school twice a week to show the younger students how to lay out the designs, mix paint, and choose colors. "It made me feel good to think that I could teach them something they didn't know," said one high school student. "They saw that art gives you a way to express yourself in ways other than words."

Riley Pagett likes the murals he helped create. "Let's say you're having a bad day," he said. "You look at something like that and you know kids your age did it. It makes you feel like you can do something special, too."

"It makes you feel like you can do something special, too."

Riley Pagett

CHAPTER 5 REVIEW

THINKING ABOUT VOCABULARY

Number a sheet of paper from 1 to 5. Next to each number write the word that best matches the definition.

culture
labor
population
powwow
Red Earth

1. A meeting of American Indians

2. The number of people who live in a place

3. An American Indian event held in Oklahoma City

4. People who make products or provide services

5. The way of life of a group of people

THINKING ABOUT FACTS

1. When did large groups of European settlers come to Oklahoma?

2. Name three parts of Oklahoma's culture.

3. Why are powwows held today?

4. What is meant by the motto "Labor Conquers All Things"?

5. About how many American Indian groups are in Oklahoma?

6. Who was Will Rogers?

7. What was some of the work early settlers had to do? Name two activities.

8. Who was Jim Thorpe?

9. Why did rodeos begin?

10. Name three American Indian groups in Oklahoma.

11. Who is Jim Shoulders?

12. What two sports are part of Oklahoma's heritage?

13. Identify three important skills used by cowhands.

14. Name two well-known ballerinas from Oklahoma.

15. Who is Charles Banks Wilson?

THINK AND WRITE

WRITING AN ADVERTISEMENT
Create an advertisement to be placed in a magazine about our state. The advertisement will encourage people to come to the Red Earth powwow. Include some of the activities that make the event special.

WRITING A LIST
Suppose you are a sports writer for a newspaper and your assignment is to interview Jim Shoulders. Write a list of three questions you might ask him. Then, think of the answers he might give.

WRITING A RESEARCH REPORT
Choose one of the people you have read about in this chapter. Do some research at the library or on the Internet to learn more about the person and his or her work or special skills. Then write a report about the person and share it with the class.

APPLYING GEOGRAPHY SKILLS

USING ROAD MAPS

Refer to the map of Oklahoma City on this page to help you answer the following questions.

1. What interstate highways go through Oklahoma City?

2. Which highway can you take from highway 40 to highway 44?

3. In which direction does highway 35 go?

4. In which direction does Interstate 40 go?

5. Which interstate highways does highway 240 meet?

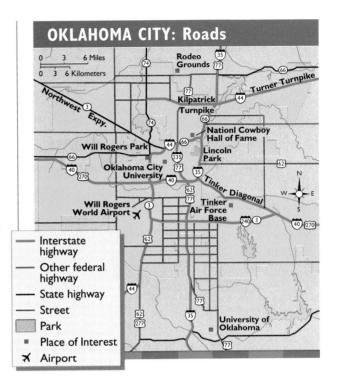

OKLAHOMA CITY: Roads

— Interstate highway
— Other federal highway
— State highway
— Street
▢ Park
▪ Place of Interest
✈ Airport

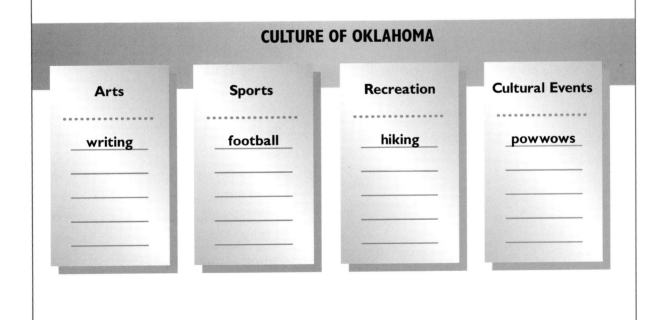

Summing Up the Chapter

Use the following horizontal organization chart to organize information from the chapter. Copy the chart on a sheet of paper. Then fill in the blank spaces on the chart. When you have filled in the chart, use it to write a paragraph answering the question, "How does the culture of Oklahoma make it a special place?"

CULTURE OF OKLAHOMA

Arts	Sports	Recreation	Cultural Events
writing	football	hiking	powwows

UNIT 2 REVIEW

THINKING ABOUT VOCABULARY

Number a sheet of paper from 1 to 10. Next to each number write the word or phrase from the list that best completes the sentence.

culture
frontier
labor
mesa
mesquite

plateau
population
powwow
prairie
Red Earth

1. A flat-topped hill with steep sides is a _____.

2. A high, flat area that rises steeply above the surrounding land is called a _____.

3. A meeting of American Indians is called a _____.

4. A type of small, thorny tree is called _____.

5. Another word for the work people do is _____.

6. The number of people who live in a place is called _____.

7. The land near where people have settled is a _____.

8. An American Indian event held in Oklahoma City is _____.

9. Grassland on a plain is a _____.

10. The way of life of a group of people is their _____.

THINK AND WRITE

WRITING A POSTER

Suppose you want to encourage people to visit Oklahoma. Write and design a poster that helps people see what makes our state great.

WRITE A SUMMARY

Write about the resources that can be found in the different countries of Oklahoma and why they are important.

WRITING AN ARTICLE

Suppose you are a writer at a newspaper. Write an article about going to a powwow. You can do research at the library or on the Internet to find out about specific powwows in Oklahoma.

BUILDING SKILLS

1. **Reading Road Maps:** Explain how a road map is different from an elevation map.

2. **Reading Road Maps:** Look at the road map of Oklahoma on page 91. How can you tell the difference between state and interstate highways?

3. **Reading Road Maps:** What is different about the even- and odd-numbered roads on a road map? How does this help you tell which direction you are going?

4. **Reading Road Maps:** Suppose you want to drive from Tulsa to Oklahoma City. Which interstate highway would you take?

5. **Reading Road Maps:** Suppose you want to drive from Tulsa to Guymon. What roads would you take?

YESTERDAY, TODAY & *TOMORROW*

Historic places help us to keep history alive. Are there any historical places in your area that have been preserved for the future? Think of a place, like your school, that you use or visit every day. What would people from the future learn about daily life today if that place were preserved.

READING ON YOUR OWN

Here are some books you might find at the library to help you learn more.

RESOURCES
by Brian Knapp
This book explores the history of natural resources such as coal and water.

WHO BELONGS HERE: AN AMERICAN STORY
by Margy Burns Knight
The author describes the story of a ten-year-old who comes to live in a new country.

OKLAHOMA
by Barbara Palmer
Read about the unique history and culture of Oklahoma.

UNIT 2 REVIEW PROJECT

Make a Community Guide

1. Take a walk around your community. What are some of the things that you see? Notice the parks, statues, and schools.

2. Research historical and cultural places in your community, such as buildings and museums. One place to look for information is your local library.

3. Then draw pictures of what you find. Cut out your pictures and glue them onto separate sheets of colored construction paper.

4. Write a desription under each picture.

5. Finally, create a cover, including the name of your community, and staple you guide together.

BISON (RIGHT); GLENN POOL OIL FIELD IN THE 1920s (MIDDLE); CAR FROM THE 1950s (BOTTOM); OPOTHLEYAHOLA (FAR RIGHT)

Oklahoma's History

> *". . . land seems well suited for buffaloes and other wild game."*
>
> from a description by explorer Major Stephen Long
> See page 132.

Why Does It Matter?

Who were the first people to live in Oklahoma? What was Oklahoma like hundreds or even thousands of years ago? How did it become part of the United States? How is it different today than long ago?

Unit 3 will answer these questions. It begins with the first people to live on the land that is now Oklahoma, tells about the people who came later and changed the history of our area, and ends with a look at our state today.

The Granger Collection

The Granger Collection

FIND OUT MORE!
Visit our website:
www.mhschool.com

inter**NET**
CONNECTION

Early Life in Oklahoma

THINKING ABOUT GEOGRAPHY AND HISTORY

Who were the first people in Oklahoma? According to many historians, the first American Indians may have lived in present-day Oklahoma beginning about 20,000 years ago. Then one day in the 1500s, strangers arrived from a distant land called Europe. They would change forever the way people lived in what is today Oklahoma. Read this chapter to find out what these newcomers did and how they changed our land.

800

SPIRO
Spiro Mound people live in Oklahoma

1541

OKLAHOMA PANHANDLE
Spanish explorer Francisco de Coronado explores areas in Oklahoma

1682

MISSISSIPPI RIVER
Robert La Salle claims lands, including Oklahoma, for France

800   1000   1200   1600

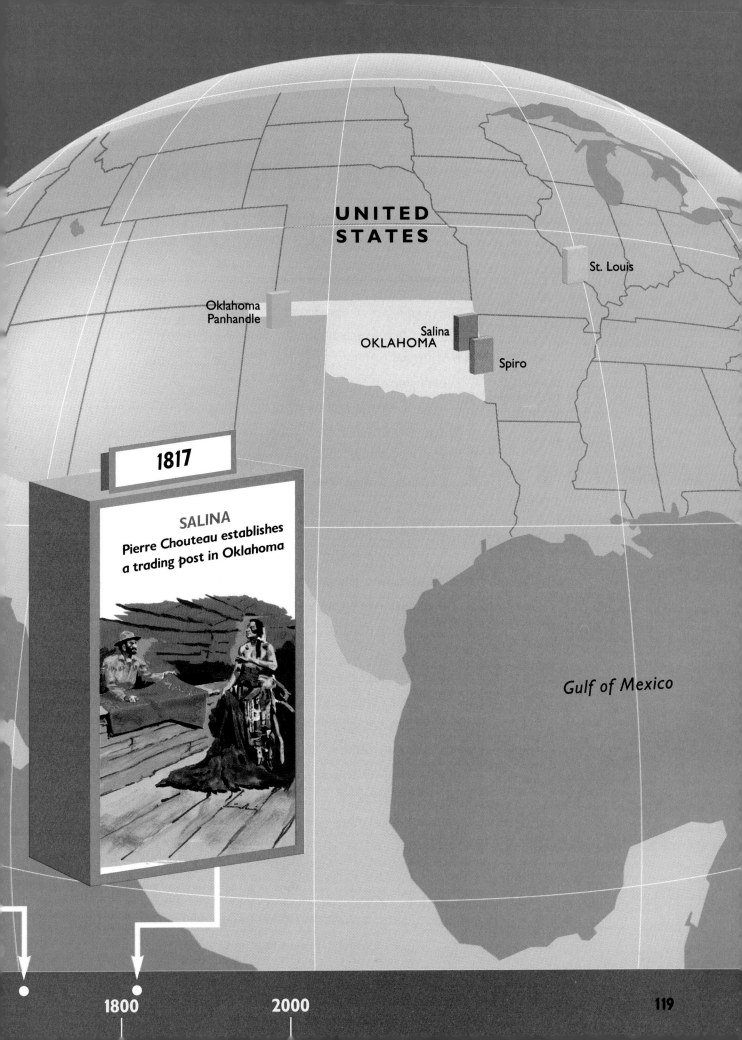

UNITED
STATES

St. Louis

Oklahoma
Panhandle

Salina
OKLAHOMA

Spiro

1817

SALINA
Pierre Chouteau establishes
a trading post in Oklahoma

Gulf of Mexico

1800

2000

| 60,000 YEARS AGO | 40,000 YEARS AGO | 20,000 YEARS AGO | 600 YEARS AGO | PRESENT |

Oklahoma's First People

Read Aloud

" . . . the Spiro Mounds show that they . . . produced pottery, textiles [clothes] . . . and metal goods."

These words tell us about an important discovery in the Arkansas River Valley in 1932. The mounds helped us learn about the early history of our state.

Focus Activity

READ TO LEARN

Who were the first people to live in Oklahoma?

VOCABULARY

- artifact
- mammoth
- Mound Builders

PLACES

- Spiro

THE BIG PICTURE

By studying items like the ones found at Spiro Mounds we can learn a lot about how early Oklahomans lived. The items left by people who lived long ago are called artifacts. Artifacts help scientists find out about life in the past. What kind of houses did these early people build? What did they make? Did they farm on our plains? Or did they hunt?

THE FIRST OKLAHOMANS

People have lived on the land of present-day Oklahoma longer than in many other places in our country. Scientists have found clues telling them that people lived here as long as 20,000 years ago.

These first Oklahomans were also the first American Indians. From artifacts that have been found, we think that these early American Indians moved from place to place hunting and gathering food.

These early Oklahomans ate fish, seeds, roots, nuts, and berries. They also ate the meat of a kind of large elephant called a mammoth (MAM uth). The plains and prairies of Oklahoma were large open spaces covered with grass. Mammoth and other large animals grazed here.

After thousands of years these early Americans learned that they could plant the seeds they gathered for food. These seeds would grow into new plants. In time they became farmers. The early people no longer moved from place to place looking for wild plants and hunting animals. They planted crops. They learned to build permanent shelters to live in. They had the time to make better weapons, tools, and baskets from natural resources such as clay, wood, and stone.

Dinosaur footprints (center). Later, at the end of the last ice age, Oklahomans hunted the woolly mammoth (below). The Spiro people produced pottery such as this jar (far left).

THE MOUND BUILDERS

From about 1,400 years ago to about 800 years ago, another farming group lived in what is today Oklahoma. These people became known as the Mound Builders. They were given this name because they built large mounds of earth. Some of these mounds still stand today. These early Americans built the mounds for different reasons. Sometimes the mounds were used as religious temples. Other times they were used to bury important leaders of the group.

Links to SCIENCE

The Dating Game

Did you know that you have something called carbon 14 inside you? All living things do. When something that is alive dies, the amount of carbon 14 starts to decrease. An archaeologist can measure how much carbon 14 is left in a very old object and tell us how old the object is. This test, called carbon dating, works for objects up to 50,000 years old!

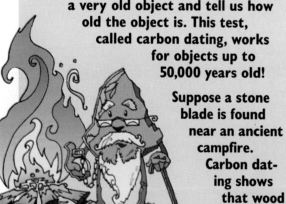

Suppose a stone blade is found near an ancient campfire. Carbon dating shows that wood from the campfire is 9,000 years old. If the same people made the blade and the fire, how old do you think the stone blade is? Explain.

Spiro Mound

During the 1930s, scientists began digging into the largest of 11 mounds near Spiro in eastern Oklahoma. The mound the scientists studied was nearly 50 feet high. It was made of both logs and tons of earth.

Scientists studied the objects they found in the mound. Among the many different objects in the mound were pottery, carved figures, baskets, cloth, and weapons. From these and other items, we have been able to tell that the Spiro people were farmers. They lived in large communities. The Spiro people also traded goods with other groups of people. Some of

the items in the mound came from faraway places. Shells and pearls came from the Gulf of Mexico. Copper came from areas in what is now the Great Lakes area of our country. A powerful group, the Spiro people controlled trade between the plains to the west and the woodlands to the east.

What Happened?

No one knows for sure what happened to the Spiro people and other Mound Builders. Some scientists believe other American Indians attacked their villages and forced them to leave. Others think that a long time without enough rain to grow crops forced the Mound Builders to move. By the time the first Europeans came to Oklahoma in 1541, the Mound Builders were gone.

WHY IT MATTERS

After the Mound Builders disappeared, groups of other American Indians came to live in the area we now call Oklahoma. For many years they were the only people to live here. In the next lesson you will see how the lives of the American Indians were forever changed.

Reviewing Facts and Ideas

MAIN IDEAS

- The first people in Oklahoma came here over 20,000 years ago.
- The early American Indians of Oklahoma were both hunters and gatherers and farmers.
- The Spiro Mound people lived in Oklahoma beginning about 1400 years ago. Scientists do not know why the Mound Builders disappeared from Oklahoma.

THINK ABOUT IT

1. How did scientists learn about the lives of the Spiro people?

2. What did the first Oklahomans eat?

3. **FOCUS** Who were the first people to live in the area that is now Oklahoma?

4. **THINKING SKILL** *Compare* and *contrast* the Mound Builders' life with your life today.

5. **GEOGRAPHY** Give two examples of natural resources in Oklahoma that were important to the American Indians of long ago.

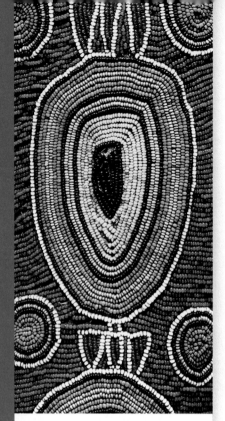

Explorers

Read Aloud

"It was said that there were cities whose walls were made of solid gold and whose people wore hats of gold and ate from golden plates."

In the 1500s some people from Europe were told about cities of gold such as the one described here. Stories of riches made them search for these "golden cities."

Focus Activity

READ TO LEARN

Who were the first Europeans to explore the land that is now Oklahoma?

VOCABULARY

- explorer
- expedition
- adobe
- trading post
- Louisiana Purchase

PEOPLE

- Francisco de Coronado
- Robert La Salle
- Thomas Jefferson

THE BIG PICTURE

A short time after the Mound Builders disappeared from Oklahoma, **explorers** from Europe came to America. An explorer is a person who travels to unknown areas. Some of them were from Spain and France. In this lesson you will read about these explorers. Their search for riches led them to what is now Oklahoma.

SPANISH EXPLORERS

While in Mexico, a Spanish explorer, Francisco de Coronado (fran SEES koh day koh roh NAH doh), heard stories that there were American Indian cities made of gold. From 1540 to 1542 he led an expedition (ek spih DISH un), or journey of exploration, to look for these cities.

Coronado's expedition traveled into the Panhandle of Oklahoma. Trace Coronado's route on the map below. As he crossed the Panhandle, Coronado became the first European to visit the area that is today Oklahoma. The first American Indians he met in our area were the Wichita, who lived in Quivira (KEE ver ah). One of the members of Coronado's expedition wrote: ". . . they were intelligent. . . and did nothing unusual when they saw [us]. . ."

No Gold

Coronado did not find golden cities. In the West, he found American Indian villages made of clay bricks, or adobe. The people he saw in Oklahoma were hunters who

sheltered in teepees covered with buffalo hides. Returning to Mexico in 1542, a disappointed Coronado sent this message to the King of Spain:

*I am sure of it that there
is not any gold nor any
other metal in that country.*

Still, Coronado claimed this land for Spain. In this way Oklahoma became Spanish territory and the Spanish flag flew over our land. A territory is land under the control of a distant government.

This painting of Coronado's expedition shows the clothing the Spanish wore and the equipment they carried.

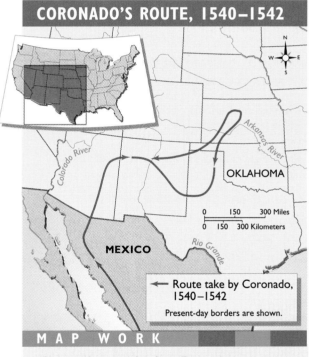

CORONADO'S ROUTE, 1540–1542

OKLAHOMA

Arkansas River

Colorado River

0   150   300 Miles
0   150   300 Kilometers

MEXICO

Rio Grande

← Route take by Coronado, 1540–1542

Present-day borders are shown.

MAP WORK

Coronado was the first European to explore the area that is now Oklahoma.

Through what part of present-day Oklahoma did Coronado travel?

FRENCH EXPLORERS

Spanish explorers were not the only Europeans to explore Oklahoma. Later, in the 1600s, French explorers and traders traveled south from Canada to the Gulf of Mexico, and then northwest to the area that is now Oklahoma.

The French were interested in the Mississippi River system. They wanted to explore the land near the rivers and meet the people who lived there. They also wanted to find places to build forts. The forts were needed by the French to protect their lands against attacks by the Spanish.

Louisiana Territory

In 1682 a French explorer, Robert La Salle (roh BAIR lah SAL), traveled with a crew of 41 men south down the Mississippi River to the Gulf of Mexico. La Salle claimed the land west of the Mississippi River for the king of France. This land included all of present-day Oklahoma. La Salle named the land he claimed the "Louisiana Territory" in honor of King Louis XIV.

The French explorers found the forests of Oklahoma filled with natural resources, especially animals with thick fur. The furs of these animals were very valuable in Europe and were sold for high prices. This caused many French to become fur traders.

The French fur traders set up buildings called trading posts near rivers and lakes. At trading posts Indians could get goods they needed in exchange for crops they had grown, furs, or things they had made.

In order to get furs, the French traded with the American Indians for such goods as guns, knives, cloth, beads, and blankets. The furs were loaded on ships and sent to Europe. There they were made into fashionable hats and clothing.

Artwork (right) by Frederic Remington shows Robert La Salle and his group exploring the Mississippi River. Robert La Salle (top).

THE LOUISIANA PURCHASE

For may years France controlled the rich lands of Louisiana. In 1803 the President of the United States, Thomas Jefferson, worried that the French might try to control even more land. They might not allow people to use the Mississippi River or to travel west through their lands. As a result President Jefferson sent James Madison to France. In 1803 Jefferson bought Louisiana from France. This land was called the Louisiana Purchase. It doubled the size of the United States.

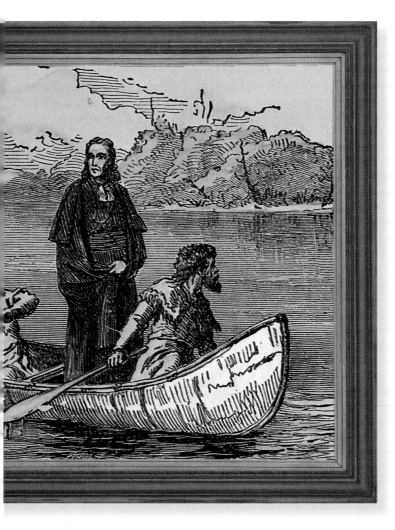

WHY IT MATTERS

The search for riches brought first the Spanish and then the French to the land of Oklahoma. They each claimed these lands to be their own at different times. Soon the United States would send explorers to the Oklahoma frontier. You will read about them in the next lesson.

✓ Reviewing Facts and Ideas

MAIN IDEAS

- The Spanish explorer Francisco de Coronado traveled through Oklahoma from 1540–1542.

- In 1682 Robert La Salle claimed the land west of the Mississippi River for France.

- In 1803, the land that was to become Oklahoma was sold to the United States as part of the Louisiana Purchase.

THINK ABOUT IT

1. What riches did the French find in Oklahoma?

2. What was the Louisiana Purchase?

3. **FOCUS** Who were the first Europeans to explore the land that is now Oklahoma?

4. **THINKING SKILL** *Predict* what might have happened if Coronado had found his cities of gold?

5. **GEOGRAPHY** Look at the Map on page 125. What river did French explorers cross to reach Oklahoma?

Reading Time Lines

VOCABULARY

Time line

WHY THE SKILL MATTERS

In the last lesson, you read about the early explorers and history of Oklahoma. You also read about the expedition of Francisco de Coronado. His expedition began in Mexico in 1540. How old was he? What else did he achieve?

To understand history, you need to know when events happened. You also need to know in which order they happened. Coronado is best remembered for exploring the Southwest. What else happened in his life? In what order did these things happen?

To help answer these questions, you can use a time line. A time line is a diagram that shows when events took place. It also shows the amount of time that passed between events. The way a time line is drawn helps to give a sense of sequence, or order, to history. The time line below shows events that occurred in the life of Francisco de Coronado.

USING THE SKILL

Look at the time line below. First look at the length of time it shows. It has two parts, and each part represents 50 years. Now look at the dates and events. As you can see, each event appears above or below the date it happened. The earliest event—Francisco de Coronado's birth—is listed on the left. The most recent—his death—is on the right.

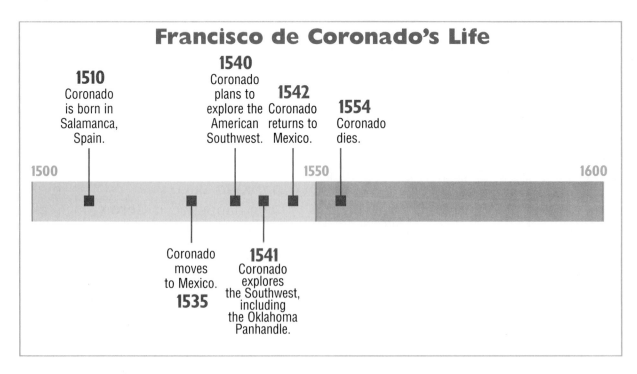

Francisco de Coronado's Life

1510
Coronado is born in Salamanca, Spain.

1540
Coronado plans to explore the American Southwest.

1542
Coronado returns to Mexico.

1554
Coronado dies.

1500   1550   1600

Coronado moves to Mexico.
1535

1541
Coronado explores the Southwest, including the Oklahoma Panhandle.

Like most time lines, this one is divided into equal parts. Each part represents a certain number of years. Each part of Coronado's time line represents 50 years.

TRYING THE SKILL

Now read the time line of Oklahoma's Early History. Use the Helping Yourself box for hints.

What period of history does the time line cover? What event on the time line happened first? In what year did La Salle claim Oklahoma for France? Did the Mound Builders disappear before or after Coronado explored Oklahoma? What happened in 1803?

Helping yourself

- A time line is a diagram that shows when historical events took place.
- Note how much time is represented by each part of the time line.
- Read the events from left to right.

REVIEWING THE SKILL

Use the information on the time line below to answer the following questions.

1. How does a time line help you to place events in the right order?
2. Which event took place in 1682?
3. How much time passed between Coronado's expedition and La Salle's?
4. Did the United States buy Oklahoma before or after La Salle?
5. Could you use a time line to show events in your life? In what other subjects would a time line be useful?

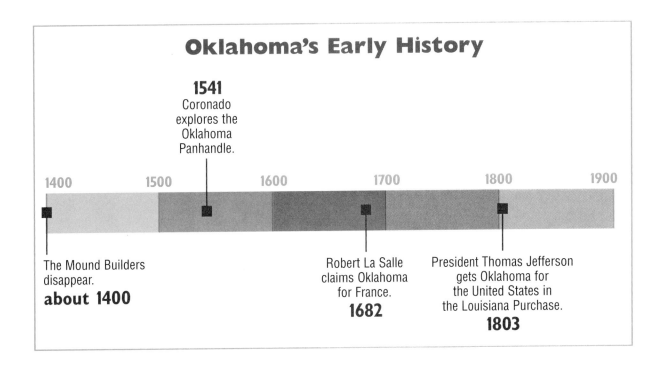

Oklahoma's Early History

1541
Coronado explores the Oklahoma Panhandle.

1400   1500   1600   1700   1800   1900

The Mound Builders disappear.
about 1400

Robert La Salle claims Oklahoma for France.
1682

President Thomas Jefferson gets Oklahoma for the United States in the Louisiana Purchase.
1803

The Granger Collection

1800	1803		1861	1880	

Pioneers and American Indians

Read Aloud

"The first village of the Osage Indians lies about 60 miles from the mouth of the Verdigris River and is said to contain 700 or 800 men and their families. Nearly the whole town . . . [was] engaged in their summer hunt, collecting buffalo meat."

These words were written by Thomas Nuttall. He was an explorer who traveled through what is now Oklahoma in 1819.

Focus Activity

READ TO LEARN

Why did American explorers go to Oklahoma?

VOCABULARY

- settlement
- teepee

PEOPLE

- Meriwether Lewis
- William Clark
- Richard Sparks
- Sacajawea
- Pierre Chouteau
- Mark Bean

THE BIG PICTURE

Like other early explorers to the West, Thomas Nuttall spent much time with American Indians. They were the first settlers of this area. In this lesson you will read more about the early explorers and American Indians of Oklahoma.

The Plains Indians depended on the buffalo they hunted. This picture was painted by an artist named Edgar Paxson.

EXPLORING THE WEST

During the early 1880s, President Jefferson ordered several explorers to map the newly gained Louisiana Territory. The first were Lewis and Clark.

Lewis and Clark

In 1803 Jefferson sent his assistant, Meriwether Lewis, and William Clark, an army officer, to explore the Louisiana Territory and find a safe route to the Pacific Ocean.

The expedition numbered 42 men, including Clark's servant, York, an enslaved African American. They spent the winter in present-day North Dakota. There they hired a French fur trapper named Toussaint Charbonneau (tou SAHN SHAHR buh noh) as a guide. His wife, Sacajawea (sah kah jah WEE uh), a Shoshone Indian, translated for the explorers when they reached Shoshone lands. After 18 months, the group reached the Pacific Ocean. They had explored and mapped over 3,000 miles of land. They had not traveled through present-day Oklahoma. But they opened the way for others.

Exploring Oklahoma

President Jefferson asked Richard Sparks to explore the Red River in 1806. His group set out for what is now southeast Oklahoma. Along the way, they drew near some Spanish soldiers. Since his group was small, Sparks turned back. It would be another 50 years before an explorer would map all of the Red River.

A third group of explorers was led by Zebulon (zehb YOO lahn) Pike and James Wilkinson. They soon separated. Pike's group headed west along the Arkansas River to Colorado. Wilkinson went southeast along the Arkansas River into what is now northeast Oklahoma.

Wilkinson's group saw several Osage (OH saj) villages. Later, they also saw Spanish soldiers. But they continued on. Finally, in 1807 they left northeast Oklahoma. They were the first to explore northeast Oklahoma for the United States.

OUR LAND LONG AGO

Many of the first American explorers to reach what is now Oklahoma were disappointed. They thought it was not good for settlers. One explorer said, "The land is poor and hilly." Another explorer, Stephen Long, wrote:

The land seems well suited for buffaloes and other wild game. But it is almost unusable by those who would want to farm it.

Long and other explorers thought that the prairies of Oklahoma were divided by "a hot dry desert." After traveling through the southwestern part of Oklahoma, Long called it "The Great American Desert." For many years, people in the United States believed Long's description.

The Long Knives

Other explorers who came to Oklahoma found that its land had much to offer. American trappers and traders came in search of one of Oklahoma's important natural resources—its animals with fur.

This painting (below) by Charles Russell shows Plains Indians and French traders meeting at a 1800s trading post. Today, people visit the Red River Trading Post in Lawton (left).

The trappers hunted in the rivers and forests of Oklahoma for animals with valuable furs. Like the French, the traders also set up trading posts. There the American Indians could trade for such goods as axes, knives, and guns.

These trappers and traders were called "Long Knives." The American Indians gave them this name because each person carried a long, sharp knife in his belt. The Long Knives started the first white settlements in Oklahoma. A settlement is a place on the frontier where people live.

Early Settlers

Pierre Chouteau (shoo TOW) and Mark Bean were two early settlers who started new lives on the Oklahoma frontier. They used what the land had to offer to set up their businesses.

Chouteau was from a rich family in the fur-trading business. He built a trading post in northeastern Oklahoma. It sent boats with furs, salt, honey, and pecans to markets in St. Louis, in modern-day Missouri. Later, they also went to New Orleans, in what is today Louisiana. The boats returned with goods for the Indians and settlers.

Mark Bean also used the land to make a living. He raised crops for his family's food. He was a salt maker. Salt was important because it was used to keep meats from spoiling.

Bean collected saltwater from a spring near his house. He boiled the saltwater in large kettles over wood fires until only the salt was left. Bean then traded or sold the salt. Salt sold for about five dollars a bushel, which was a good sum of money at this time.

Chouteau and Bean made a lot of money in their businesses. Their success encouraged other Americans to explore the Oklahoma frontier.

Pierre Chouteau (below) started a trading post in Oklahoma. He sold a variety of goods, including kettles like this one.

OKLAHOMA'S INDIANS

When the Long Knives and American traders came to Oklahoma in the early 1800s, it was the home of several different American Indian groups. These included the Osage, Kiowa (KI oh wah), Comanche (ku MAN chee), Wichita (WICH ih tah), Apache and groups from the southeast and north.

Apache, Kiowa, and Comanche are called Plains Indians because they lived in the Great Plains area of our country. These American Indians were hunters. They moved from place to place hunting and gathering food. The Osage were Woodland Indians and lived in farming villages. The Wichita both farmed and hunted.

A Valuable Resource

The buffalo, or bison, was very important to the Plains Indians. It was their main source of food and clothing. Parts of it were also used for tools such as needles and weapons such as arrowheads. Horses were also

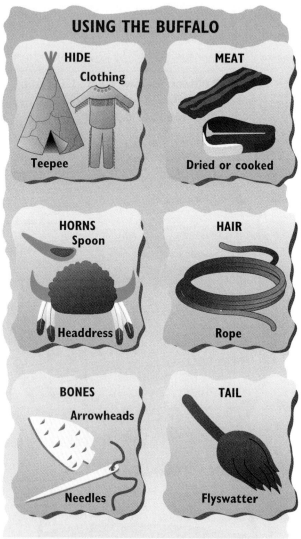

USING THE BUFFALO

HIDE
Clothing
Teepee

MEAT
Dried or cooked

HORNS
Spoon
Headdress

HAIR
Rope

BONES
Arrowheads
Needles

TAIL
Flyswatter

CHART WORK

The American Indians did not waste any part of the buffalo.

1. How did the American Indians make use of the hair of the buffalo?
2. Why do you think the American Indians needed to make needles from the bones?
3. Why do you think the buffalo were important to the American Indians?

This photo shows a Comanche winter camp from around 1875.

important. The Spanish first brought horses to what is now our country in the 1500s. Before that time, the Plains Indians hunted on foot. Horses allowed them to move about faster and farther. The Plains Indians were skilled horse riders. They used horses to hunt buffalo over the long, flat plains.

Look at the chart on page 134. From it you can see that the Plains Indians used the hides of the buffalo to build teepees (TEE peez). A teepee is a cone-shaped tent made with wooden poles and animal skins.

WHY IT MATTERS

Plains and Woodlands Indians, trappers, traders, and business people found the area that is today Oklahoma to be a good place to live. However, just as many people began coming to this land, the United States government made plans that totally changed Oklahoma's future. You will read about these plans in the next chapter.

✓ Reviewing Facts and Ideas

MAIN IDEAS

- In the early 1800s, Americans began to explore land throughout the Louisiana Purchase.
- Lewis and Clark explored the Louisiana Territory. Richard Sparks explored parts of the area that is today Oklahoma.
- Pierre Chouteau and Mark Bean were two early European American traders in Oklahoma.
- Long before the Americans arrived, the Plains and Woodland Indians had lived in the area for many years.
- The Plains Indians were skilled buffalo hunters.

THINK ABOUT IT

1. Who was Richard Sparks?
2. What are some of the American Indian groups that lived in Oklahoma when American explorers and settlers first came?
3. **FOCUS** Why did American explorers go to Oklahoma?
4. **THINKING SKILL** *Classify* into groups the different uses of the buffalo by the Plains Indians.
5. **WRITE** Suppose you were a settler in Oklahoma in the early 1800s. Write a short letter to your family describing your new life in Oklahoma.

CHAPTER 6 REVIEW

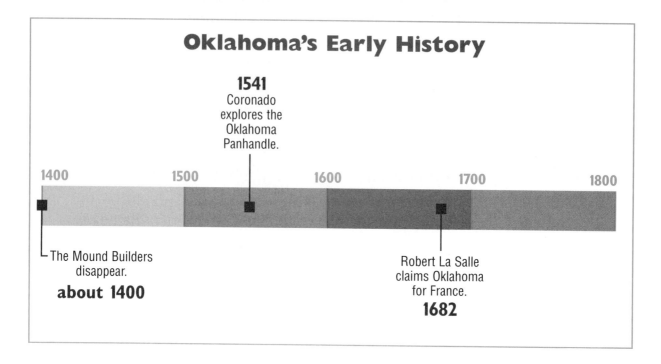

Oklahoma's Early History

1541
Coronado explores the Oklahoma Panhandle.

1400   1500   1600   1700   1800

The Mound Builders disappear.
about 1400

Robert La Salle claims Oklahoma for France.
1682

THINKING ABOUT VOCABULARY

Number a sheet of paper from 1 to 10. Beside each number write **C** if the underlined word or phrase is used correctly. If it is not, write the word that would correctly complete the sentence.

1. A Spiro was a large elephant that lived long ago.

2. A cone-shaped tent made with wooden poles and animal skins is called a settlement.

3. An explorer is a journey of exploration.

4. Clay bricks are called adobe.

5. Artifacts are items left by people who lived long ago.

6. A place where people could exchange goods was called a teepee.

7. A time line is a diagram that shows when events in history took place.

8. An expedition is someone who travels to unknown areas.

9. A trading post is a place on a frontier where people hunt.

10. Mound Builders were American Indians who built large mounds of earth.

THINKING ABOUT FACTS

1. Who was the first European to visit Oklahoma?

2. Why did the Spanish originally come to Oklahoma?

3. What were scientists able to tell about the Mound Builders?

4. Why was James Wilkinson important?

5. Why did the French become fur traders?

THINK AND WRITE

WRITING AN EXPLANATION
Explain why Thomas Jefferson wanted to purchase Louisiana from the French.

WRITING A COMPARISON
Write a comparison of the reasons why the Spanish, French, and Americans explored the land that became Oklahoma.

WRITING A LIST
Suppose you were to interview one of the early settlers in Oklahoma such as Pierre Chouteau and Mark Bean. Write three questions you would ask. Then, write answers they might give.

APPLYING STUDY SKILLS

USING TIME LINES
Use the time line on the opposite page to answer the following questions.

1. How many years does the time line cover?

2. When did Francisco de Coronado reach Oklahoma?

3. About how many years had the Mound Builders been gone when Coronado reached Oklahoma?

4. How many years after Coronado's expedition did La Salle claim Oklahoma?

5. How are some time lines useful for studying history?

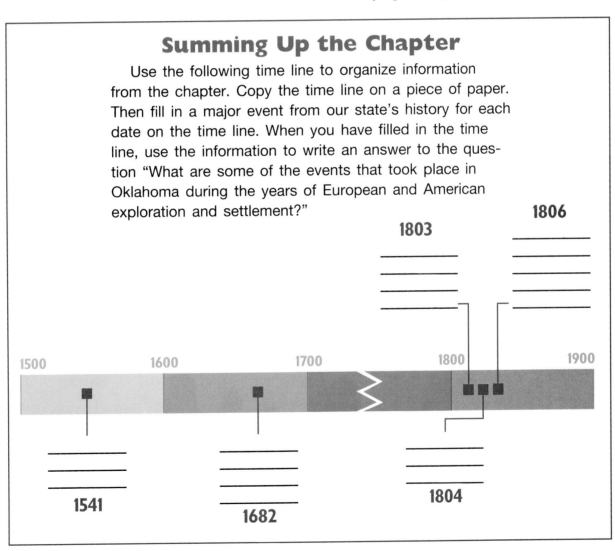

Summing Up the Chapter

Use the following time line to organize information from the chapter. Copy the time line on a piece of paper. Then fill in a major event from our state's history for each date on the time line. When you have filled in the time line, use the information to write an answer to the question "What are some of the events that took place in Oklahoma during the years of European and American exploration and settlement?"

1803

1806

1500   1600   1700   1800   1900

1541

1682

1804

Territorial Days

THINKING ABOUT GEOGRAPHY AND HISTORY

You have just read that people have lived in Oklahoma for thousands of years. In this chapter you will read why many American Indians were forced to move to Oklahoma from other areas. Soon they were followed by settlers who claimed these same lands. Read on to learn about conflicts and challenges facing different groups of people in Oklahoma.

1838

FORT GIBSON
Cherokee travel Trail of Tears

1861

ROUND MOUNTAIN
Opothleyahola leads Muskogee (Creek) in fight against Confederates

1860s

RINGLING
Millions of cattle are driven across Oklahoma from Texas

1825   1850   1875

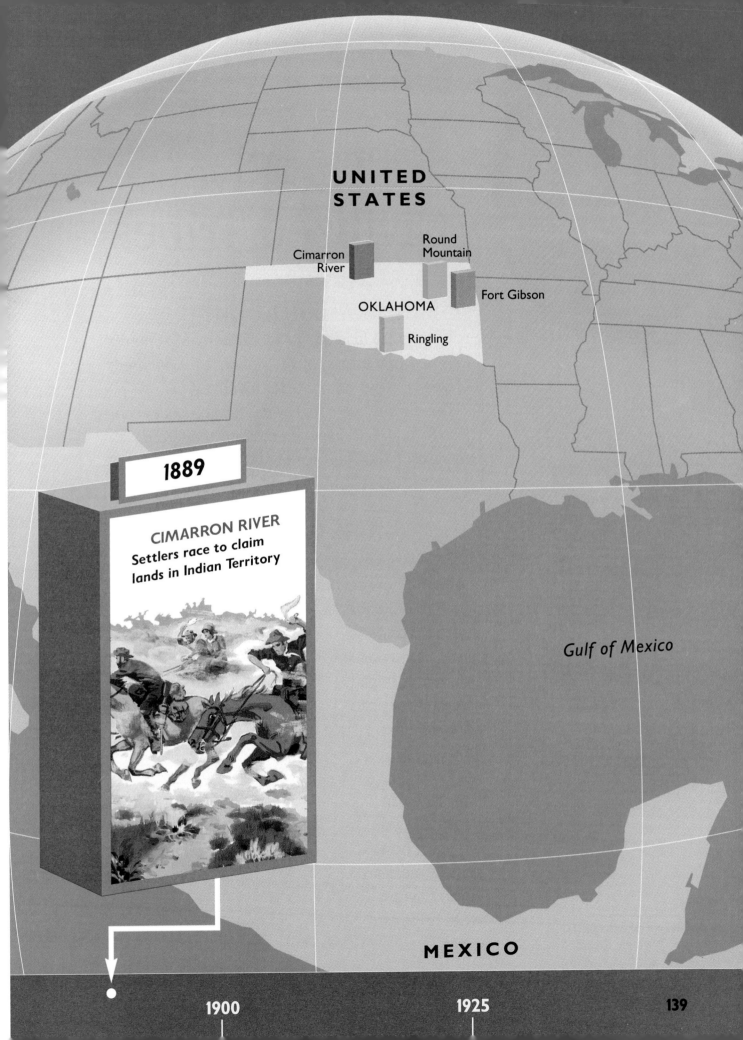

UNITED
STATES

Round
Mountain

Cimarron
River

Fort Gibson

OKLAHOMA

Ringling

1889

CIMARRON RIVER
Settlers race to claim
lands in Indian Territory

Gulf of Mexico

MEXICO

1825 1831 1838 1840

The Five Civilized Tribes

Read Aloud

"This is the land of our forefathers. My Cherokee kinsmen [ancestors] have lived on it for hundreds of years . . . we do not want to leave."

These words were said by a Cherokee leader named John Ross in 1835. He was describing the forced removal of the Cherokee people from their lands.

Focus Activity

READ TO LEARN

How did the Trail of Tears change the lives of American Indians?

VOCABULARY

- Five Civilized Tribes
- treaty
- Trail of Tears
- constitution

PEOPLE

- Andrew Jackson
- John Ross
- Sequoyah

PLACES

- Indian Territory

Pictured at right is a Cherokee drum.

THE BIG PICTURE

In the last chapter you learned about the new settlers who moved to Oklahoma. By 1831 President Andrew Jackson and others began forcing American Indians in the Southeast Region to leave their lands. In this lesson you will learn how some American Indians' lives were forever changed.

INDIAN TERRITORY

In return for the lands they would lose, the Choctaw, Cherokee, Creek, Chickasaw, and Seminole would receive land in Indian Territory. This was the name of Oklahoma at this time. These people were known as the Five Civilized Tribes. They were called 'civilized' because they had learned the ways of the white settlers. They lived in Georgia, Alabama, Mississippi, Florida, and Tennessee.

The Five Civilized Tribes had lived among European settlers for more than 150 years. But new settlers kept moving into the Southern states. They wanted the Indians' land.

The Treaties

The United States government encouraged the Five Civilized Tribes to move to Indian Territory. Small groups of leaders from each of the tribes agreed to sign treaties. A treaty is an agreement among nations.

In these treaties the American Indians agreed to give up their lands in the Southeast. For their lands they would receive new land, in Indian Territory. The United States government promised the tribes that this land would be theirs forever. It also promised to protect these American Indians forever.

Leaders from the Five Civilized Tribes in the 1800s included Allen Wright, Campbell Le Flore, Julius Folsom, and F. Battiste of the Choctaw (left); Nelson Chigley of the Chickasaw (center); and Chitto Harjo of the Creek (right).

THE TRAIL OF TEARS

Most American Indians did not support these treaties. They fought to stay in their homes. Led by their chief John Ross in Georgia, the Cherokee took their case to the Supreme Court. The court ruled that, "the laws of Georgia can have no force" on Cherokee lands.

Despite the Supreme Court's ruling, in 1838, United States soldiers rounded up the Cherokee. Then they burned their towns and villages. The soldiers then forced the Cherokee to march 800 miles to Indian Territory.

"The Place Where They Cried"

The American Indians suffered terribly during their march west. It took more than a year. Sometimes they had to walk in freezing cold weather through deep snow. At night they had little or no shelter for protection. Diseases spread quickly. About 4,000 out of 15,000 Cherokee died along the way. In their own language, the Cherokee called this march "the place where they cried." Over time the Cherokee's journey became known as the Trail of Tears.

Read the words at right. They were said by a soldier named John Burnett. He grew up among the Cherokee in Tennessee in the 1800s. How does he describe the Trail of Tears?

The Granger Collection

PRIMARY SOURCE

Excerpt from an Account, by John G. Burnett, published in 1890.

[In] May 1838, [I] witnessed the execution of the most brutal order in the History of American Warfare. I saw helpless Cherokees arrested and dragged from their homes . . . I saw them loaded like cattle or sheep into six hundred and forty-five wagons and started toward the west . . . [When] the bugle sounded and the wagons started rolling many of the children rose to their feet and waved their little hands good-by to their mountain homes, knowing they were leaving them forever. Many of these helpless people did not have blankets and many of them had been driven from home barefooted.

———————
execution: carrying out

LIVING IN A STRANGE LAND

By the late 1830s, most of the people in the Five Civilized Tribes had been moved to Indian Territory. On the map below you can see in which parts of the Territory each of these groups settled.

Building New Lives

The people of the Five Civilized Tribes had given up almost everything they owned. They also had lost many family members and friends. Still, they did not lose hope.

Once in Indian Territory, the five tribes did not waste any time starting new lives. Each group used the natural resources in their adopted land. They planted crops and raised farm animals. They built houses, schools, and churches. They also set up new businesses, created new governments, and traded goods. It was hard work, but they learned to live in their new homelands.

Four of the five groups drew up their own constitution. A constitution is a plan for a government. It was not until later in the 1880s that the Seminole wrote one. All of the constitutions were similar to the Constitution of the United States. Soon the five tribes built very successful communities.

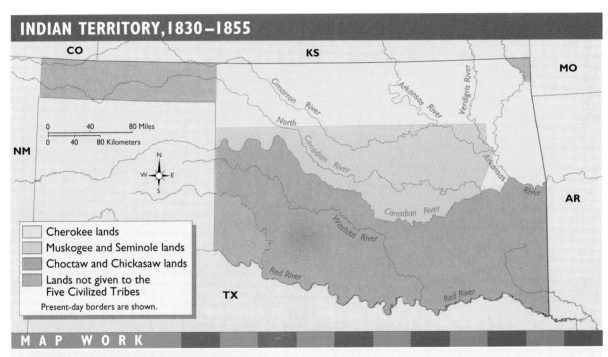

INDIAN TERRITORY, 1830–1855

CO   KS   MO

Cimarron River

North Canadian River

Arkansas River

Verdigris River

NM

0   40   80 Miles
0   40   80 Kilometers

N W E S

Canadian River

AR

Canadian River

Washita River

Red River

TX

Red River

Cherokee lands
Muskogee and Seminole lands
Choctaw and Chickasaw lands
Lands not given to the Five Civilized Tribes
Present-day borders are shown.

M A P   W O R K

The Five Civilized Tribes were given lands in Indian Territory by the United States government.
1. Which group lived farthest north?
2. The Canadian River forms the border between the lands of which groups?
3. What part of Oklahoma was not given to the Five Civilized Tribes?

SEQUOYAH

Sequoyah was a member of the Cherokee nation. He was born in eastern Tennessee in about 1770. He worked for many years as a silversmith. Sequoyah also was a remarkable person who created a system of writing although he had never gone to school. As an adult he met many white settlers. He came to love their books, or "talking leaves," as he called them. However, he could not read or write English.

Sequoyah wanted his people to learn how to read and write in their own language. It would help his people keep their heritage alive. Being able to read would also help the Cherokee find out about the treaties and plans of the United States government.

A New System of Writing

The Cherokee language is very difficult. Also, it had never been written down. For 12 years Sequoyah worked hard at sorting out the many sounds of his language. In about 1824 he finally decided that there were 86 sounds in Cherokee language. For each sound he created a written symbol. In this way he made a type of alphabet called a syllabary.

Sequoyah's alphabet was a great success. The Cherokee people learned to read and write in their own language. Soon the Cherokee also began to print their own newspaper. They began to write books.

Sequoyah was the inventor of the Cherokee alphabet.

144

The *Cherokee Phoenix* was printed in 1828. Today, some signs are in Creek (top, left) and Cherokee (top, right).

WHY IT MATTERS

You have read that in spite of great suffering along the Trail of Tears, the Five Civilized Tribes built new lives in Indian Territory. Soon however, their lives, as well as the lives of the Indians who had lived in the area before them, would be changed again. In the next lesson you will read about this event and its effect on the American Indians.

✓✓ **Reviewing Facts and Ideas**

MAIN IDEAS

- American Indians in the Southeast were forced to move west on the Trail of Tears.
- Many American Indians died while traveling the Trail of Tears.
- Despite hardship and loss, the Five Civilized Tribes quickly built new lives in Indian Territory.
- Sequoyah created a written form of Cherokee language.

THINK ABOUT IT

1. Name the five tribes that were forced to move to the Indian Territory.

2. What is the Trail of Tears?

3. **FOCUS** How did the Trail of Tears change the lives of the American Indians in the Southeast?

4. **THINKING SKILL** What *effect* did Sequoyah's alphabet have on the lives of the Cherokee?

5. **GEOGRAPHY** In what direction did the Five Civilized Tribes move along the Trail of Tears to reach Indian Territory?

The Granger Collection

1855   1861   1865   1870

The Civil War

Read Aloud

"Now their pride is gone, their wealth is gone, and they are defeated. They must begin again with what they can make and save; they will have nothing more."

These words were used to describe the Cherokee during the 1860s. A great war had been fought that changed people's lives forever.

Focus Activity

READ TO LEARN

In what ways did the Civil War affect the Indian Territory?

VOCABULARY

- Civil War
- Slavery
- States' rights
- Union
- Confederacy

PLACES

- Round Mountain
- Honey Springs

PEOPLE

- Opothleyahola
- Robert E. Lee
- Ulysses S. Grant

Today, people act out many Civil War battles (right). Opothleyahola (above right) did not want to take sides in the Civil War.

THE BIG PICTURE

In 1861 the United States was torn in half by the **Civil War** or the "War Between the States." The North and South had become divided over the question of **slavery**. The North wanted to end it, while the South did not. Slavery is the practice of making one person the property of another. They also fought over the question of **states' rights**. This was the right of states to make laws over anything not given to Congress by the U.S. Constitution.

DIVIDED LOYALTIES

Abraham Lincoln became President of the United States in 1861. This led 11 states in the South to break away from the United States, which was called the Union. Worried that Lincoln would end slavery, these states decided to form a government of their own called the Confederacy.

In Indian Territory the Five Civilized Tribes were caught in the middle of the war. Many Indian groups supported the South. They had lived in the South and had learned Southern ways of life. Also, they did not trust the Union because the Union government had forced them off their lands.

Other American Indians stayed loyal to the Union because of the treaties they had signed. Still others did not want to take sides.

Opothleyahola

In 1861 some Indian groups decided to take sides with the South. A Muskogee leader, Opothleyahola,

The Granger Collection

(oh puh thlee yuh HOH lah) did not want to join the North or the South. He gathered his people and headed north. About 7,000 Muskogee left. Most did not want to leave their new home, but they were willing to do so to find peace. Soon other groups joined them.

The First Battle

On November 19, 1861, a group of 1,400 Confederate soldiers drew near the Muskogee and their followers, who were very tired. They had been building a camp. Some Indians believe they set up camp at Round Mountain in what is now north central Oklahoma. Others believe they camped at Twin Mounds on the Cimarron River.

The fighting that broke out was the first Civil War battle to be fought in Indian Territory. The Muskogee successfully fought off the Confederates, even though they were outnumbered two to one. Late that night Opothleyahola's group headed north.

Opothleyahola and his followers fought the Confederates at Round Mountain. This cannon was used in the Civil War.

DEFEAT

Over the next few weeks the Confederate soldiers attacked Opothleyahola's group two more times. Finally the Indians fell back. Some of Opothleyahola's follower's escaped to Kansas.

A Long Journey

In all about 600 of Opothleyahola's followers were killed. Many others were captured. Those who escaped set out north to Kansas, the nearest Union state. However, soon they were caught in a bitter snowstorm. Families that weeks earlier had hundreds of horses and thousands of head of cattle now had nothing to eat. Many froze to death.

Battle at Honey Springs

Once in Kansas, Opothleyahola's men joined the Union army. They hoped to return to the Indian Territory to fight the Confederates and their Indian allies.

Over the next two years more than 100 battles were fought in Indian Territory. In July 1863, the Union defeated the Confederates in a battle at Honey Springs in eastern Oklahoma. The Union Army included American Indians and African Americans. Following this victory, the Union controlled much of Indian Territory, even though fighting continued.

THE UNION WINS

On April 9, 1865, Confederate General Robert E. Lee surrendered to Union General Ulysses S. Grant. The Civil War was over. In all, about 620,000 people died in the war. Following the war, many Indian groups returned home to Indian Territory. Soon the territory became a mixture of many American Indian groups. Much had been destroyed in the war. The task of rebuilding was great.

The United States government also decided to punish the Five Civilized Tribes. Many of their people had fought for the Confederacy. The government demanded that the Indians give up much of their lands.

WHY IT MATTERS

Our country had survived after the Civil War, but the cost was great. The difficult task of rebuilding the country lay ahead. In the next lessons you will see how people in the Southwest built new lives.

✓✓ Reviewing Facts and Ideas

THE MAIN IDEAS

- The Civil War was fought between the North and South from 1861 to 1865. When the war began, the Five Civilized Tribes had divided loyalties.
- Opothleyahola led a force of American Indians who refused to take sides during the Civil War.
- Opothleyahola won the first Civil War battle in Indian Territory.
- When the Civil War ended, the U.S. Government took away land from the Five Civilized Tribes.

THINK ABOUT IT

1. How did the Civil War divide the loyalties of the American Indians?

2. Who was Opothleyahola?

3. **FOCUS** In what ways did the Civil War affect Indian Territory?

4. **THINKING SKILL** In what ways could you *classify* the loyalties of the Indians in the Civil War?

5. **WRITE** Suppose you are a Confederate soldier. Write a letter home describing the first battle in Indian Territory.

Lee (right) surrendered to Grant in Virginia on April 9, 1865.

CITIZENSHIP
VIEWPOINTS

Should the Five Civilized Tribes join the Union or the Confederacy?

As chances of a Civil War grew, Arkansas and other Confederate states began to demand that the Five Civilized Tribes join them. Most American Indian groups did not want to take sides in the war. They feared that if they joined the losing side, the winners would take away their land and rights.

Muskogee (Creek) chief Opothleyahola urged President Lincoln to support the treaties that the American Indians had signed with the government to protect Indian Territory.

Others like John Ross, the Cherokee chief, feared the Cherokees would fight among themselves and lose everything if they did not join the Confederacy. The Chickasaw also decided they had much in common with the Confederate states. They joined them against the Union.

Consider three different viewpoints on this issue from history. Then answer the questions that follow.

Three DIFFERENT Viewpoints

1 CHICKASAW DELEGATE
Excerpt from speech, May 25, 1861

[Our] feelings and sympathies, all attach us to our Southern friends . . . . [We] have . . . confidence that all our rights . . . will be fully recognized, guaranteed, and protected by our friends of the Confederate States and . . . as a Southern people we consider their cause our own.

"...as a Southern people we consider their cause our own."

2 OPOTHLEYAHOLA
Muskogee (Creek) leader
Excerpt from a letter to President Abraham Lincoln, August 15, 1861

You said that in our new homes we should be defended . . . from any people . . . and should we be injured by anybody you would come with your soldiers and punish them. But now . . . men who are strangers tread our soil, our children are frightened, and the mothers cannot sleep for fear . . . . Keep off the intruder and make our homes again happy as they used to be.

"...make our homes again happy as they used to be."

3 JOHN ROSS
Cherokee Chief
Excerpt from address to the Cherokee people, August 21, 1861

The [split] of the United States into two governments is now probable. Arkansas and the Indian Nations have . . . joined the Confederate states. Our interest [cannot be separated] from theirs and . . . it is not [good for us] that we should stand alone . . . . [We must make] an alliance with the Confederate States.

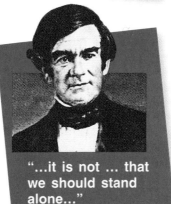

"...it is not ... that we should stand alone..."

BUILDING CITIZENSHIP

1. What is the viewpoint of each person?
2. What reasons did each give for the position taken?
3. What other viewpoints might people have on this issue?

SHARING VIEWPOINTS

Discuss what you agree with or disagree with about these and other viewpoints. Then as a class, write three statements about the Five Civilized Tribes and the Civil War.

1820   1840   1860   **1866**   **1886**   1900

Life on the Trails

Read Aloud

*"We'll ride the range from sun to sun,
For a cowboy's work is never done,
He's up and gone at the break of day,
Drivin' the dogies [calves] on their weary way."*
These words are from a cowboy song. Cowboys often sang during the late hours of the night as they sat on their horses guarding their cattle. A few hours later they would be up before sunrise to begin a long, hard day.

Focus Activity

READ TO LEARN

What was life like for the cowboys along the cattle trails?

VOCABULARY

- cattle drive
- cow town
- stampede

PLACES

- Shawnee Trail
- Chisholm Trail

THE BIG PICTURE

After the Civil War ended in 1865, the southern part of our country lay in ruins. Destroyed homes and buildings in the South had to be rebuilt. Crops had to be replanted. In the North, as industries grew, so did the population. This population growth created a great need for food, like beef.

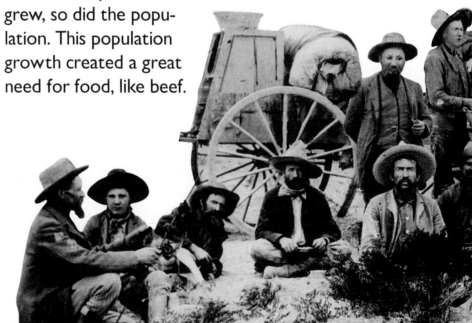

THE GREAT CATTLE DRIVES

The Five Civilized Tribes returned to the Indian Territory from Texas and Kansas in the 1860s. They found their land destroyed and their cattle gone.

Farther south, in Texas, there were large numbers of cattle. Texas cattle ranchers wanted to sell their cattle to Northerners. A steer could be sold for about $5 in Texas. In the North it could be sold for $40. Texas ranchers needed a way to move their cattle to Kansas and Missouri, where railroads could take the cattle north to the meatpacking plants.

The ranchers began to use cattle drives. A cattle drive is the herding of large numbers of cattle by cowboys and leading them along trails to railroad shipping stations.

Who were these cowboys? They came from many different parts of our country. Many were Texans. Some were American Indians. At least one out of seven of them were African Americans.

Ranchers hired cowboys to move and keep track of their herds. They also protected the cattle from thieves and wild animals. Read how one rancher described the way cowboys talked about their horses. Why do you think this was a favorite topic for them?

MANY VOICES
PRIMARY SOURCE

Excerpt from *The Story of the S.M.S. Ranch*, by Frank S. Hastings, 1919.

Every horse has a name and every man on the ranch knows every horse by name. . . . A man who does not love his mount [horse] does not last long in the cow business. . . . Cowboys' principal topic is their horses or of men who ride, and every night about the camp fire, they trade horses, run imaginary horse races, or romance [invent stories] about their pet ponies.

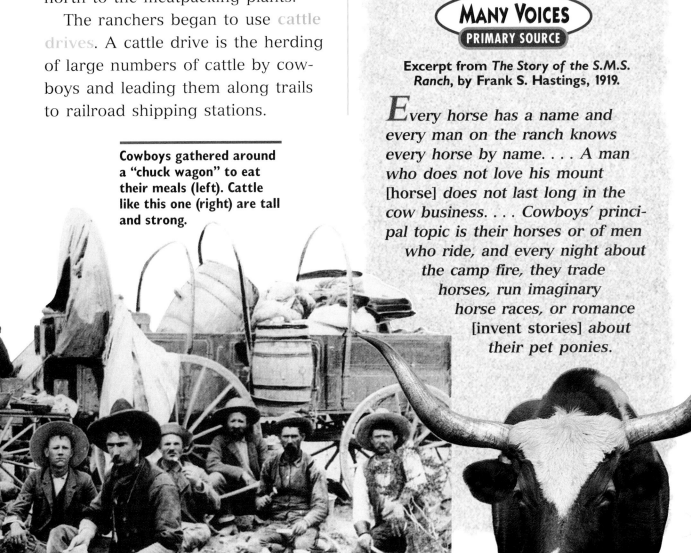

Cowboys gathered around a "chuck wagon" to eat their meals (left). Cattle like this one (right) are tall and strong.

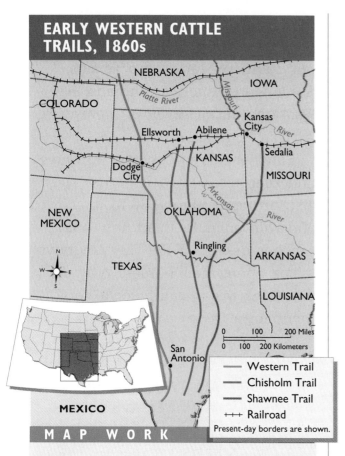

EARLY WESTERN CATTLE TRAILS, 1860s

Western Trail
Chisholm Trail
Shawnee Trail
+++ Railroad

Present-day borders are shown.

MAP WORK

Millions of cattle were driven through Oklahoma from the 1860s–1880s.

1. Which trail ran from Ringling to Abilene?
2. Which trails passed through Kansas?

CATTLE TRAILS

Beginning in the 1860s, cowboys traveled long distances on cattle drives. Sometimes they traveled over 1,000 miles.

Shawnee Trail

From the map you can see that Texas cattle were taken on the Shawnee Trail through the Indian Territory on their way to Missouri. Travel on the Shawnee trail was dangerous. Using the trail could also be costly. In Indian Territory some Indian nations charged a fee for the cattle crossing and grazing on their land.

The Chisholm Trail

Difficulties along the Shawnee Trail made the cattle ranchers look for a new trail. In 1866, Joseph McCoy set up a shipping station in Abilene, Kansas. Now cattle drivers were able to drive their cattle to Abilene. They used a trail known as the Chisholm Trail. In 1867 35,000 head of cattle reached Abilene. A year later about 75,000 cattle were moved there.

McCoy built a type of town in Abilene called a cow town. These were towns with pens for the cattle and hotels for the cowboys.

The Chisholm Trail also had problems. Outlaws called rustlers sometimes caused the herds to stampede (stam PEED), or run wild. Then they offered to help with the roundup— for a price. Cowboys might also be attacked by Indians who did not want them on their land.

Bacon, beans, biscuits and coffee were all part of a cowboy's breakfast.

LIFE ON THE TRAIL

The following story will take you into a day in the life of Luke, a cowboy who is herding cattle along the Chisholm Trail in the 1870s.

Luke's Story

"Rise and shine! Come and get it!" The cook calls to the sleeping cowboys. Luke rubs his eyes as he crawls from his bedroll. He pulls on his boots and stumbles toward the good smells coming from the chuck wagon.

Today they will cross the Red River into Indian Territory. Many of the cattle will have to be pushed off the banks into the water. Some will have to be pulled out of the mud and onto the banks on the other side. Luke hopes the storm is over and the river will be calm.

The cattle drive started in Texas more than a month ago. Stormy nights like last night made Luke feel as if he has been on the trail forever.

The cattle drive travels only about 10 miles a day. Cattle need a lot of time to graze along the way and to fatten up. It will take them almost 3 months to reach Abilene 400 miles away.

Luke can hardly wait to reach the end of the trail. First he will sleep on a real bed and take a bath! Then he will buy new clothes and look for a place to eat good food. Then he will buy a new horse to take him back to Texas. It will be a long ride.

WHY IT MATTERS

For about 12 years, cowboys drove many thousands of cattle across Indian Territory to cow towns in the North. Then railroad lines were built and took the place of the cattle trails. Soon people began to move into Indian Territory to settle.

✓/ Reviewing Facts and Ideas

MAIN IDEAS

- Texas cattle ranchers wanted to sell their cattle to Northerners. Cowboys traveled long distances in cattle drives to towns to the north.

- The Shawnee and Chisholm trails were important cattle trails. Life along the trails was hard and often dangerous. Outlaws sometimes threatened the cowboys.

- Cattle drives often took about 3 months and traveled only about 10 miles a day. Cowboys looked forward to resting and eating well after each cattle drive.

THINK ABOUT IT

1. Why did Texas ranchers want to drive their cattle north?

2. What did Joseph McCoy do to help the cattle drivers?

3. **FOCUS** What was life like for the cowboys along the cattle trails?

4. **THINKING SKILL** *Compare* and *contrast* your life with that of the cowboy Luke.

5. **GEOGRAPHY** Using the map on page 154, list the important cattle trails and the towns where they ended.

1820   1840   1860   1879   1889

Boomers and Sooners

Focus Activity

READ TO LEARN

Why are the Boomers and Sooners important to the history of Oklahoma?

VOCABULARY

- Unassigned Lands
- Boomer
- Homestead Act
- claim
- Land Run
- Sooner

PEOPLE

- Elias C. Boudinot
- David L. Payne
- Benjamin Harrison

Thousands of homesteaders traveled to Indian Territory. David L. Payne (right) claimed land that is now Oklahoma City.

Read Aloud

"These lands are among the richest in the world. . . . The people . . . will go down there and occupy and cultivate [farm] these lands."

These words were said in 1879. The speaker believed that parts of the Indian Territory belonged to any homesteader [settler] who wished to live there.

THE BIG PICTURE

By 1880 much of the good land in the West had been settled. In Kansas and Texas farmers wanted to find new rich lands to grow their crops. They looked towards land in the Indian Territory on which to build new homes. But this land could not be used because it belonged to the American Indians.

BOOMERS

In 1879 a lawyer named Elias C. Boudinot (BOO deh noh), who was a Cherokee citizen, spoke about the land in the Indian Territory on which no one lived. He said it was really public land. He believed this land should be open to all for settlement. These areas were called the Unassigned Lands because they had not been assigned, or given, to a tribe, like all the other land. They were located in the central western part of the Indian Territory.

Boudinot's words caught the attention of newspapers throughout the country. Soon people demanded that these lands be opened to settlers. Farmers and others who planned to push their way onto the Unassigned Lands and who talked a lot about it were called Boomers.

David L. Payne

The most famous Boomer was David L. Payne. He was called the "Prince of Boomers." Payne was a colorful leader and speaker. One man described him as being able to "talk a bird right out of a tree."

In 1880 Payne led a group of 21 Boomers into Indian Territory, to the area that is now Oklahoma City. They had no right to be there. When government soldiers found Payne and his "Boomers," they arrested Payne and drove the Boomers back to Kansas and Texas.

When the Boomers were arrested, they said that they had the right to settle the land under the Homestead Act of 1862. The Homestead Act allowed United States settlers to have 160 acres of land for free. This was called a claim. The homesteaders had to build homes and live on the claim for five years in order to own it.

Boomers called Indian Territory the "last frontier." They often told exaggerated stories about the land to encourage more people to go there. One poster said, "The grass is green the year round," with "no flies or mosquitoes!"

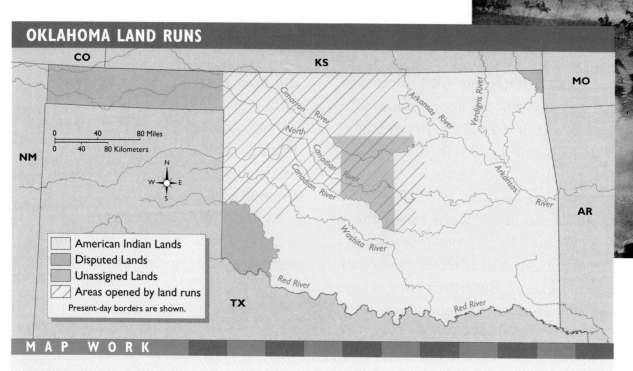

CO

KS

MO

NM

Cimarron River

North

Canadian River

Canadian River

Arkansas River

Verdigris River

Arkansas River

River

AR

Washita River

Red River

TX

Red River

0 40 80 Miles
0 40 80 Kilometers

N
W E
S

American Indian Lands
Disputed Lands
Unassigned Lands
Areas opened by land runs
Present-day borders are shown.

MAP WORK

Thousands of homesteaders raced to claim lands during the 1880s.

1. What parts of our present-day state were opened by land runs?

2. Where were the Unassigned Lands located?

3. If you were in Kansas during the 1880s, where in present-day Oklahoma would you most likely stake a claim?

UNASSIGNED LANDS SOLD

The Boomers failed to settle in the Indian Territory. But they made people aware of the issue of who had the right to live on the Unassigned Lands. By 1885 the United States government started to listen to the Boomers.

Other people thought it would be wrong to allow homesteaders into Indian Territory. They felt that American Indians had been promised this land "as long as grass grows and water flows." No one was supposed to live on the land without the permission of the Indians.

Finally, in 1889 Chief Pleasant Porter, the Principal Chief of the Muskogee (Creek), agreed to sell their

Unassigned Lands. He would give it to the United States government for about $2,200,000. Soon after, the Seminole sold claims to their lands for about $1,900,000.

The Land Runs

On March 23, 1889, United States President Benjamin Harrison signed an order opening the Unassigned Lands to settlement. The order said that no one would be allowed to settle there until noon on April 22, 1889. People were told to line up on the borders of the lands and wait for the signal to take off. The first person to reach a place could claim it.

On that day homesteaders from around the country waited nervously along the border of the newly

The Granger Collection

On September 16, 1893, homesteaders raced to claim lands in the Oklahoma Territory.

WHY IT MATTERS

The Boomers and Sooners are a part of our state's history. Today we show our pride in our history in many ways. For example, Oklahoma is called the "Sooner State" because many Oklahomans would "sooner" live here than anywhere else.

opened lands. At noon the race was on! Thousands of people ran on foot, by horse, bicycle or any other way they could to get to an area to claim. This race was called a land run. Soon there would be other land runs into Indian Territory. Look at the map on page 158. What part of our state was opened by land runs?

The Sooners

Some people did not wait until noon on April 22 to claim their land. They entered the Unassigned Lands ahead of time. Hiding in bushes or trees, they waited until noon and then grabbed the best claims. These people were called "Sooners." If it could be proved that someone was a Sooner, his or her land claim would be taken away.

Lands that were claimed during the land run are now our cities of Guthrie, Kingfisher, Norman, Moore, Edmund, Seward, Stillwater, and Oklahoma City. If you visit our capital today, try to think what it must have looked like on that day over 100 years ago!

Reviewing Facts and Ideas

MAIN IDEAS

- In the 1880s many people claimed that the Unassigned Lands in the Indian Territory should be opened to all. The Boomers were determined to claim these lands.

- The Muscogee and Seminole nations sold their lands to the United States in 1889. President Benjamin Harrison then opened them to settlement.

- The Sooners tried to unfairly take the best claims.

THINK ABOUT IT

1. How did the Boomers get their name?

2. Why were some people called Sooners?

3. **FOCUS** Why are the Boomers and Sooners important to our history?

4. **THINKING SKILL** What were some of the *causes* and *effects* of the land runs?

5. **GEOGRAPHY** Look at the map on page 158. What states were next to the areas opened by the Land Runs?

CHAPTER 7 REVIEW

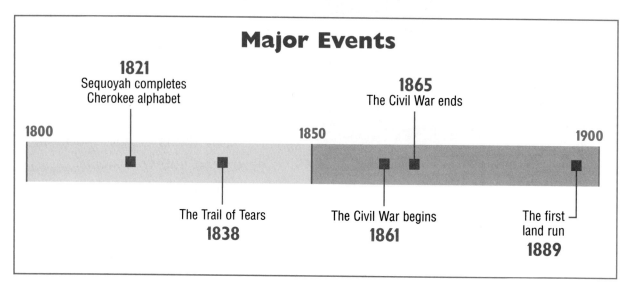

Major Events

1821
Sequoyah completes
Cherokee alphabet

1865
The Civil War ends

1800

1850

1900

The Trail of Tears
1838

The Civil War begins
1861

The first
land run
1889

THINKING ABOUT VOCABULARY

Number a sheet of paper from 1 to 10. Beside each number write the word from the list that best matches the description.

Boomers	cow town
Civil War	land run
claim	Trail of Tears
Confederacy	treaty
constitution	Union

1. Forced march of the Cherokee and other American Indians in 1838.

2. Land given to a homesteader

3. The northern states during the Civil War

4. A plan for a government

5. The war between the North and South

6. The name taken by the South during the Civil War

7. Farmers who illegally took Unassigned Lands

8. An agreement among nations

9. A race for land

10. Place with pens for cattle and hotels for cowhands during the 1860s–1880s

THINKING ABOUT FACTS

1. What is the present-day name of Indian Territory?

2. What did American Indians agree to do when they signed treaties?

3. About how many American Indians died during the Trail of Tears?

4. What was Sequoyah's accomplishment? Why was it important?

5. Why did the Muskogee (Creek) want to leave Indian Territory during the Civil War?

6. What did the Boomers want?

7. Name two Civil War battles that took place in Indian Territory. What happened during these battles?

8. Why were the Five Civilized Tribes punished after the Civil War?

9. Why did ranchers need cattle drives?

10. What was the Chisholm Trail? Why was it created?

THINK AND WRITE

WRITING A JOURNAL ENTRY

Suppose you were a Boomer moving to the Unassigned Lands. Write a journal entry describing what it might have been like.

WRITING A POSTER

Write and design a poster that tells people about the Land Run in Indian Territory.

WRITING A SUMMARY

Write a summary of the different sides in the Civil War. Be sure to include the Union and Confederate views as well as those of the American Indians in Indian Territory.

APPLYING STUDY SKILLS

USING TIME LINES

Use the Major Events time line on the opposite page to answer the following questions.

1. What is a time line?
2. How much time is represented by each section of the time line?
3. How long did the Civil War last?
4. About how many years passed between the Trail of Tears and the first land run?
5. In what portion of the time line would you put the Battle at Round Mountain?

Summing Up the Chapter

Use the vertical organization chart to organize information from the chapter. Copy the chart on a sheet of paper and fill in the blank spaces. Then use it to write a paragraph that answers the question, "How were movements of people into Oklahoma both good and bad?"

FIVE CIVILIZED TRIBES

Why they came:

What they did here:

UNION AND CONFEDERATE ARMIES

Why they came:

What they did here:

HOMESTEADERS

Why they came:

What they did here:

CHAPTER 8

Oklahoma Grows

THINKING ABOUT
GEOGRAPHY AND HISTORY

People who came to Oklahoma to build new lives had to work hard to survive. Soon Oklahoma became our country's forty-sixth state. Oklahoma's fortunes changed greatly with the discovery of rich oilfields. In this chapter you will read about our state's good times and hard times. It is the story of people who worked hard to help our state grow.

1890s

STILLWATER

Homesteaders use Oklahoma's resources to help build better lives

1907

GUTHRIE

Oklahoma becomes the forty-sixth state

1920s

BARTLESVILLE

An oil boom begins as large oil fields are discovered

1880　　　　　　1900　　　　　　1920

UNITED STATES

Dust Bowl

Stillwater

Guthrie

Bartlesville
Tulsa

OKLAHOMA

1930s

DUST BOWL

A long drought forces
Oklahomans to move west

1950s

TULSA

Many Oklahomans move
to suburbs after WWII

Gulf of Mexico

MEXICO

1940

1960

1840   1860   1880 1889   1907   1920

Life on the Frontier

Focus Activity

READ TO LEARN

What was life like for homesteaders on the Oklahoma prairie?

VOCABULARY

- dugout
- sod house
- windmill
- drought

Read Aloud

*"Picking up bones to keep from starving,
Picking up chips to keep from freezing,
Picking up courage to keep from leaving,
Way out West, in No Man's Land."*
This song tells the story of the hardships homesteaders faced when they settled in the Oklahoma Territory.

THE BIG PICTURE

As you read in Chapter 7, the land runs of the late 1800s brought thousands of homesteaders to the Indian Territory. They faced long, cold winters. There were also floods, sandstorms, tornadoes, and dry periods. But the homesteaders worked hard. By the time of the fifth, and last, land run in May 1895, almost all of the lands had been claimed.

LOG CABINS AND DUGOUTS

The homesteaders who came to Oklahoma wanted better lives for themselves and their families. To make their dreams come true, they would have to work very hard. The first thing they did when they arrived on their new lands was to find shelter.

Families worked together to build shelters. Often neighbors helped, too. In areas where there were many trees, they built log cabins. The settlers cut down the trees with axes. Then they cut the logs to their correct lengths. Log by log the walls grew higher. The men added a roof when the log walls were high enough. Next, the settlers filled the cracks between the logs with mud and grass. Floors were usually made of dirt, or sometimes of wood.

In western areas with few trees, homesteaders had to find other materials for building their homes. They used natural resources such as soil, rocks, and wild plants to meet their needs. But they hoped to replace these temporary shelters with permanent homes.

Dugouts

Some of the homesteaders built dugouts. A dugout was a large hole dug into the ground or into the side of a hill, like a cave. It usually had a wooden front with a door and a window. Dugouts were warmer in winter and cooler in summer than other kinds of houses.

Inside the dugout, the dirt walls were often covered with newspapers. The floors were usually of dirt. Rats sometimes made their homes in the dirt walls. When it was cold, snakes, field mice, and other animals also sheltered there.

Many homesteaders lived in log cabins (below). Even before homes could be built, blacksmiths (right) were busy making things people needed.

203

SOD HOUSES

In areas where there were few trees, homesteaders often built sod houses. These houses were made from tangled grass roots in the soil. The grass roots held the soil together so tightly that the settlers could cut the soil into blocks. Blocks of this soil were stacked like bricks to build the walls. Poles held up the sod-covered roof. During the warm days of summer and spring, grass and flower seeds in the roof would sometimes grow into colorful flowers.

Plenty of Leaks

Sod houses were often called *soddies*. They had more light and air than dugouts. But they leaked when it rained. Bits of dirt fell from the ceiling. Some families cooked under an umbrella to keep dirt out of the food. Bugs, snakes, and mice were also found in the soddies.

Dugouts and sod houses were small and overcrowded. Sometimes a whole family slept in one bed. During the day beds were also used to store clothes and other items. In spite of these conditions, the homesteaders were often willing to share their homes with relatives and travelers.

Read below the words of a homesteader who describes the difficulty of living in a sod house. What was it like inside?

. . . nearly everything in the house was soaked and the fuel gone. I went to a neighbor's and found haven [shelter] . . . . But before morning there was six inches of water in it, so we had to make another move.

HARDSHIPS

Finding water and fuel for cooking food and heating houses were problems faced by many homesteaders.

"Prairie Coal"

Homesteaders often had to travel long distances to find wood to build fires. Stalks from large plants were sometimes used. But these stalks produced too much smoke inside the settlers' homes.

Homesteaders had to find something else to burn. They used dried cow or buffalo manure to heat their foods and homes. The manure was often called *prairie coal, buffalo chips,* or *cow chips.* Gathering the chips was often a chore given to children.

Rainwater

Many areas did not have enough water to use for washing, cooking, or drinking. Many families were far from a river or stream. To get water, they left barrels outdoors to catch rainwater. Sometimes they used windmills to gather water. Windmills used wind power to pump underground water up from wells to the surface.

Fire and Weather

The homesteaders also faced the danger of prairie fires and changing weather. The dry prairie grass could easily catch fire and destroy everything in its path. Homesteaders learned to dig ditches around their homes and fields. This slowed the spread of fires. Tornadoes, blizzards, and floods were other dangers. They could take lives and ruin homes and crops. Droughts also caused settlers to lose their homes, animals, and crops. A drought is a long period of time with little or no rain.

"Cow chips" (right) were used to make fires for cooking. Windmills pumped water from deep below the dry prairies (below).

167

LIFE ON THE FARM

Homesteaders worked from sunrise to sunset. Every member of the family was expected to help. Children went to school for only about three months a year. The rest of the time they were needed to help with farming, hunting, and daily chores. Children raked the land and planted seeds in the spring. In the fall they helped harvest the crops. Crops included corn, cotton, wheat, and oats. A scythe, a tool with a big, curved blade, was used to cut down the crops.

Boys and girls learned to hunt and fish at an early age. Both men and women were often skillful with a gun. The homesteaders mostly hunted deer, opossums, wild turkeys, and prairie chickens.

Clothing

Homesteaders made many of their own clothes. They also made beautiful quilts. Some women and girls spun the yarn or cloth they used. Sometimes they dyed them beautiful colors. The dyes came from the plants and trees around them. Brown was made from walnut hulls, red from berries, blue from indigo, and yellow dye came from peach tree bark.

Religion

Religion was an important part of the homesteaders' lives. Many

Homesteaders made their own quilts (above). This photo (below) shows homesteaders enjoying a picnic in 1906.

families read the Bible and made time each day to pray. During the early years, schools were often used as churches. Many communities also used schools as a place to hold all-day meetings. Later, churches and meeting halls would be built.

Having Fun

Children had fun by riding horses, walking on wooden stilts, and swimming. When picnics or parties were given, families came in wagons and buggies from miles around to visit. Homesteaders often danced and sang at these events. Sometimes children fell asleep on piles of quilts, while adults continued to dance and sing until the next morning.

Childrens' toys (above) included wooden boats and stuffed animals.

WHY IT MATTERS

During the late 1800s many homesteaders came to what is now our state. They worked hard to build their communities and improve their lives. As you will read in the next lesson, this growth continued when Oklahoma became a state.

Reviewing Facts and Ideas

MAIN IDEAS

- Some of the early homesteaders built log cabins. Others had to build dugouts.
- In areas with few trees, many homesteaders built sod houses. These houses often leaked.
- Among the hardships the homesteaders faced were fire, lack of water, tornadoes, blizzards, floods, and droughts.
- Homesteaders worked hard. Children went to school only about three months a year. However, families also took time for religious services and having fun.

THINK ABOUT IT

1. What did many homesteaders often use as fuel?
2. What did homestead families do for fun?
3. **FOCUS** What were some challenges that homesteaders faced?
4. **THINKING SKILL** *Compare* and *contrast* a homesteader's home with a small house in Oklahoma today.
5. **WRITE** List three questions you would like to ask a homesteader to find out more about what his or her daily life was like.

Geography Skills

Using Latitude and Longitude

VOCABULARY

latitude
parallel
degree
longitude
prime meridian
meridian
global grid

WHY THE SKILL MATTERS

In the last lesson you read about homesteaders in Oklahoma. Suppose you are looking for a treasure buried by homesteaders long ago. The only clue you have is an old map. The writing on the map is faded, but you can just make out some lines that cross each other a little like a tic-tac-toe grid. Each line has a number on it.

You discover that these are imaginary lines invented long ago by mapmakers. The lines describe the location of a particular place. They provide an "address" for every place on Earth.

Airline pilots use this system of lines to keep track of where they are. Up among the clouds a pilot must be sure of a plane's location at all times. Pilots also need an exact way to explain where they are going. These lines will also help you to find the treasure. You will use this system of imaginary lines on maps in this book and in many others.

USING LATITUDE

Let's study these imaginary lines. Look at the map on this page and place your finger on the equator. This is the starting point for measuring latitude. Latitude is a measure of how far north or south a place is from the equator.

Lines of latitude are also called parallels because they are parallel lines. Parallel lines always remain the same distance apart.

Each line of latitude has a number. You can see that the equator is labeled 0°, meaning zero degrees. Degrees are used to measure the distance on Earth's

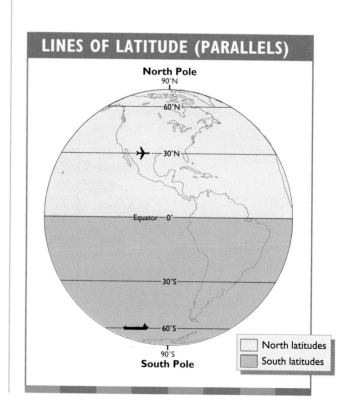

LINES OF LATITUDE (PARALLELS)

North Pole
90°N
60°N
30°N
Equator—0°
30°S
60°S
90°S
South Pole

North latitudes
South latitudes

surface. The symbol ° stands for degrees. What is the latitude of the equator?

Now look at the lines of latitude north of the equator. Notice that these parallels are labeled N for "north." The North Pole has a latitude, too, which is 90°N. The parallels south of the equator are labeled S for "south." The latitude of the South Pole is 90°S.

Find the ship on the map on page 170. The ship is moving west. It is located at 60°S. Now find the small airplane on the map. Along which parallel is it flying?

USING LONGITUDE

Now look at the map on this page. It shows lines of longitude. Like parallels, these are imaginary lines on a map or globe. But instead of measuring distance north or south, they measure distance east or west of the prime meridian. Prime means "first." Lines of longitude are also called meridians. The prime meridian is the first line, or starting place, for measuring lines of longitude. That's why the prime meridian is marked 0° on the map. Put your finger on the prime meridian. It runs through the western parts of Europe and Africa.

Look at the meridians to the west of the prime meridian. These lines are labeled W for "west." The lines to the east of the prime meridian are labeled E for "east." Longitude is measured up to 180° east of the prime meridian and up to 180° west of the prime meridian.

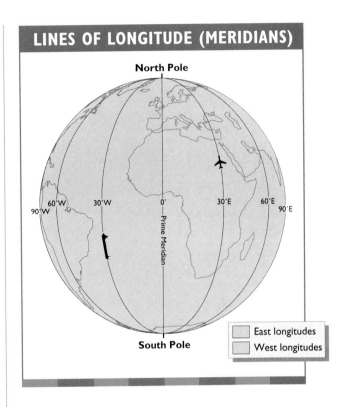

LINES OF LONGITUDE (MERIDIANS)

North Pole

60°W 30°W 0° 30°E 60°E
90°W 90°E

Prime Meridian

South Pole

East longitudes
West longitudes

Since 180°E and 180°W fall on the same line, this line is marked neither E nor W. This line runs through the Pacific Ocean.

Unlike lines of latitude, meridians are not parallel to one another. Look at the map on this page again. As you can see, the meridians are far apart at the equator. They meet, however, at the North Pole and the South Pole.

Lines of longitude measure degrees east and west. Look at the ship on the map. It is traveling along latitude 30°W. Now look at the airplane on the same map. It is flying over the continent of Africa. In which direction is the airplane traveling?

Geography Skills

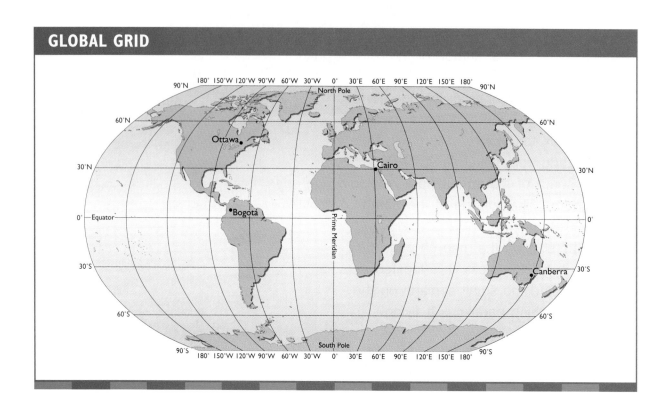

FINDING PLACES ON A MAP

In order to use latitude lines and longitude lines to find places, you must combine them on the same map. Look at the map of the world on this page. You can see that the lines of latitude and the lines of longitude cross to form a grid. A grid is a set of crisscrossing lines, such as a tic-tac-toe board.

The grid on this map is called a **global grid** because it covers the entire Earth. By using the global grid, you are able to locate the "address" of any spot in the world.

Look at the map above. Find Canberra, Australia, and Bogotá, Colombia. Which of these two cities is closer to the equator? How can you tell?

Now find Ottawa, Canada. Is this city east or west of the prime meridian? Find Cairo, Egypt. Is Cairo east or west of the prime meridian? Is it north or south of the equator?

Look at the map of the 48 states. Find Trenton, New Jersey. As you can see, it is located at about 40°N latitude. It is also located at 75°W longitude. So we say that its location—or its "address"—is 40°N, 75°W.

Remember that when you locate a place on a map, you always give latitude first and longitude second. You also must remember to give north or south for the latitude, east or west for the longitude. To describe a place that is not exactly at the point where two lines cross, you must use the closest lines.

TRYING THE SKILL

Try to find a city by its "address." This city is located at 40°N, 105°W. What city is it? Now describe the location of Oklahoma City, using latitude and longitude.

On your faded buried-treasure map, you found the following numbers: 45°N, 70°W. Do you understand what those numbers mean now? In what state is the treasure located? In what part of the state? Start digging!

REVIEWING THE SKILL

Most maps include a grid of latitude and longitude. Use the 48 States map below to answer these questions.

1. What are lines of latitude and longitude? How can they be helpful?

2. Describe the location of Tulsa, using latitude and longitude.

3. Name two cities on the map that share the same latitude. Then name two cities that share the same longitude.

4. How did you find the answer to the last question?

LATITUDE AND LONGITUDE: 48 States

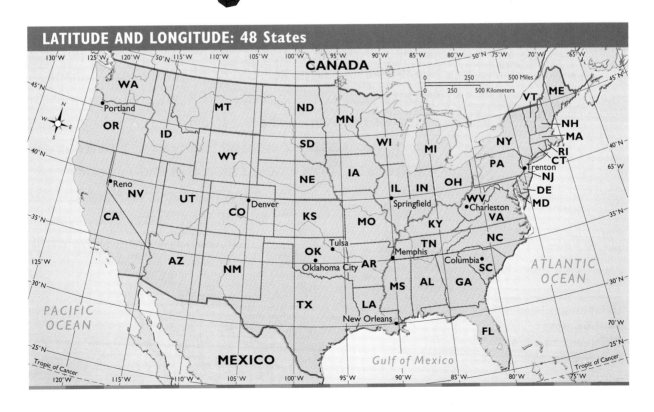

1880   1889   1907 1910   1920

Oklahoma Becomes a State

Read Aloud

"When the brilliant rays of this morning's sun spread over our land, it lighted forty-five strong states between the two oceans. The sun will set tonight and its last rays will light a grander nation now grown to forty-six states."

These words were spoken by Charles Haskell, as he took office on the day that Oklahoma became a state. He was Oklahoma's first governor.

Focus Activity

READ TO LEARN

How did Oklahoma become a state?

VOCABULARY

- Organic Act
- Curtis Act
- Enabling Act

PEOPLE

- Charles Haskell

PLACES

- Oklahoma Territory
- Twin Territories
- Guthrie

THE BIG PICTURE

Despite many hardships, homesteaders slowly built successful communities in the western part of what is now Oklahoma. The American Indians continued to live in eastern Oklahoma, with a smaller number in the western area. As the number of homesteaders increased, many of the newcomers wanted to form a new state. But the American Indians wanted to govern themselves in their own state. They wanted their own laws and ways of life.

Oklahomans heading to southwest Oklahoma to build new lives in 1901.

OKLAHOMA TERRITORY

In the last chapter, you read about the land runs of 1889. They opened up the Unassigned Lands to settlement. However, as communities grew, homesteaders wanted more land.

In 1887 the United States government began making land agreements with the American Indians in Oklahoma's western areas. Each adult was given a small plot of about 160 acres of land. Each child received 80 acres. The rest of the Indians' land in the west was opened to homesteaders.

As homesteaders began to build their communities, they formed local governments. Still, many people made their own laws. They often protected each other by forming peacekeeping groups.

Organic Act

By 1890, there was a need for a larger government to oversee Oklahoma's communities. On May 2, 1890, the United States Congress passed the Organic Act. It ordered that a new government be formed for an area to be called Oklahoma Territory. This territory would include the western part of the old Indian Territory and was west of where the Five Civilized Tribes lived.

Look at the map below. From it you can see that what is today Oklahoma was made up of two territories in 1900. They were Indian Territory and Oklahoma Territory. They became known as the Twin Territories.

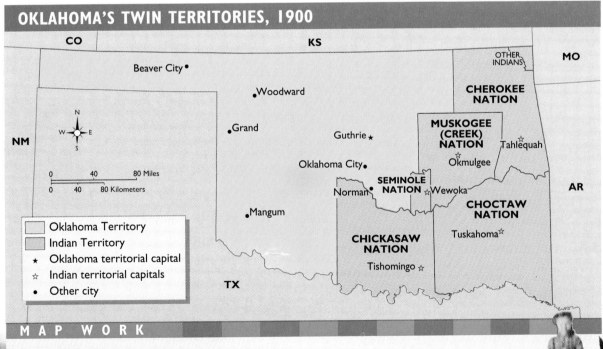

OKLAHOMA'S TWIN TERRITORIES, 1900

CO   KS   OTHER INDIANS   MO

Beaver City•   •Woodward   CHEROKEE NATION

NM   N W E S   •Grand   Guthrie ★   MUSKOGEE (CREEK) NATION   ☆Tahlequah

0 40 80 Miles   Oklahoma City•   ☆Okmulgee
0 40 80 Kilometers   SEMINOLE NATION ☆Wewoka   AR
Norman•   CHOCTAW NATION

•Mangum   Tuskahoma☆

Oklahoma Territory
Indian Territory   CHICKASAW NATION
★ Oklahoma territorial capital
☆ Indian territorial capitals   Tishomingo ☆
• Other city   TX

M A P   W O R K

Before it became a state in 1907, Oklahoma was divided into two territories.
1. What were the capitals of Indian Territory?
2. What part of the Twin Territories was Oklahoma Territory?
3. Why do you think there were several capitals in Indian Territory?

President Theodore Roosevelt used this pen (right) to sign the bill that made Oklahoma a state. This ribbon (far right) was worn on statehood day, November 16, 1907.

INDIANS THREATENED

Life for the Five Civilized Tribes changed greatly with the creation of the Twin Territories. Now the American Indians in Indian Territory realized that their lands would soon be taken by homesteaders. They felt they did not have much choice about their future.

What they feared began to happen. The United States government passed the Curtis Act. This act said that American Indians had to live by the laws of the United States government. In addition, Indian lands in the Indian Territory would be divided into small plots. The American Indians who received plots of land would become citizens of the United States.

The homesteaders wanted the Twin Territories to become a state. But most American Indians wanted to govern themselves in the Indian Territory. They did not want to be joined with Oklahoma Territory as a single state. They wanted "double statehood." This meant that Indian Territory would become a separate state from Oklahoma Territory.

A Place Called Sequoyah

On August 21, 1905 the principal chiefs of the Five Civilized Tribes met to draw up a constitution for their state. They named the state *Sequoyah* after the famous creator of the Cherokee writing system. On November 7, the people of Indian Territory voted to accept the constitution. The American Indian leaders went to Washington, D.C., to ask Congress to accept their state.

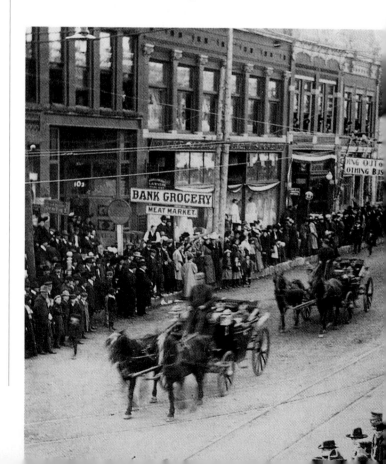

Enabling Act

Congress did not accept the plan for the state of Sequoyah. It wanted the Twin Territories to become one state. In 1906 Congress passed a law called the Enabling Act. This law said the Twin Territories should be joined to form the state of Oklahoma.

A New State

On November 16, 1907, President Theodore Roosevelt proclaimed Oklahoma as our country's forty-sixth state. A huge crowd gathered in Guthrie. They were waiting for the official message announcing that Oklahoma was a new state. When the news came, people cheered. Soon a big parade started. Charles Haskell was chosen to be our state's first governor. Guthrie was our first capital city.

In Guthrie and other towns, people celebrated when Oklahoma became the forty-sixth state.

WHY IT MATTERS

By 1907 about one and a half million people lived in the new state of Oklahoma. As our young state grew, many people felt good about its future. However the American Indians and some other Oklahomans felt less sure about the future. In the next lesson you will read about an event that changed Oklahoma's future.

✔ Reviewing Facts and Ideas

MAIN IDEAS

- The United States Congress created Oklahoma Territory in 1890.
- The Curtis Act of 1898 said that American Indians in Indian Territory who received plots of land were United States citizens.
- American Indians in the Indian Territory asked Congress to allow them to form their own state.
- The Enabling Act said the Twin Territories should be joined to form the state of Oklahoma.
- On November 16, 1907, Oklahoma became our country's 46th state.

THINK ABOUT IT

1. What was the Organic Act?
2. What were the Twin Territories?
3. **FOCUS** How was the state of Oklahoma formed?
4. **THINKING SKILL** What *effects* did the creation of the Oklahoma Territory have on the Five Civilized Tribes?
5. **GEOGRAPHY** What part of our present-day state formed Oklahoma Territory?

177

CITIZENSHIP
VIEWPOINTS

In 1890 the Chickasaw were one of the Five Civilized Tribes whose leaders met to discuss statehood.

Should the Twin Territories Become One State or Two?

As soon the Oklahoma Territory was formed in 1890, settlers began to think about it becoming a state. Before this could happen a question had to be answered. Should the Twin Territories—Oklahoma Territory and Indian Territory—be separate states? Or should they be joined to form a single state?

Most American Indians in the Twin Territories did not want to be joined into one state. Creek leader Roley McIntosh pointed out that the Five Civilized Tribes had their own governments and their land was guaranteed by treaties. Indian Territory resident Gideon Morgan did not want the Oklahoma Territory to make laws for Indian Territory.

Charles B. Ames believed that joining the territories would help the area's economy. Consider three viewpoints on this issue. Then answer the questions that follow.

Three DIFFERENT Viewpoints

1 CHARLES B. AMES
Attorney
Excerpt from the resolutions of the Oklahoma City Commercial Club in 1903

The resources of the two territories cry aloud for union. Oklahoma is almost [entirely] agricultural. The great wealth of the Indian Territory is in her mines and forests. With the product of the farm, the forest, and the mine [working together] . . . immediate success and immense achievements are sure to follow.

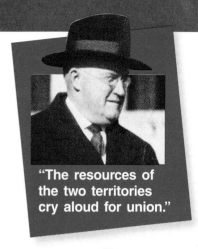

"The resources of the two territories cry aloud for union."

2 ROLEY MCINTOSH
Creek Indian leader
Excerpt from *Roley McIntosh Gives Good Reasons* in 1894

If [the people of Oklahoma] want a state . . . let them go on and do that for themselves; but let them leave us out. We have a free system of government and have had it for years, and we must insist upon not being included in the proposed State of Oklahoma.

"...let them leave us out."

3 GIDEON MORGAN
Resident of Indian Territory
Excerpt from a statement to the United States Senate, 1903

[Giving Oklahoma Territory] . . . the right to [make] the law and organize the state government . . . and then to attach . . . [Indian Territory, which has] equal population, equal taxable wealth, and equal resources is [very unfair] to . . . the people [of Indian Territory].

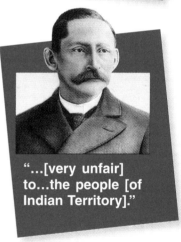

"...[very unfair] to...the people [of Indian Territory]."

BUILDING CITIZENSHIP

1. What is the viewpoint of each person?
2. What reasons did each give for their position?
3. What other viewpoints might people have on this issue?

SHARING VIEWPOINTS

Discuss what you agree with or disagree with about these and other viewpoints. Then as a class, write three statements about the one-state plan for the Twin Territories.

1880   1897   1929 1940   1960

The Oil Boom

Read Aloud

". . . when they first heard the gurglin' and roarin' down in the hole, they all . . . ran just as far and fast as they could. 'Thar she blows!' "

This is how one man described an important event of the early 1900s. It would change the lives of many Oklahomans.

Focus Activity

READ TO LEARN

How did the discovery of oil change people's lives in our state?

VOCABULARY

- fossil fuel
- boom town
- gusher
- discrimination

PEOPLE

- Dick Rowland
- Sarah Page

PLACES

- Greenwood

THE BIG PICTURE

In 1897 Oklahomans discovered a valuable natural resource—oil, or petroleum. It is formed from the remains of plants and animals that lived millions of years ago. The remains of once living things are known as fossils. As a result, oil is called a fossil fuel. In this lesson you will learn how this natural resource changed Oklahoma.

Boom towns like Three Sands grew around oil fields.

BLACK GOLD

On April 15, 1897, the first productive oil well in Oklahoma was discovered near Bartlesville. It was named the "Nellie Johnstone," after a Cherokee girl. Her father had helped to drill the well. The oil was called "black gold" because it was valuable, like gold.

By 1904 oil had been struck around towns and cities in our state. In all about 1 million gallons of oil were produced in 1904.

In 1905 a huge oil field was found at Glenn Pool near Tulsa. Towns that grew near places like Glenn Pool became known as boom towns. These are communities that grow rapidly. Within days of hearing of an oil find, many people would arrive. They hoped to get rich.

Gusher!

The 1920s brought another oil boom. Look at the map below. You can see that there were several sites of oil discoveries. For example, by 1923 rich oil wells were discovered in the Burbank field. In that year, about 32 million barrels of oil were produced at the Burbank field.

Some oil wells were called gushers. Gushers are wells that spray large amounts of oil into the air without being pumped. Many of them are hard to stop.

One gusher named "Wild Mary Sudick" sprayed thousands of gallons of oil into the air. The oil sprayed so high that it rained oil almost 20 miles away. "Wild Mary" rained oil for 11 days before it could be safely capped, or closed up.

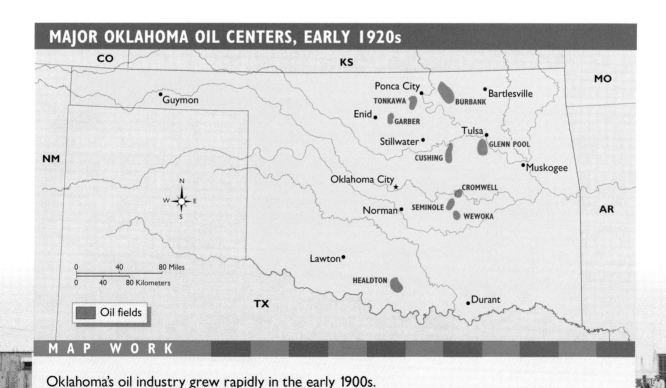

MAJOR OKLAHOMA OIL CENTERS, EARLY 1920s

MAP WORK

Oklahoma's oil industry grew rapidly in the early 1900s.

1. In what part of Oklahoma were most oil fields located?
2. What oil fields were discovered near Tulsa?

GOOD TIMES, HARD TIMES

In the early 1900s Oklahoma oil wells produced thousands of barrels of black gold daily. Everyone had oil fever. The oil boom, like the land runs before it, brought many people to Oklahoma. However, as cities grew, conflicts arose between different groups of people.

Oil Capital of the World

By 1920 Oklahoma had become our country's leading producer of oil. Over 1 billion barrels of oil were produced in 1920 alone. Oil helped almost everyone make money. It created many good paying jobs, which helped our state's economy.

Farmers considered oil to be a "crop" when oil companies paid to drill on their farms. Refineries were built, giving people more jobs. The transportation of the oil products made in refineries also became an important business.

Bartlesville and Ponca City started as oil towns. Big cities like Tulsa grew as they became important business centers for oil companies. Tulsa became known as the "Oil Capital of the World."

Discrimination

During the oil boom many people in cities like Tulsa lived well. Like others, many African Americans had come to Oklahoma in the 1920s. They came to work in the oil industry and at other jobs. They hoped that Oklahoma would be free from discrimination, the unfair difference in the treatment of people. They worked hard. Within a few years they had built strong communities, like Greenwood in Tulsa.

Tulsa was a busy oil center in the early 1900s (below), but a race riot in 1921 almost completely destroyed the Greenwood section (right).

Tulsa Race Riots

On May 30, 1921, an event occurred that changed the lives of many people in Oklahoma. An African American man named Dick Rowland was accused of attacking a white woman in Tulsa. Her name was Sarah Page. Many people believed that Rowland was innocent. Even so, he was arrested the next day.

A crowd of white citizens gathered outside the jail. Many people feared that they planned to harm Rowland. To prevent this, a group of African Americans armed with guns went to the jail. Violence broke out. For a few days, angry whites killed over 100 African Americans. They also destroyed Greenwood.

For many years, people have argued over who should be held responsible for the deaths and destruction. In 1998, a Tulsa race riot commission began studying the event. From its findings Oklahomans hope to finally understand what really happened.

WHY IT MATTERS

The discovery of oil changed Oklahoma forever. Boom towns appeared almost overnight. The history of Oklahoma is the story of people who have worked hard to make lives better for others. At the same time, Oklahomans had to struggle with discrimination and conflicts like the Tulsa Race Riots. In the next lesson you will read about other struggles that affected Oklahomans.

✓ Reviewing Facts and Ideas

MAIN IDEAS

- The discovery of oil in the late 1800s led to the rapid growth of Oklahoma. Following the discovery of oil, boom towns grew rapidly.

- By 1920 Oklahoma had become the largest oil-producing state in our country.

- As Oklahoma's cities grew, conflicts between groups also grew. In 1921 over 100 African Americans were killed during the Tulsa Race Riots.

THINK ABOUT IT

1. What was the "Nellie Johnstone"?

2. What is a gusher?

3. **FOCUS** How did the discovery of oil change people's lives in Oklahoma?

4. **THINKING SKILL** *Predict* what would happen if there were an oil strike in Tulsa today.

5. **WRITE** Suppose you were a newspaper reporter at the site of an oil gusher. Write a brief article describing what you have seen.

Wildcatters

When they struck "black gold," "wildcatters" smiled. A wildcatter is someone who digs for oil in hopes of finding a rich well. Wildcatters in the early 1900s often had to guess where oil might be found.

The early wildcatters traveled around Oklahoma looking for places that might have oil. If they found one, they would buy a land lease. This lease gave them the right to any oil that was under the ground. A land lease could cost a lot. Wildcatters also had to pay for equipment and people to dig for the oil.

If they did not find oil, wildcatters often ended up without any money. But many wildcatters enjoyed taking risks. If one place had no oil, they searched for others. The legacy of taking risks to reach one's dreams lives on in Oklahoma today.

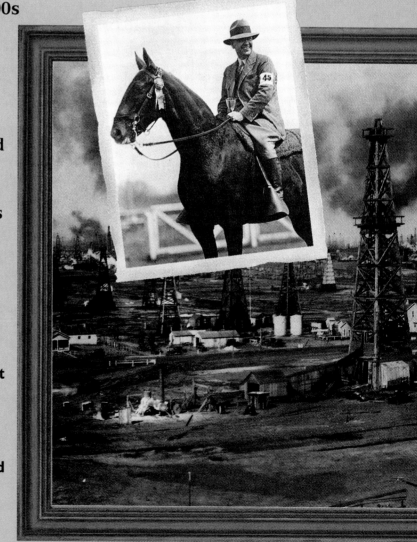

Thomas Gilcrease (top) was part Muskogee (Creek). By 1905, he held rich oil leases in the Glenn Pool oil field. E.W. Marland (above right) struck oil in 1911. By 1920, his company controlled the Tonkawa oil field (right).

Frank Phillips (inset) started with one small oil refinery in 1927 (above). Today, Phillips' oil company is one of the largest in Oklahoma. Many products we use today (below) are made from petroleum.

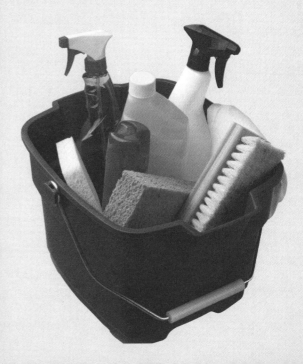

| 1920 | 1929 | 1939 | 1950 |

The Great Depression

Read Aloud

"Dust filtered [spread] into everything. It gritted between our teeth when we tried to eat. It muddied a glass of water before we could drink."

This is what one Oklahoman had to say about life in the Dust Bowl during the Great Depression.

Focus Activity

READ TO LEARN

What happened in Oklahoma during the Great Depression?

VOCABULARY

- stocks
- Great Depression
- New Deal

PEOPLE

- Franklin D. Roosevelt
- "Alfalfa" Bill Murray

THE BIG PICTURE

In the last lesson you read how the oil booms helped Oklahoma grow quickly. However, the good times did not last. In this lesson you will learn how Oklahomans struggled through some very hard times.

THE GREAT DEPRESSION

As you read, the 1920s were a time of growth in our state. Oil discoveries created jobs for many Oklahomans. The 1920s were also good years for the stock market. Stocks are shares, or parts, of ownership in a company. In the 1920s many people in our country bought stocks. They hoped to earn money as businesses boomed and stock prices went up.

Stock Market Crash

On October 24, 1929, stock prices fell suddenly and sharply. People across the country rushed to sell their stocks. The stock market "crashed." This marked the beginning of hard times for the people of our state and our country. A long period of hardships called the Great Depression had begun.

By 1932 more than 5,000 United States banks had failed. About 32,000 companies and stores had closed. More than 12 million Americans were out of work. This meant that one out of every four adults had no jobs. In Oklahoma, factories and mines closed. Oil prices fell to 15 cents a barrel.

In 1932 Americans elected a president with a plan to help end the Depression. This President, was Franklin D. Roosevelt (ROH zuh velt). He introduced a program called the New Deal. It included many government programs to help poor, jobless, disabled, and retired Americans. It also formed a government agency to control the stock market.

People lined up for food (below, left) during the Great Depression. President Franklin Roosevelt (below) worked to help Americans.

DROUGHT AND DUST

As you read, cities developed and grew after the land runs and the oil boom. Even so, most Oklahomans lived in rural communities in the 1930s. Many were farmers.

Farming in Oklahoma had always been very hard work. Farmers worked from dawn to dusk. Strong winds and heavy rains often made farm work harder. By the 1930s the Depression caused the prices for Oklahoma's agricultural products to drop greatly. Crops like cotton were now worth only four cents a pound. Many farmers lost their farms.

The Dust Bowl

Life in Oklahoma grew even worse. Years of drought in the 1930s turned more than 150,000 square miles of the Great Plains into dust. As you read earlier, this area became known as the *Dust Bowl.*

Farmers could do almost nothing. There was very little rain. Without water, crops dried up. The winds picked up the dry soil and blew it across their fields.

The drought continued until the soil turned into black or red dust. Read below the words of a well-known Oklahoma singer named Woody Guthrie. How does he describe the dust storms that destroyed our lands in the 1930s?

A dust storm hit and it hit like thunder,
It dusted us over and it covered us under:
Blocked out the traffic and blocked out the sun,
Straight for home all the people did run.

Woody Guthrie (below) wrote songs about the hardships of the Depression. Dust storms could even bury cars (left). Governor "Alfalfa" Bill Murray (right) tried to help Oklahomans during the drought years.

"Alfalfa" Bill Murray

During the difficult drought years from 1930-1935, Oklahoma was led by a governor named "Alfalfa" Bill Murray. Many people believed that he was called "Alfalfa Bill" because he was the first person to grow alfalfa in the Chickasaw Nation. He had often represented the Chickasaw at government meetings.

As governor, Murray tried to help Oklahomans who were affected by the Great Depression and droughts. Murray asked rich citizens to pay more taxes. He also wanted to stop oil production. The large amount of oil being produced was forcing its price to drop. The governor also made state officials control the money they spent for government.

WHY IT MATTERS

The Great Depression was a time of terrible hardship. Through hard work and determination, the people of Oklahoma helped each other through to better times. Many of the government agencies set up during the New Deal to help the poor are still in place today.

✓// Reviewing Facts and Ideas

MAIN IDEAS

- The Great Depression brought great hardship to all Americans. To help those who were suffering, President Franklin D. Roosevelt started the New Deal.

- The Dust Bowl covered large areas of the Great Plains in dust. Crops dried up and many farm animals died.

- Governor "Alfalfa" Bill Murray tried to help Oklahomans during the Great Depression.

THINK ABOUT IT

1. What are stocks?

2. Who was elected President of the United States in 1932?

3. **FOCUS** What happened in Oklahoma during the Great Depression?

4. **THINKING SKILL** *Compare* and *contrast* Oklahoma today and during the Great Depression.

5. **WRITE** Suppose you were a singer like Woody Guthrie. Write a song about life during the Great Depression.

1900　　1920　　1939　　　1965　1980

World War II and After

Read Aloud

"The 45th is one of the best, if not actually the best division in the history of American Arms."

These words were said by United States General George S. Patton, Jr. He was describing a well-known World War II army division that included many Oklahomans.

Focus Activity

READ TO LEARN

What effects did World War II have on Oklahoma's growth?

VOCABULARY

- Axis Powers
- Allies
- urban
- suburb
- turnpike
- segregation
- civil rights
- Civil Rights Act of 1964

PEOPLE

- Roy Turner
- Rosa Parks
- Clara Luper
- Martin Luther King, Jr.

PLACES

- Pearl Harbor, Hawaii
- Tinker Air Force Base
- Turner Turnpike
- Montgomery, Alabama

THE BIG PICTURE

People like President Roosevelt and Governor "Alfalfa" Bill Murray worked hard to end the Great Depression. Even with their efforts, the difficult times continued. Then, before good times could return, the country was thrown into another crisis, World War II.

190

WORLD WAR II

World War II began in 1939. It started when German soldiers marched into the nearby country of Poland. Soon the war spread around the world. Germany, Italy, and Japan formed the Axis Powers. They fought against the Allies, led by Great Britain, France, China, and the Soviet Union.

At first, The United States stayed out of the war. But on December 7, 1941, Japanese planes bombed the United States naval base at Pearl Harbor, Hawaii. The attack came without warning, and 2,403 people died. The next day the United States declared war on Japan. Germany and Italy, in turn, declared war on the United States.

During the war, more than 14 million Americans served in the military. This number included about 500,000 Oklahomans. Among the Oklahoman officers were Lieutenant General Raymond S. McClain and Major General Clarence L. Tinker, an Osage Indian.

The War at Home

Americans worked hard to produce goods for the war. Oklahomans worked to build airplanes and other things needed to fight the war. They also helped to train soldiers and sailors. Twenty-eight army camps and 13 naval bases were built in our state. Tinker Air Force Base was built in 1942 in Oklahoma City. It became one of the most important air depots in the country. A depot is a place to store equipment

The war helped the United States economy. The industries building weapons, planes, and ships created new jobs for Americans. This ended the Great Depression. The war effort continued until the Japanese surrendered, on August 14, 1945.

On June 6, 1944, American soldiers landed in France. (left) At home (below, right), Oklahoma's Women's Naval Reserve members helped our country during World War II.

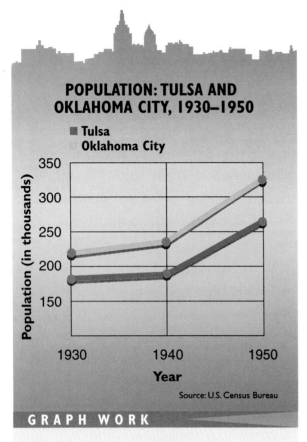

POPULATION: TULSA AND OKLAHOMA CITY, 1930–1950

■ Tulsa
■ Oklahoma City

Population (in thousands)

350
300
250
200
150

1930   1940   1950

Year

Source: U.S. Census Bureau

GRAPH WORK

The population of Oklahoma City and Tulsa grew between 1930 and 1950.

1. When did Tulsa's population reach 200,000 people?
2. Which city had more people in 1930?

AFTER THE WAR

Following WWII, Americans stopped manufacturing products for the war. Instead they made many different kinds of products like cars, stoves, and refrigerators. Around the country and in Oklahoma people began to put the war behind them and build new lives.

Urban Communities

After the war, Oklahomans looked for better jobs and new opportunities. Some moved from their farms to find higher paying work in urban areas. Urban means city or like a city. In the cities many people found jobs in factories. They also started small businesses. Others went to school to learn new skills.

City population grew quickly. Look at the graph on this page. Tulsa and Oklahoma City are Oklahoma's two largest cities. How did their population increase between 1930 and 1950?

Before World War II, most of the land outside of Oklahoma's cities had been used mostly for farming. Now, with the growing city population, people began to build homes outside the cities. The new communities were called suburbs. Suburbs are communities just outside of a city.

In 1953, the Turner Turnpike was opened to traffic between Tulsa and Oklahoma City.

LIFE IN THE SUBURBS

Better roads and cheaper cars made it possible for people to live farther from their jobs in the cities. Houses in the suburbs were larger. They often cost less than houses in the cities. New shopping centers made the suburbs comfortable places to live in and to raise families.

Some Oklahomans missed life on the farm, but many others did not. Here's what a farmer named Harold A. Todd said:

I was born on a farm in 1921 and was pretty good working a team of mules. But after joining the army in World War II . . . I realized that I just couldn't go back to the farm. I had seen too much of the world.

On the Road

As many Oklahomans moved to suburbs and cities, the sale of cars increased. By 1950 there were over 830,000 cars in Oklahoma. More gasoline and oil were needed to fuel and keep these cars running.

A New Oil Boom

The discovery of new oil fields in Oklahoma caused an oil boom in the 1950s. New oil refineries were built. This created many new jobs. Large cities like Tulsa and Oklahoma City became important business centers for the oil industry. Oklahomans bought even more cars.

Soon our roads and highways were crowded with cars carrying people and products to cities and towns around Oklahoma and our country. Traffic jams began to clog the roads. Businesses began to suffer because it took trucks longer to transport goods between places.

Governor Roy Turner

Governor Roy Turner was governor of our state from 1947 to 1951. It was his idea to build a turnpike from Oklahoma City to Tulsa. A turnpike is a highway that charges a toll for traveling on it. In 1953 the Turner Turnpike opened. Trucks and cars on the turnpike could quickly carry people and products to Oklahoma's cities.

Governor Turner brought other changes to our state as well. For example, he improved education for children. He also worked to bring new businesses to Oklahoma.

SEPARATE BUT NOT EQUAL

After World War II, one of the most serious problems facing our country was segregation. Segregation is the keeping of one group apart from another by law. In Oklahoma and many other parts of the United States, blacks were not allowed to eat in the same restaurants as white people. They could not attend the same schools as whites either. Even restrooms and drinking fountains were segregated. On buses, black passengers had to sit in back.

African Americans in Oklahoma and much of the rest of our country were being denied their basic civil rights. Civil rights are the rights of all people to be treated equally under the law.

Rosa Parks

In the 1950s events in other states and in Oklahoma would begin to end segregation. One African American who demanded her civil rights at this time was a woman named Rosa Parks. In December of 1955, she boarded a bus in Montgomery, Alabama. When the bus filled up, the driver told her to give up her seat to a white person. When she refused, she was arrested. Hundreds of African Americans in the city refused to ride the buses. A civil rights group in Montgomery took their demands to court. A year later the United States Supreme Court ordered Montgomery to end segregation on buses.

Working to End Segregation

Around the country blacks and whites worked together to end other kinds of segregation. In Oklahoma City in 1958 an African American teacher named Clara Luper and a group of teenagers started a sit-in. They refused to move from a section of a restaurant set aside for whites. They decided to continue sitting there even though they were not served. Here's what she said about her role in fighting segregation:

I am an agitator [someone who arouses the public to make changes]. But it's my understanding that an agitator is what gets the clothes clean in a washing machine.

Rosa Parks was arrested and fingerprinted (above) in Montgomery, Alabama, in 1959.

Civil Rights Act

During the 1950s and 1960s leaders like Martin Luther King, Jr. worked with others to gain equal rights for all Americans. Finally, his work led to the United States Congress passing the Civil Rights Act of 1964. It made it illegal for businesses to discriminate against anyone because of their race, sex or religion. It also required restaurants and hotels to admit African Americans. A year later, Congress passed The Voting Rights Act. This outlawed any action that prevented African Americans from voting.

WHY IT MATTERS

During World War II Americans worked hard at home and overseas to defeat the Axis Powers. After the war, our country entered a period of great growth. At this time many Oklahomans moved to cities and suburbs. Problems such as segregation caused a movement for equal rights throughout the country. Today, the struggle to make sure all people are treated fairly continues.

Today, Clara Luper is still working to make sure that all Oklahomans have equal rights.

✔// Reviewing Facts and Ideas

MAIN IDEAS

- The United States entered World War II in 1941. The war ended on August 14, 1945, when Japan surrendered to the United States.

- Following the war, cities and suburbs grew rapidly. Oklahomans left their farms and took jobs in urban areas.

- One of the problems facing Americans after the war was segregation. The Civil Rights Act of 1964 made it illegal for businesses to discriminate against anyone because of race, sex, or religion.

THINK ABOUT IT

1. How did World War II help end the Great Depression?

2. Who was Clara Luper?

3. **FOCUS** How did World War II affect Oklahoma's growth?

4. **THINKING SKILL** Identify one *cause* and one *effect* of the fight against discrimination by African Americans in the 1950s and 1960s.

5. **WRITE** Suppose that you are a leader in the fight for civil rights. Write a speech to convince Oklahomans to end segregation.

CHAPTER 8 REVIEW

THINKING ABOUT VOCABULARY

Number a sheet of paper from 1 to 10. Next to each number write the word from the list that best completes the sentence.

Civil Rights	segregation
discrimination	stocks
drought	suburb
fossil fuel	turnpike
New Deal	urban

1. A _____ is a highway that charges a toll for traveling on it.

2. Oil is formed from the remains of plants and animals that lived millions of years ago. That is why it is also called _____.

3. Separating one group of people from another by law is called _____.

4. A long period of time with little or no rainfall is a _____.

5. An unfair difference in the treatment of people is _____.

6. Government programs to help Americans during the Great Depression were part of the _____.

7. An _____ area is a city or part of a city.

8. Shares, or parts, of ownership in a company are called _____.

9. _____ are the rights of all people to be treated equally under the law.

10. A community just outside a city is called a _____.

THINKING ABOUT FACTS

1. When did Oklahoma become a state?

2. What kinds of homes did the homesteaders build?

3. What was one thing Governor Turner was known for?

4. In 1900 Oklahoma was made up of two territories. What was each territory's name? Who lived in each territory?

5. Why was oil called "Black Gold"?

6. How did oil help Oklahoma?

7. Who was "Alfalfa" Bill Murray? How did he help Oklahomans?

8. Name two things that happened as a result of the Great Depression.

9. How did World War II help to end the Great Depression?

10. Why did people move from farms to cities after World War II?

THINK AND WRITE

WRITE A DESCRIPTION

Write a paragraph about what life was like in Oklahoma for the children of homesteaders.

WRITE A LETTER

Most American Indians did not want the Twin Territories to become a single state. Write a letter from a member of the Five Civilized Tribes to a member of U.S. Congress to explain the views of American Indians.

WRITE AN ARTICLE

Suppose you are a reporter at the time of the Tulsa Race Riots. Write an article describing what happened during the race riot.

APPLYING STUDY SKILLS

LONGITUDE AND LATITUDE

Answer the following questions about the map on this page.

1. What are lines of latitude and lines of longitude?

2. Cushing is closest to which line of latitude?

3. Tulsa is closest to which line of longitude?

4. What is the approximate location of Stillwater?

5. Why is it important to understand latitude and longitude?

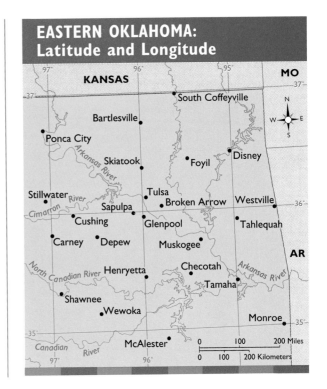

EASTERN OKLAHOMA: Latitude and Longitude

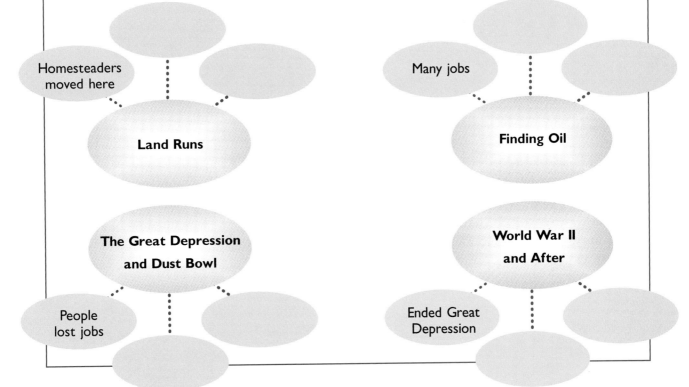

Summing Up the Chapter

Use the following semantic map to organize information from the chapter. Copy the map on a sheet of paper. Then write at least one piece of information from the chapter in each blank circle. Lastly, write a paragraph that answers the question "How did these important events change Oklahoma?"

Homesteaders moved here

Land Runs

Many jobs

Finding Oil

The Great Depression and Dust Bowl

World War II and After

People lost jobs

Ended Great Depression

UNIT 3 REVIEW

THINKING ABOUT VOCABULARY

Number a sheet of paper from 1 to 10. Beside each number write the word from the list that best matches the description.

artifacts	explorer
constitution	segregation
drought	slavery
dugout	time line
expedition	treaty

1. A diagram that shows when events in history took place

2. Someone who travels to unknown areas

3. Separating one group from another by law

4. A journey of exploration

5. Items left by people who lived long ago

6. A plan for a government

7. An agreement among nations

8. Shelter built into the side of a hill

9. The practice of making one person the property of another

10. Long period with very little rain

THINK AND WRITE

WRITING A JOURNAL ENTRY

It is after World War II and you have just moved from your family's farm to the city of Tulsa to take a job there. You are living in the suburbs. Describe what your new life is like.

WRITING A NEWSPAPER ARTICLE

Reread page 159. Then, write an article for your school newspaper describing the "Sooners."

WRITING A REPORT

Write a report about farmers in Oklahoma during the Great Depression and drought years. Do some research at the library or on the Internet to learn more about this period and what was done to help the farmers.

BUILDING SKILLS

1. **Time lines** Draw a time line that begins with 1850 and ends with 1960. Place five events that you read about in Unit 3 on the time line.

2. **Time lines** Draw a time line that begins with your birth year and ends with this year. Place three events from your life on the time line.

3. **Latitude and Longitude** Look at the map on page 197. What is the latitude of Monroe?

4. **Latitude and Longitude:** Look at the map on page 197. What is the longitude of Henryetta?

5. **Latitude and Longitude** Look at the map on page 197. What large city is located at 36°N, 96°W?

YESTERDAY, TODAY &
TOMORROW

Some Oklahomans do not know that our state was once divided into two territories. Do you think it is important for Oklahomans to know about events from the past? Do you think it will be important for people living in Oklahoma fifty years from now to learn our state's history? Why or why not?

READING ON YOUR OWN
Here are some books you might find at the library to help you learn more.

THE GREAT DEPRESSION
by R. Conrad Stein
Read about the 1929 stock market crash and its affect on urban and rural Americans.

LONGWALKER'S JOURNEY: A NOVEL OF THE CHOCKTAW TRAIL OF TEARS
by Beatrice Orcutt Harrell
A father and son on the forced march to Indian Territory travel ahead of the rest of their people to prepare a home.

PIONEERS
by Martin W. Sandler
American pioneer life is presented with fascinating details, quotes, and art.

UNIT 3 REVIEW PROJECT

Write a Historical Diary

1. Suppose you were one of the following people:
   - a french fur trader in the 1600s
   - an Oklahoma homesteader in the late 1800s
   - a member of the Five Civilized Tribes in the early 1900s
2. Gather information from your textbook and your school library about the person you chose.
3. Write a diary page that might have been written by that person. You may write about your home life, family, or thoughts on the new or changing world around you.
4. Trade papers with a partner.
5. Challenge your partner to guess which person from the list wrote the diary.

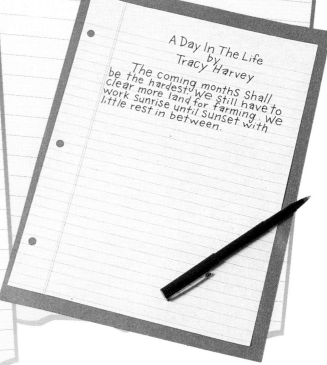

A Day In The Life
by Tracy Harvey
The coming months shall be the hardest. We still have to clear more land for farming. We work sunrise until sunset with little rest in between.

HIGH-TECH WORKER (RIGHT);
INDIAN BLANKET WILDFLOWER
(FAR RIGHT); OKLAHOMA'S
STATE FLAG (BELOW LEFT);
THE STATE CAPITOL BUILDING
IN OKLAHOMA CITY (BELOW);
STATUE OF CARL ALBERT
IN MCALESTER (FAR RIGHT)

OKLAHOMA

Oklahoma Today

"We stand on the mountaintop of a new millennium."

from a speech by President Bill Clinton
See page 256.

Why Does It Matter?

What kinds of work do Oklahomans do? How have the economy and government of our state continued to be successful? What do you think Oklahoma will be like in the next century?

As you read Unit 4 you will see how Oklahoma has much to celebrate as it faces the twenty-first century. We are lucky to live in a state where a blending of cultures gives us the opportunity to better understand the world we live in. In this unit you will learn about the ways Oklahoma is special both as a state and as a part of our country.

FIND OUT MORE!
Visit our website:
www.mhschool.com

inter**NET**
CONNECTION

CARL ALBERT
COAL MINER'S SON
UNITED STATES REPRESENTATIVE
3RD DISTRICT OF OKLAHOMA
1947 TO 1977

46TH SPEAKER OF THE
U.S. HOUSE OF REPRESENTATIVES
1971 TO 1977

Oklahoma's Economy

THINKING ABOUT GEOGRAPHY AND HISTORY

Oklahoma contributes many important goods and services to the economy of the United States. We are lucky to be rich in natural resources and to have many skilled workers. In this chapter, we will learn many of the ways Oklahomans today work to keep the economy of Oklahoma strong.

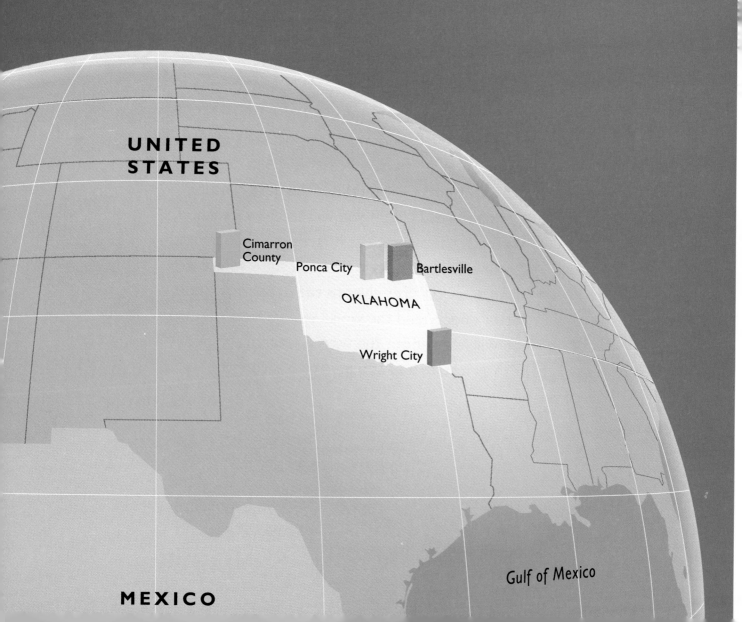

UNITED STATES

Cimarron County

Ponca City

Bartlesville

OKLAHOMA

Wright City

Gulf of Mexico

MEXICO

Wheat Farm
BARTLESVILLE

Wheat is a major crop in Oklahoma. Vast wheat fields can be seen stretching over northern Oklahoma.

Cattle Ranch
CIMARRON COUNTY

Cattle are also another important agricultural product in Oklahoma. The rolling plains of the Panhandle provide rich grazing land.

Oil Refinery
PONCA CITY

Oil, or "Black Gold," has been an important industry in our state since the early 1900s.

Lumber Mill
WRIGHT CITY

The forests of southeastern Oklahoma provide timber for lumber mills in our state.

Local and Regional Economies

Focus Activity

How does the free enterprise system work in Oklahoma?

- entrepreneur
- raw material
- labor
- supply
- demand

Read Aloud

"Yourtown T-shirt Design Contest
Design a T-shirt describing our community.
Winning T-shirts will be sold at the School Fair."
Suppose that this sign was posted at Yourtown Elementary School in Oklahoma. Also suppose that your friend Maria entered and won the contest. Her T-shirts sold quickly at the school fair. She then decided to try and sell them to a local store.

THE BIG PICTURE

By making and selling her T-shirts, Maria was taking part in our country's free enterprise system. People who form and run a business, like Maria, are called **entrepreneurs** (ahn truh pruh NURZ). In this economic system, entrepreneurs are free to produce, or make, different kinds of goods or services. People are also free to choose the goods and services they want to consume, or buy and use.

Local businesses provide important goods and services to communities.

LOCAL ECONOMIES

As you have read, our country's free enterprise system is made up of many state and regional economies. These economies are interdependent. Oil produced in Oklahoma may be sold in Florida. In the same way, oranges grown in Florida may be sold in stores in Oklahoma.

Oklahoma's Economies

Oklahoma's regional and local economies work in much the same way. Most local economies include different kinds of small businesses. Maria's community, for example, would have a print shop to help her produce her T-shirts. However, the equipment in the shop probably would be bought in a nearby city.

Geography and the Economy

As you read, each of Oklahoma's regions has special geographical features and natural resources. This makes it easier for Oklahomans to raise certain crops and make specific products.

Wheat, for example, is grown in northern Oklahoma, where the climate is cooler. Farmers grow peanuts and cotton in the southern part of Oklahoma, where the climate is warmer.

Oklahoma City is the largest city in our state. Its location in the middle of our state has helped it grow quickly. From Oklahoma City, it is easy to travel to and from other communities in the state. Think again about Yourtown. Suppose it is on a lake. As you might expect, Yourtown has stores selling equipment and bait to people who fish. It also has a marina. Small boats can dock there and be repaired.

STARTING A LOCAL BUSINESS

As you have read, most communities are made up of small businesses like the print shop Maria uses in her T-shirt business. They have small businesses like those in your town or city. Does you community have a coffee shop? A grocery store? Most towns also have a lawn-mowing or machine-repair service, a grocery store, a bank, and a bookstore. These businesses serve the different needs of people in the community.

Getting Enough Money

Starting and running a business is a lot of work. First, a business needs money. A business cannot get started without money. It is needed to pay for rent or to buy a building, to buy tools or materials, to pay workers, and for transportation. There are also other costs.

Most businesses have to borrow money to get started. Often they borrow money from their investors. As you learned earlier, an investor is someone who puts money into a business. In return, most investors expect to get some of the profit the business earns.

Suppose Maria's teacher, some of her classmates, and her parents were all investors in Maria's business. Without their help, Maria would not have had enough money to buy the T-shirts and other things she needed.

Before Maria could start producing her T-shirts, she sat down and began to think about what she would have to do to make a profit. She knew she would have to buy T-shirts. She would also have to pay the print shop that would print her design onto the T-shirts. She began to make a list of all her costs.

Towns like Broken Arrow have many different types of small businesses.

COSTS AND PRICES

All businesses, large and small have to figure out how much a product will cost to make. One cost for Maria's business is the raw materials she will need. The raw material is the resource a business uses to make a finished product. Businesses use different types of raw materials. For example, a furniture maker would use wood and steel. A shoe maker would need leather and rubber. In Maria's small business, the raw materials would be the undecorated shirts and the paper and colored pens she used to draw her designs.

Maria would also have to pay for labor. Labor is the people who use their strength and skills to make a product. As you read, Maria would have to pay the print shop. She also would have to pay the people who help her deliver the T-shirts to the local store selling the shirts. Maria probably would decide that her total cost will include the cost of raw materials, labor, and perhaps transportation.

Deciding on the Price

Maria adds up the cost of producing her T-shirts. She then would decide on the selling price. Suppose Maria sells her T-shirts for more money than it costs to make them. Then she will make a profit. Profit is the money a business earns after it pays for its costs. If she spends more than she makes, Maria and the investors in her business will lose money.

In a free enterprise system, the price of goods is partly decided by supply. Price is also decided by demand. Supply is the amount of an item a business is willing to make. Demand is the amount of an item that people are willing to buy.

Maria's supply is the number of T-shirts she will make to sell. The demand is the number of T-shirts that people are willing to buy at the price she sets. Running a business is hard work. But by working hard, Oklahomans have built many businesses. In the Infographic on the next page you will read about some of these businesses.

The hard work of business people like the store owner above helps to keep our economy strong.

infographic

Local Businesses

The local economy of any area can include many different businesses. These pages show different local businesses that are common in Oklahoma. What business or businesses are in your community?

Whether constructing large buildings (left) or making boots in a shop (below), Oklahomans work hard to provide the things we need.

Local businesses sell the food you will eat today. This baker is selling today's fresh bread.

Many small businesses support the high tech industry in Oklahoma. A computer technician repairs a computer (above). Some Oklahomans enjoy working outdoors, like this rancher (below).

WHY IT MATTERS

Maria made some good decisions and created a local Oklahoma business. Like Maria, you may one day start a business and play an important part in our state's economy. By buying or selling products, you too are helping Oklahoma's free enterprise system work.

✔ Reviewing Facts and Ideas

MAIN IDEAS

- In a free enterprise system, people are free to choose the products they make and consume. Geography is important to a community's economy.

- Investors provide money in order to help start businesses.

- Labor, raw materials, and transportation are among the costs of businesses. The price of goods and services depend on supply and demand.

THINK ABOUT IT

1. What is labor?

2. How does a business make a profit?

3. FOCUS How does the free enterprise system work in Oklahoma?

4. THINKING SKILL What *decisions* would you have to make before going into business?

5. GEOGRAPHY In what ways can the geography of Oklahoma affect its economy?

Oklahoma Industry

Focus Activity

READ TO LEARN

What are some important industries in Oklahoma?

VOCABULARY

- industry
- high tech
- software
- assembly line
- robot
- mining
- tourism

Read Aloud

"We're building quality cars here and the attitude of the people is probably the most important thing. They are . . . determined to do the job right."

These words were spoken by a worker at a large automobile plant in Oklahoma City. They show his pride in his job and the place he works.

THE BIG PICTURE

Oklahoma's economy is diverse. Some people in our state are farmers. Some are factory workers. Others are doctors, lawyers, teachers, police officers, and firefighters. The list is long. Thanks to our state's hard-working people and our natural resources, Oklahoma has helped the free enterprise economy of the United States stay strong.

A VARIETY OF INDUSTRIES

Today Oklahomans work in many different industries. Industry is all the businesses that make one kind of goods or provide one kind of service. The automobile industry, for example, includes the factories making cars. It also includes factories making tires, windshield wipers, engines, and other parts.

The oil industry has long been an important industry in our state. A growing new industry is the high tech industry. High tech, or high technology, is the use of computers and other electronics to meet people's needs. Another growing industry in Oklahoma is telecommunications. Telecommunications is the sending of messages by radio, telephone, the Internet, or satellite. You can find other industries in our state on the map on this page.

The Computer Industry

Think about the computer you may use. Like you, many people use the computer to find information on the Internet. It is a network that connects computers all over the world.

Oklahoma has a growing computer industry. Some of its businesses make computers. Others make computer parts and programs for computers. Our state also has companies that design websites. A website is a place on the Internet where people can find information.

Some companies in Oklahoma make software. Software is a program that tells a computer what to do. Software lets you use your computer to write a school paper, add numbers, or play games. Companies also use software to keep track of bills, to send messages, and to store information.

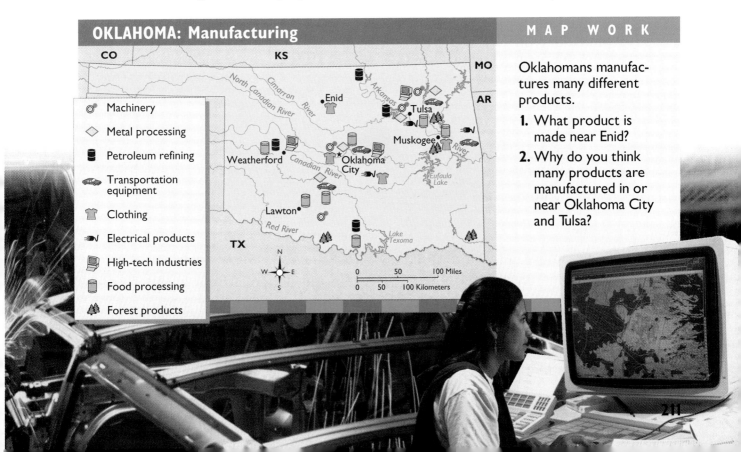

OKLAHOMA: Manufacturing

Legend:
- Machinery
- Metal processing
- Petroleum refining
- Transportation equipment
- Clothing
- Electrical products
- High-tech industries
- Food processing
- Forest products

CO, KS, MO, AR, TX

North Canadian River, Cimarron River, Arkansas River, Canadian River, Red River, Lake Texoma, Eufaula Lake

Enid, Tulsa, Muskogee, Weatherford, Oklahoma City, Lawton

N W E S

0 50 100 Miles
0 50 100 Kilometers

MAP WORK

Oklahomans manufactures many different products.

1. What product is made near Enid?
2. Why do you think many products are manufactured in or near Oklahoma City and Tulsa?

211

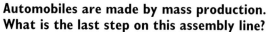

Automobiles are made by mass production. What is the last step on this assembly line?

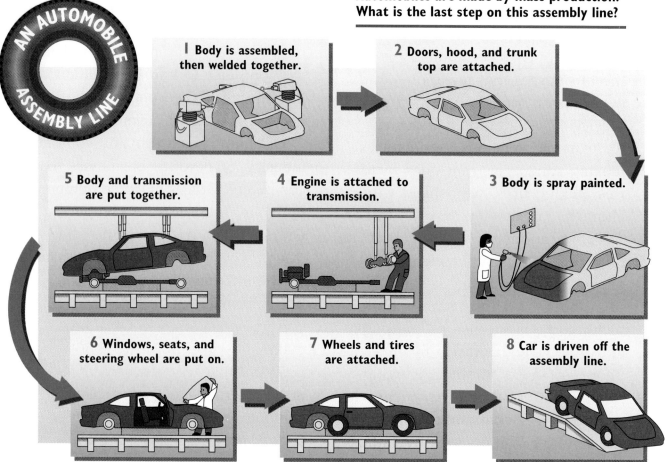

AN AUTOMOBILE ASSEMBLY LINE

1 Body is assembled, then welded together.

2 Doors, hood, and trunk top are attached.

3 Body is spray painted.

4 Engine is attached to transmission.

5 Body and transmission are put together.

6 Windows, seats, and steering wheel are put on.

7 Wheels and tires are attached.

8 Car is driven off the assembly line.

MANUFACTURING INDUSTRIES

Manufacturing industries are very important to our state. Today about 150,000 Oklahomans work in manufacturing industries. Among the goods produced are automobiles, oil field equipment transportation equipment, food products, and various metal products.

Automobiles

One of our state's largest manufacturing plants is an automobile factory in Oklahoma City. What do you think happens there?

The first thing you might see in the factory are the long belts running down the assembly lines. An assembly line is a line of workers and machines that put together the parts of a product as they move past them.

In many factories, some car parts are put together by robots. A robot is a machine that is controlled by computers. The chart above shows you which car parts are put together by robots.

At the factory you may also see the car's body being spray painted. You may see the wheels and tires being attached. In all, about 75 cars are built in an hour in this way. Workers at this plant in Oklahoma will make about 500 cars while you are in school today.

THE MINING INDUSTRY

Mining is also an important industry in Oklahoma. Mining is the business of digging valuable natural resources out of the earth. Oil, natural gas, coal, stone, sand, and salt are some of the important mining industries in our state.

Oil and Natural Gas

As you read earlier, oil is one of Oklahoma's most important resources. Oklahoma is a leading state in the production of oil and natural gas. These industries give many Oklahomans jobs. They also provide a large amount of money to our state's economy.

Central Oklahoma produces much of the oil in our state. Western Oklahoma produces natural gas. It is used for cooking foods and heating buildings.

Non-metals

Non-metal minerals are minerals found in the earth that cannot be melted, carry electricity, or made into thin sheets or wires. Non-metals include fossil fuels, such as coal, and crystals, such as iodine. Other non-metal minerals are sand, crushed stone, and gravel.

Today some coal is mined in Oklahoma. Sand and gravel are mined around Tulsa and Oklahoma City. Southwest Oklahoma supplies crushed stone.

Oklahoma is the only state that mines iodine. It is mined in the northwest part of our state. Iodine is an important mineral. Plants, animals, and people need small amounts of iodine to grow.

Oklahoma has about 25 working mines. Over 500,000 oil and gas wells have been drilled.

213

SERVICES

Oklahoma's service industry is the largest industry in our state. The service industry is made up of all the people whose jobs are to help other people rather than to make things. Today, about one–third of Oklahoma's workers are in the service industry.

Cooks, doctors, salespeople, and teachers work in the service industry. Government workers such as police officers, postal workers, and firefighters are also service workers. Most service industry jobs are in areas like Oklahoma City and Tulsa.

Oklahoma's 122 airports provide service jobs for pilots and other airport workers.

The Tourist Industry

One of the leading service industries in our state today is tourism. Tourism is all the different businesses that sell goods and services to people who travel on vacations. About 62,000 people in Oklahoma work in the tourist industry. They work as airline pilots, hotel workers, and travel agents.

Each year about 14 million tourists visit Oklahoma. Tourists spend over $3.2 billion each year in Oklahoma. This money is spent on transportation, hotels, food, and entertainment. Look at the map below. It shows some of the places in our state that tourists might visit. Have you visited any of these sites?

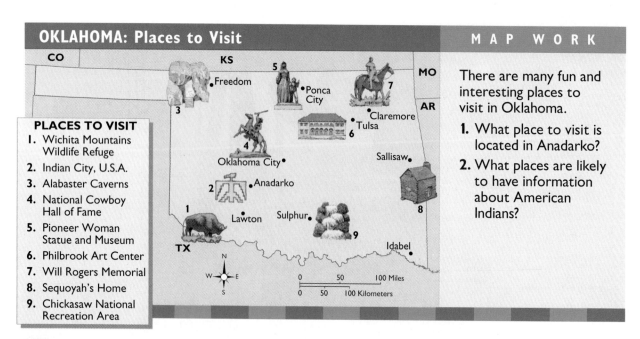

OKLAHOMA: Places to Visit

PLACES TO VISIT
1. Wichita Mountains Wildlife Refuge
2. Indian City, U.S.A.
3. Alabaster Caverns
4. National Cowboy Hall of Fame
5. Pioneer Woman Statue and Museum
6. Philbrook Art Center
7. Will Rogers Memorial
8. Sequoyah's Home
9. Chickasaw National Recreation Area

CO   KS   MO   AR   TX
Freedom   Ponca City   Claremore   Tulsa   Sallisaw   Oklahoma City   Anadarko   Lawton   Sulphur   Idabel

N W E S
0   50   100 Miles
0   50   100 Kilometers

M A P   W O R K

There are many fun and interesting places to visit in Oklahoma.

1. What place to visit is located in Anadarko?
2. What places are likely to have information about American Indians?

Service workers enrich
our lives in many ways.

Other Services

Radio and television stations also provide services. They give the news, weather reports, and music everyday. Different kinds of services are given by banks. Banks keep, save, and lend money. Did you know that writers, musicians, painters, and athletes also provide services?

WHY IT MATTERS

You have read about some of the industries in which Oklahomans work. Many people in our state have jobs in high-tech manufacturing industries. They may make products as different as computer software and airplanes. Other Oklahomans work in the mining or service industries. What do you think you would like to do for a living? Before you answer, read the next lesson to learn about other types of jobs people have in Oklahoma.

✓// Reviewing Facts and Ideas

MAIN IDEAS

- Oklahoma's manufacturing industries make a wide range of products. Their factories often use high-tech robots to assemble parts.

- Important mining industries in Oklahoma include the production of oil, natural gas, and non-metallic minerals.

- The service industry is the largest industry in our state.

THINK ABOUT IT

1. What is an industry?

2. Name three products manufactured in our state.

3. **FOCUS** What are some important industries in Oklahoma?

4. **THINKING SKILL** *Compare* and *contrast* the service industry and the manufacturing industry.

5. **GEOGRAPHY SKILL** Look at the map on page 214. Which tourist sites would you like to visit?

Oklahoma Agriculture

Focus Activity

READ TO LEARN

How does agriculture provide jobs for people in Oklahoma today?

VOCABULARY

- food processing
- combine
- livestock
- poultry

Read Aloud

"So long as there are people on earth, they must be fed, and the farms of the world will see to it they are. The farmers of Oklahoma will continue to do their part in this great task."

These words were written many years ago to describe farming in Oklahoma. Today, farming is still important to Oklahomans.

THE BIG PICTURE

Today, there are about 83,000 farms and ranches in our state. Many of them grow wheat and raise beef cattle. Other important products are cotton, hay, corn, peanuts, peaches, hogs, and chickens. In this lesson you will read how modern equipment has made agriculture, or the business of growing crops and raising animals, a high-tech industry.

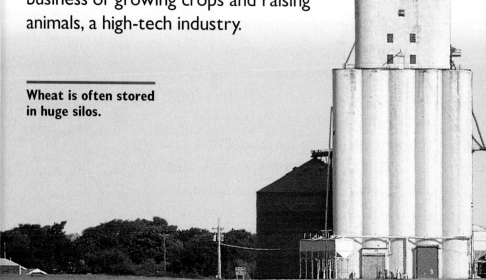

Wheat is often stored in huge silos.

216

FARMING TODAY

Most Oklahomans were farmers until the middle of the 1900s. Today Oklahomans have many kinds of jobs. One of the reasons for this change is technology. Most of the work on farms used to be done by people and animals. Now machines do much of this work. With machines, it takes fewer people to run farms and ranches, even though they are larger in size.

Food Processing

Many of the people who left the farms found jobs in industries using modern technology to make agricultural products. The map below shows that our state has different agricultural products. Some of them are made by food processing businesses. Food processing is the turning of crops and animal products into different products.

A food-processing company might take wheat from northwest Oklahoma and turn it into flour. Dairy workers in towns like Chandler may use milk to make products like ice cream, butter, and cheese.

The Move Back to Farms

The chart on the next page shows that the number of farms in Oklahoma is increasing. This is happening mainly near large cities like Tulsa and Oklahoma City. Many Oklahomans who are moving to farms like the slower pace of rural life.

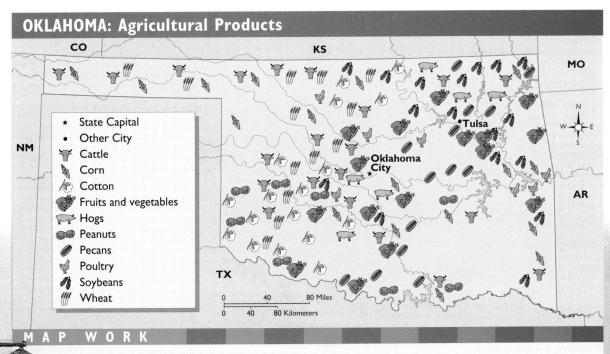

OKLAHOMA: Agricultural Products

Legend:
- ★ State Capital
- • Other City
- Cattle
- Corn
- Cotton
- Fruits and vegetables
- Hogs
- Peanuts
- Pecans
- Poultry
- Soybeans
- Wheat

0 40 80 Miles
0 40 80 Kilometers

MAP WORK

Agriculture is an important industry in Oklahoma.

1. In what part of Oklahoma are wheat and cotton grown?
2. Why do you think fruits and vegetables are grown near river areas?
3. What are some agricultural products from the area where you live?

OKLAHOMA'S CROPS

Oklahoma's most valuable crop is wheat. Wheat is mostly grown in the northwest and north central areas of our state.

More wheat is planted in Oklahoma than any other crop. Today, Oklahoma is one of the largest wheat-growing states in our country. Wheat is harvested early each summer by large machines called combines. Combines cut the stalks of wheat. They also separate the kernels, or seed, of the grain from the rest of the plant.

Oklahoma's wheat is mostly used to make flour. Did you know that the bread that you and children in other countries eat could be made from wheat grown on a farm in Oklahoma? This is true because some of the wheat that is grown in Oklahoma is sold to other countries.

Other Crops, Other Products

Another important crop grown in Oklahoma is cotton. Cotton is grown in the southwestern part of our state. It is used to make clothing. Manufacturing clothes is an important industry in our state.

Hay is another important crop. It is grown around the state. Corn is also grown in Oklahoma, mostly in the Panhandle. Most of our state's corn

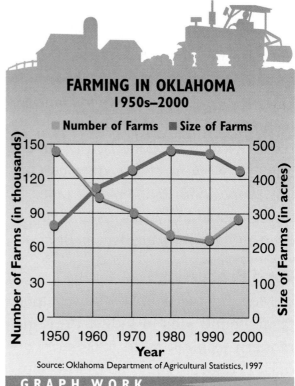

FARMING IN OKLAHOMA
1950s–2000

■ Number of Farms   ■ Size of Farms

Number of Farms (in thousands) — left axis: 0, 30, 60, 90, 120, 150
Size of Farms (in acres) — right axis: 0, 100, 200, 300, 400, 500
Year — 1950 1960 1970 1980 1990 2000

Source: Oklahoma Department of Agricultural Statistics, 1997

GRAPH WORK

Farming has always been important to Oklahomans.
1. About how many farms were in Oklahoma in 1970?
2. In what years did the number of farms increase as the size of farms decreased?

is used to feed animals. Corn can be made into many products. They include a sweet syrup that is used to make foods like candy canes. Peanuts, soybeans, and pecans are other crops grown in our state.

Farmers harvest wheat fields with large machines called combines.

218

WEATHER AND RANCHING

Farmers must pay attention to the growing season and the plants that grow in the climate they live in. A growing season is the number of days in a year when the weather is warm enough for crops to grow.

Two Growing Seasons

All areas of Oklahoma do not have the same growing season. The southern part of our state has a long growing season of about 240 days. The growing season in northern Oklahoma is shorter. It is about 168 days.

Some crops grow well in the cooler climate in the northern parts of our state. There, wheat is an important crop. The type of wheat grown by farmers in the north can be planted in the fall and harvested in the spring. Cotton, on the other hand, needs warm temperatures most of the year. It is grown in southwest Oklahoma.

Livestock and Poultry

One very important part of agriculture in our state is the raising of livestock (LIV stahk) and poultry (POHL tree). Livestock are animals such as cattle, horses, sheep, or pigs. Birds, such as chickens or turkeys, are called poultry when they are raised for their meat or eggs. Livestock and poultry are raised in the Panhandle and other parts of Oklahoma.

Livestock ranches in Oklahoma raise hogs, sheep, horses, beef cattle, and dairy cattle. Oklahoma's most important livestock are beef cattle. Beef cattle are raised by ranchers in the Panhandle and other parts of Oklahoma.

Dairy cattle are raised on farms in many different parts of our state. The milk these cattle produce is used to make cheese, ice cream, and other foods.

ON THE RANCH

Ranchers work hard to raise live-stock. There is much work to do on a ranch every day. Both men and women feed the livestock and repair the farm equipment. They also use computers to decide when and where they will sell their animals. One rancher is Mike Brooks of Ringling, Oklahoma. Here's what he says about working on a cattle ranch.

"Our ranch is about 15,000 acres," he explains. "And the only thing we raise is cattle. Some of these are born on the ranch. But we also buy extra cattle from as far away as Florida."

Their ranch has been in the Brooks family since the 1870s. "These days I run the place with my two brothers and my father-in-law," says Brooks. "My son Carson helps to put up the hay and crops."

Cattle stay at the ranch until they are fat enough to be sold. By then they weigh about 700 pounds. Then they are sent to large pens called feedlots in Kansas. At these feed-lots, the cattle are fat-tened further. Then they are sold.

"A modern rancher has to be educated in many areas," Brooks points out. "We use computers to test soil samples. In my garage I'm also

building a helicopter, which I'll use to round up cattle."

Old and New

The computer and the helicopter are not the only changes for modern ranching. In the past, cowboys on horseback rounded up the cattle. Now ranchers are more likely to ride trucks than horses. Rounding up the cattle is also different. Brooks explains, "These days cattle are called by siren. There's no more of that horn-honking and hollering going on."

Mike Brooks (left) is a cattle rancher. He uses a helicopter to help round up his cattle.

Shoppers enjoy the pick of the harvest at an Oklahoma farm stand.

Today's ranchers are also more aware that natural resources are limited. "We're committed to conserving the environment," Brooks says. "We guard against soil erosion. We protect endangered species. We try to make our ranch a better place."

Cars, helicopters, telephones, and computers make ranch life less lonely. Yet much of the old cowboy spirit remains. "The freedom, the way of life we have in the country, is still exciting," Brooks admits.

WHY IT MATTERS

Agriculture is important to Oklahoma's economy. It provides jobs for farmers and ranchers. Agriculture also provides jobs in related industries like food processing. For rancher Mike Brooks, agriculture is also an exciting way of life. However, the most important role of Oklahoma's agriculture is to help feed people both in our country and around the world.

✓ Reviewing Facts and Ideas

MAIN IDEAS

- In the past, most Oklahomans made their living from agriculture. Because of modern equipment, Oklahomans can now work in industries using technology to make agricultural products.

- Oklahoma's most important crop is wheat. Farmers also grow crops such as cotton and corn.

- Because of its two growing season, Oklahoma can grow different types of crops.

- Beef cattle is Oklahoma's most important livestock.

THINK ABOUT IT

1. How can people who are not farmers or ranchers make a living from agriculture?

2. How has farming changed in Oklahoma over the years?

3. **FOCUS** How does the agriculture industry provide jobs for people in Oklahoma?

4. **THINKING SKILL** *Classify* Oklahoma's agricultural products. Which come from ranches? Which come from farms?

5. **WRITE** Suppose you are a rancher in Oklahoma today. Write two paragraphs describing a day on the ranch.

Study Skills

Reading Newspapers

VOCABULARY

news article

feature article

editorial

headline

byline

dateline

WHY THE SKILL MATTERS

You just read about Oklahoma's agricultural industry. What if you wanted to find out what is happening right now to farmers—that is, current events? A good way would be to read a newspaper.

Reading a newspaper is often the best way to get information about what is happening today. Many newspapers cover events from all over our country and around the world. Some focus on events from a state, city, or town. Use the Helping Yourself box to guide you in reading newspapers.

USING A NEWSPAPER

When you read a newspaper, it is useful to know the different parts. The front section of a paper is made up mostly of news articles. These are news stories based on facts about recent events. Sometimes you may also find some of the writer's opinions in a news article, however.

Another kind of newspaper article is a feature article. A feature article takes a detailed look at a specific person, subject, or event.

Newspapers also include sports articles, cartoons, letters to the editor, and editorials. In an editorial, the editors—the people who run the paper—share their ideas about an issue. Unlike a news article, an editorial gives opinions, rather than facts.

Farmers Asked to Grow New Products

By Gary Brown

STILLWATER, November 5—"You work your heads off from June through October, and then you spend the winter staring at the walls," said Steve Jones, a wheat farmer and rancher from Billings.

At a meeting last Wednesday, government leaders encouraged farmers like Jones to spend those months out of the fields developing alternative products. Then, they said, if the farmers have a poor harvest or if livestock prices tumble, they will have other sources of income.

While wheat, cotton, and peanuts will remain Oklahoma's major crops, leaders urged more farmers to grow crops like pears and apples. They also suggested that cattle ranchers also raise poultry, goats, sheep, and hogs.

USING A NEWS ARTICLE

A news article usually begins with a headline—a title printed in large letters at the top of the story. The headline gives the main idea of the story.

Look at the news article on the facing page. As you can see, the headline is "Farmers Asked to Grow New Products".

In addition, news articles often have a byline. The byline tells the reader who wrote the story. The author of that story is Gary Brown.

Finally, many news articles include a dateline. This tells when and where the story was written. As you can see, the dateline in the story tells that it was written in Stillwater on November 5.

A good news article should answer five questions: (1) *Who* was involved in the story? (2) *What* took place? (3) *When* did the event happen? (4) *Where* did it happen? (5) *Why* did it happen?

Read the news article on the facing page. Does it answer the five questions? The answer to the first question, for example, might be "Oklahoma Farmers." Can you explain *what* happened in your own words?

TRYING THE SKILL

You just read a news article about a debate in the state legislature. Why do you think that reading a newspaper is a good way to learn about such an event? Can you think of any other sources for this kind of information?

Now suppose that your class is curious about a different topic: the construction of a new state highway. An article in the newspaper is called "Highway Opening Delayed." What kind of article do you think this is? Why do you think so? Another is called "New Highway Is a Step in the Right Direction." What kind of article do you think this is? Why do you think so?

REVIEWING THE SKILL

1. Name three different kinds of articles that appear in newspapers.

2. How can you tell that the article below is a news article instead of an editorial?

3. Why is it important for some news articles to have a dateline?

4. How would a newspaper help you learn about your state?

CHAPTER 9 REVIEW

THINKING ABOUT VOCABULARY

A. Write a sentence for each pair of words below. Include details that give clues to the meaning of the first term in the pair.

1. tourism, mining
2. software, high-tech
3. poultry, livestock
4. raw materials, manufacturing
5. entrepreneurs, industry

B. Number a sheet of paper from 1 to 10. Beside each number write the word or phrase from Part A that best matches the statement.

1. All the businesses that make one kind of product or provide one kind of service
2. Making large amounts of good in factories
3. The use of computers and other electronics to meet people's needs
4. A program that tells a computer what to do
5. People who form and run businesses
6. The resources a business uses to make a finished product
7. Animals such as cattle, horses, sheep, and pigs
8. The business of digging valuable natural resources out of the earth
9. The different businesses that sell goods and services to people who travel on vacations
10. Birds, such as chickens or turkeys, that are raised for their meat or eggs

THINKING ABOUT FACTS

1. What is Oklahoma's most important crop?
2. What are some of the first steps in starting a business?
3. What is a profit and why is it important to a business?
4. Name some business expenses.
5. How are food processing and farming linked? Provide an example of this link using wheat.
6. How has technology changed farming in Oklahoma? Provide an example.
7. What is the Internet?
8. How do Oklahoma's land, climate, and natural resources help its economy?
9. What are some examples of service jobs? Think of one kind of service job that is not listed in the chapter.
10. Explain supply and demand.

THINK AND WRITE ◂ ⫍⫍⫍▸

WRITING A JOB DESCRIPTION
Choose an industry in our state that you might like to work in some day. Write a description of a job in that industry that you might enjoy doing.

WRITING A BUSINESS PLAN
Think of a product or service that people might buy. Write a business plan for your idea. Include the things you would need to get started such as time, money, tools, and supplies. In addition, name your company.

WRITING A POSTER
Write and illustrate a poster advertising your business idea.

APPLYING STUDY SKILLS

READING NEWSPAPERS
1. What five questions should a well-written news article answer?
2. Look at the news article on page 222. Identify the headline, byline, and dateline.
3. What is an editorial? How does it differ from a news article?
4. Look again at the news article. How would you change the article to an editorial?
5. What can you learn from reading newspapers?

Summing Up the Chapter

Use the horizontal organization chart below to organize information from the chapter. Copy the chart on a sheet of paper. Use the words in the box below to fill in the blanks in the columns. When you have filled in the chart, use it to help you write a paragraph that answers the question, "What kinds of jobs do Oklahoma's industries and businesses provide for Oklahomans?"

OKLAHOMA'S IMPORTANT INDUSTRIES

Industry	Business	Jobs
service		travel agent
manufacturing	automobile maker	
	software maker	programmer
mining		miner
	cattle ranch	

The Government of Oklahoma

THINKING ABOUT GEOGRAPHY AND CITIZENSHIP

Have you ever wondered how you could help make changes in your community? Have you ever thought about ways you would like to help our state? Do you know what your responsibilities are as a citizen of the United States? Read on in this chapter to discover how our local, state, and national governments work.

UNITED STATES

Oklahoma City

OKLAHOMA

MEXICO

Gulf of Mexico

OKLAHOMA CITY

Oklahoma's state legislature (left) meets in the Capitol Building (above).

Local Government

Focus Activity

READ TO LEARN

What role does local government play in the life of Oklahomans?

VOCABULARY

- citizen
- municipal
- elect
- taxes
- mayor
- city council
- county
- commissioner

Read Aloud

"Lots of people think of a police officer as a person in a uniform . . . chasing a lawbreaker. Catching thieves and murderers is not as exciting as you see in the movies. What really makes my day is finding a lost child."

This is what one Oklahoma police officer said when asked about the service law officers perform for the local community.

THE BIG PICTURE

You already know that Oklahoma is part of the United States. Oklahomans are proud to be citizens of the United States. Citizens are people who are born in a country or who have earned the right to become members of a country. United States citizens have special rights and freedoms. They also have responsibilities, or duties.

COMMUNITY GOVERNMENT

Why is it important to have a government in the community where you live? Community governments are needed to make decisions about things that affect all the people in a community. For example, a community government usually makes decisions about where and how a park in your community will be built.

Local Government

The city or town where you live has a local government. It is called a municipal (myoo NIHS I pul) government. The citizens of a city elect their municipal leaders. To elect is to choose by voting.

A municipal government provides many services. Citizens pay taxes to help pay for these services. A tax is the money people pay to the government so that it can carry out public

services. These include fixing roads and building new schools. Many municipal governments decide where new homes and businesses should be built. They run libraries, parks, and local police departments. A municipal department is responsible for fixing public streets. When there is a fire, the municipal fire department puts it out.

Another type of community government in Oklahoma is the tribal government. Many American Indian groups in our state have their own government. Some have a constitution, elected officials, and a tribal council. The tribal governments are responsible for education and for improving the health, well-being, and economy of the community. They also work to solve problems.

American Indians in Oklahoma vote at a tribal council meeting (above). Oklahoma's county governments take care of roads (below).

OKLAHOMA MUNICIPAL GOVERNMENT

Mayor	City Manager	City Council
• elected by the citizens of the city or town	• chosen by city council	• elected by citizens of the city • number of members varies from city to city

CHART WORK

Most city governments in Oklahoma have a mayor and a city council. Some also have a city manager.

1. Who chooses the mayor and the council members?

2. Who chooses the city manager?

3. How many members are in a council?

CITY GOVERNMENT

Oklahoma has more than one kind of municipal government. These different city and town governments have similar responsibilities.

Mayor and City Council

Most cities in Oklahoma are governed by mayors. Cities also have city councils. The city council is the group that makes the local laws. The mayor is the head of the municipal government. The mayor and the council members are usually elected to serve for four years.

The mayor is often the leader of the city. He or she is responsible for carrying out city laws and for making the city budget. The budget is a plan for spending the city's money.

The city council makes laws for issues like crime, public safety, and health. It is also responsible for raising and collecting taxes. In addition, council members spend the money that is listed in the city budget and set the salaries of the mayor, city manager, judges, and other public leaders.

City Managers and City Courts

Oklahoma City and some other large Oklahoma cities are run by city managers. A city manager is a person hired by the city council to help take care of the city's business. He or she is not elected. The city manager is in charge of hiring most city employees, such as the police chief. He or she also supervises all city services and reports on the budget.

Most cities in Oklahoma have city courts. These courts define the law. They also decide how people who commit crimes should be punished.

COUNTY GOVERNMENT

The county government is an important part of local government. Look at the map below. From it you can see that our state is divided into 77 sections called counties. Did you know that most of Oklahoma's counties were named after famous people or American Indians? For example, can you guess who Lincoln County was named for? Lincoln County was named for Abraham Lincoln. Choctaw County was named after the Choctaw group of American Indians. Among those that were not named after people or American Indians are Beaver and Cimarron counties. They were named after rivers. What do you think Texas and Coal counties were named after?

Each county includes cities or towns, each of which usually has its own municipal government. The place where the county government is located is called the county seat.

County Commissioners

Each county has three leaders called commissioners, who are elected by the citizens of the county. Commissioners approve how much county money can be spent on things like police cars and schools. Citizens also elect other officials, such as the county clerk and the county sheriff. The county clerk keeps the legal records of the county, such as birth certificates and marriage licenses. The sheriff makes sure the laws of the county are followed.

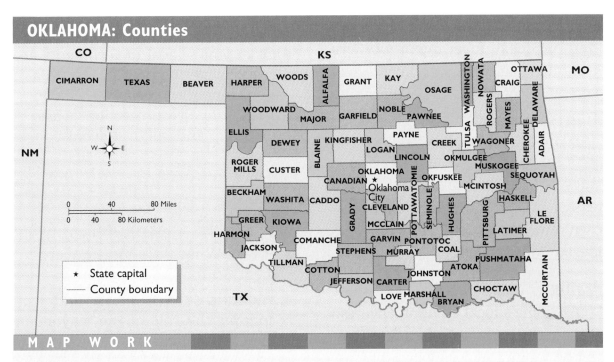

OKLAHOMA: Counties

★ State capital
— County boundary

MAP WORK

Oklahoma has 77 counties. Each county is an important part of local government.

1. What county is at the northwest tip of the panhandle?

2. What county is Oklahoma City located in?

3. In what county do you live?

Emergency workers rescue citizens from danger.

COMMUNITY SERVICES

Local governments perform many important services. When an emergency happens, the first people to arrive on the scene to help are often our local government workers. Firefighters and police officers, for example, protect the lives and property of all citizens.

Oklahoma's local governments also remove garbage and provide water service for homes and businesses. In addition, they repair town and city streets. They also operate local buses.

Having Fun

Oklahoma's local governments also take care of parks and libraries. They support cultural events like public concerts and sporting events. What events in your community does your local government support?

WHY IT MATTERS

Local governments make decisions that affect the health, safety, and education of our communities. But some problems cannot be solved by local governments. Oklahoma's local governments also work with our state government to solve problems. In the next lesson you will learn about Oklahoma's state government.

✓ Reviewing Facts and Ideas

MAIN IDEAS

- Citizens vote for local government leaders. They also pay taxes to pay for local government services.
- Oklahoma's municipal government leaders include mayors, city councils, and city managers.
- Each of Oklahoma's 77 counties elect three county commissioners.
- Oklahoma's local governments are responsible for providing education, repairing roads, for public safety, for fire protection, waste disposal, and cultural events.

THINK ABOUT IT

1. What is a county?
2. What does a mayor do?
3. **FOCUS** What does local government do for Oklahomans?
4. **THINKING SKILL** *Compare* and *contrast* the role of the mayor and the city council.
5. **GEOGRAPHY** Find the county in which you live on the map on page 231. Make a list of the names of the counties that surround it.

MAKING A DIFFERENCE

Speaking Out for Books

SEMINOLE, OKLAHOMA— Students at Varnum Public School had a problem. They were getting ready for a science fair and needed books to help research their projects. "Most of the [library] books were out-of-date and there weren't really enough of them," said one student, Stephanie Sims. So, a group of students at the school decided to solve this problem.

Some students talked to people in the community, telling them about the need for books. "Most people we talked to had never thought much about the school library," said a student, Whitney Quinalty. "We're making the community more aware of the problem."

Other students met with school officials. They wanted to know how much money was spent on books for the library. They learned that although their school bought many new computers, it did not spend much on new books. Other students received information about state laws explaining how much could be spent on materials for school libraries.

Then the students got together to share what they learned and write a report. "[We] recommended that the school make buying new books one of its top goals," said Stephanie. "We felt we would all read more books and use the library more if it had more books we were interested in." After reading the report, the principal agreed and ordered many new books.

The students decided to take more action. First they held a schoolwide read-a-thon to raise money for new library books. A local company agreed to match all the money that the students raised. Soon they had enough money to buy the new books the school needed.

"We made people more aware of the need for books," Whitney said. "People actually listen if you speak up a little bit. If you work hard enough, you can make a difference."

"If you work hard enough, you can make a difference."

Stephanie Sims

State Government

Focus Activity

READ TO LEARN

What are the jobs of the three branches of our state government?

VOCABULARY

- checks and balances
- executive branch
- legislative branch
- bill
- veto
- judicial branch

PEOPLE

- Larry Rice
- Hannah Atkins

PLACES

- Oklahoma City

Read Aloud

"To be a good public servant a person must be honest and caring. You must . . . listen to the ideas of others. I have tried to do this."

These words were said by Hannah Atkins, a former leader in Oklahoma's state government.

THE BIG PICTURE

The Oklahoma Constitution is like the United States Constitution. It explains the three branches, or parts, of state government and the duties of each one. Oklahoma's constitution also describes the rights of our state's citizens.

Our state's Capitol Building is in Oklahoma City.

234

THREE BRANCHES OF STATE GOVERNMENT

EXECUTIVE
Governor

- Signs or vetoes bills
- Carries out laws
- Nominates justices to the state Supreme Court

LEGISLATIVE
**Legislature
(101 Representatives, 48 Senators)**

- Makes laws for our state
- Decides how much money to spend

JUDICIAL
**Supreme Court
(9 Judges)**

- Makes sure our laws follow the state constitution

CHART WORK

Our state government is located in Oklahoma City. It has three branches.

1. How many Representatives are there? How many senators?

2. Who leads the **executive branch**?

3. What are the duties of the **State Supreme Court**?

4. Which branch makes laws?

OUR STATE AND YOU

Have you ever visited Oklahoma City? It is our state capital. Many important decisions are made there. These decisions affect the lives of every Oklahoman—including you!

Our state government is divided into three branches. That way, no person or group of people will have too much power. Each branch of government keeps watch over the other two branches. This is called the principle of checks and balances.

The Executive Branch

The executive (eg ZEK yoo tihv) branch of Oklahoma's government carries out the laws of our state. The governor is the head of the executive branch. The governor is elected by the people of our state to serve for four years. He or she may be reelected once. The governor's office is in Oklahoma City.

The governor helps set goals for our state. He or she chooses people to run our state departments. These include the Tourism and Recreation Department and the Department of Transportation. They care for state parks and highways.

Oklahomans pay taxes that make it possible for the state government to perform these services. The governor helps to prepare a budget. Like the city budget, the state budget is a plan that shows how the money will be used.

HOW A BILL BECOMES A LAW

1 Citizens develop an idea for a bill.

2 Members of the House of Representatives or the Senate propose the bill.

3 The House of Representatives and the Senate vote to approve the bill.

4 The governor signs the bill.
OR
The governor vetoes the bill.

5 If the bill is vetoed, another vote can be taken. If 27 senators and 54 representatives vote to approve it, the bill becomes a law.

LAW
The bill becomes a law.

THE LEGISLATIVE BRANCH

The legislative (LEJ is lay tiv) branch of government makes our state's laws. It has two parts. They are the Senate and the House of Representatives. Oklahoma voters elect our 48 Senators and 101 Representatives. Senators serve for four years and Representatives serve for two years.

From Bill to Law

Senators and Representatives create and vote on bills. A bill is a written idea for a law. Did you know that you can help make a new law in Oklahoma?

Suppose you want your community to protect the environment and save natural resources. You think of one way the state government can help. It can start a program for recycling aluminum cans. Follow the arrows in the chart on the left of this page to find out how this happens.

First, you would write to your state representative and senator. You would ask them to write a bill to start a recycling plan.

The Senate and House of Representatives will then vote to pass the bill. If it passes, the bill will go to the governor for approval. If the governor disagrees with the bill, he or she could veto, or not approve, it. However, in this case the governor signed the bill. Thanks to your idea, the plan for recycling aluminum cans is now a law!

OKLAHOMA LAWMAKERS

In the history of our state there have been many representatives who have made a difference to Oklahomans. Our state has become a better place to live because of their efforts.

Larry Rice

Larry Rice is a state representative in Oklahoma. He works hard to make sure that Oklahomans recycle wastes. Here's what he says about working to improve Oklahoma:

State and local governments in recent years have worked hard to encourage businesses and people in Oklahoma to recycle. Through state and local efforts, many cities and towns have implemented important recycling programs.

He and other state representatives work together to protect our environment and natural resources.

Hannah Atkins

At the beginning of this lesson, you read the words of well-known state representative, Hannah Atkins. She served for 12 years. One bill she wrote became an important law. It states that your parents or guardians must have records showing you have had shots to protect you from certain diseases. If you don't have these shots, you can't go to school. She believed this law was needed so that diseases would not spread among schoolchildren.

Every year our state representatives pass new bills. In 1953, they passed a bill making "Oklahoma" our official state song. You can sing along with it on the next page.

Larry Rice (top) and Hannah Atkins (bottom) have both worked to make Oklahoma a better place to live.

237

OKLAHOMA!

from the musical *Oklahoma!*
Music by Richard Rodgers
Lyrics by Oscar Hammerstein II

O____ o____ k - la - ho-ma, where the wind comes sweep-in' down the

plain, _____ And the wav - in' wheat can sure smell

sweet, When the wind comes right be - hind the rain _____

O_____ o____ k - la - ho - ma, ev - 'ry night my

hon - ey lamb and I_____ Sit a - lone and talk and

watch a hawk mak-in' la - zy cir - cles in the sky ____

____ We know we be - long to the land ____ And the

land we be - long to is grand! ____ And when we say: ____

____ Yeow! A - yip - i - o - ee - ay! ____

____ We're on - ly say - in', "You're do - in' fine, Ok - la - ho -

ma! Ok - la - ho - ma! ____ O. K." ____

Oklahoma's Supreme Court has nine judges.

THE JUDICIAL BRANCH

The judicial (joo DISH uhl) branch of state government interprets, or explains, our state's laws. This branch is made up of judges. They are people who hear cases in courts. The highest court in Oklahoma is the Supreme Court. It has nine judges.

The Supreme Court hears cases from lower courts. It may also decide to hear any case that it considers to be very important. Suppose the Supreme Court judges decide that a law goes against the Oklahoma Constitution. They can then get rid of the law.

Oklahoma's judges work hard to make sure all Oklahomans are treated fairly in court. What does the leader of the Supreme Court, Chief Justice Hardy Summers, say about our judicial system?

MANY VOICES
PRIMARY SOURCE

Excerpt from an interview with Hardy Summers, Chief Justice of the Oklahoma Supreme Court, 2000

Our courts must be open . . . to all persons. Our judges must always apply the laws uniformly [fairly], without regard to position, wealth, race, or other status [standing] of anyone who comes to court. We must devote ourselves, as judges, to deciding the cases correctly, and within a time period that is reasonable [fair] under the circumstances.

Programs like Girls State help Oklahoma's students learn about our government.

LEARN ABOUT YOUR GOVERNMENT

Every year about 1,200 high school students in Oklahoma are chosen to take part in a program called American Legion Auxiliary Girls State. At selected places throughout the state students learn what it is like to be a government leader. They can even vote on their own bills. When you are 18, you will be able to vote for government leaders. But don't wait until then to take part!

WHY IT MATTERS

A government works well when its citizens take an interest in issues that affect its citizens. There are many ways to take part in government. What issues interest you? How can Oklahoma become a better place to live? Write letters to your representatives. Elected officials need to hear from citizens in order to represent their view.

✓/ Reviewing Facts and Ideas

MAIN IDEAS

- The checks and balances system makes sure no one branch of government has too much power.
- Our executive branch carries out the laws of our state.
- The legislative branch makes the laws of our state. It is made up of the Senate and House of Representatives.
- Oklahoma's judicial branch interprets our state laws.

THINK ABOUT IT

1. Who heads our executive branch?

2. In what way does our state government affect how we live every day?

3. FOCUS What are the jobs of the three branches of the state government?

4. THINKING SKILL *List* the steps a bill has to go through to become a law.

5. WRITE Think of a bill you would like to see passed in Oklahoma. Write a short paragraph explaining why you think this bill would make a good law.

Oklahoma and the National Government

Focus Activity

What are the rights and responsibilities we have as people of the United States?

- democracy
- democratic republic
- candidate
- political party
- United States Congress

- Washington, D.C.

- Carl Albert

Read Aloud

"The fact that a country boy from Bugtussle, Oklahoma, can reach this goal points to the greatness of America and the opportunity the United States gives all its people."

An Oklahoman named Carl Albert used these words to describe a goal he had. He was an important leader in our national government.

THE BIG PICTURE

Running a country is not easy. The United States became an independent country in 1776. Then, our first leaders faced the tough job of governing it. In 1787, they created the United States Constitution, the plan for running our government.

THE UNITED STATES GOVERNMENT

The United States Constitution begins with the words, "We the people of the United States . . ." These words remind us that we have a democracy. This is a government in which the power to rule come from the country's people. But the United States is a big country. Not every person can directly take part in every decision. This led the writers of the Constitution to make our country a democratic republic. In a democratic republic people pick representatives to run the government and make decisions for them. Citizens do this by voting in elections.

The right to vote is an important right given to us by the Constitution. Yet many people do not use this right. Did you know that in our country only five out of every ten people who can vote do so?

Electing Officials

In an election, voters choose between candidates. These are the people running for office. Usually candidates are members of a political party. A political party is a group of citizens who share many of the same ideas about government. The Democratic and Republican parties are the largest political parties in the United States.

Our country's Capitol Building (below) in Washington, D.C. President Bill Clinton (left) speaks to Oklahoma schoolchildren following a bombing in Oklahoma City in 1995. J.C. Watts (above) is a leader in the Republican party.

NATIONAL GOVERNMENT: Three Branches

EXECUTIVE President	LEGISLATIVE Congress (100 Senators, 435 Representatives)	JUDICIAL Supreme Court (9 Judges)
● Carries out laws ● Meets with leaders of other countries ● Leads military	● Makes laws for our country ● Decides how much money to spend	● Makes sure our laws follow the Constitution

CHART WORK

Our national government, located in Washington, D.C., has three branches.

1. How many senators does Congress have? How many representatives?

2. Which branch does the President head?

3. What are the President's duties?

4. Who are the highest officials of the judicial branch of our government?

THE THREE BRANCHES

Our national government is located in Washington, D.C. Like our state government, the United States government has three branches. Each branch has different duties. Find these branches on the chart above.

The Legislative Branch

The legislative branch of our national government is called the United States Congress. Congress makes laws for the entire country. Congress is made of the Senate and the House of Representatives.

Voters in each state elect two senators to the Senate. The number of representatives voters elect depends on how many people live in their state. Oklahoma elects six people to the United States House of Representatives.

The Executive Branch

The leader of the executive branch is the president. Voters elect the president every four years. The president makes sure that our country's laws are carried out. The president chooses people to head national departments in charge of areas such as the environment and transportation. The president is the leader of our military forces.

The Judicial Branch

The president also selects the justices of the United States Supreme Court. The Supreme Court is the highest court in our country. It heads the judicial branch of government. Its judges hear cases from the lower courts. They also decide whether laws agree with the United States Constitution.

SPEAKER OF THE HOUSE

Carl Albert was born in the eastern Oklahoma town of Bugtussle in 1908. He worked hard from a young age and became one the most important leaders in our national government. He served as Speaker of the United States House of Representatives from 1971 to 1976. The Speaker is the leader of the House. Suppose both the president and vice president were unable to serve. The Speaker would then become president.

Thinking about his success and how much the people of our state helped him, Carl Albert once said:

"All I want to do is serve . . . Oklahoma and the United States."

Carl Albert served as a Congressman for many years. He died in 2000.

WHY IT MATTERS

The United States is a democratic republic. Citizens elect leaders to serve in our national government and to make decisions and laws for them. When you are 18, you will be able to vote for national, state, and local leaders. Voting in elections will be your right and responsibility.

✓ Reviewing Facts and Ideas

MAIN IDEAS

- The United States is a democratic republic.
- Like Oklahoma's government, the United States government is made up of a legislative, an executive, and a judicial branch.
- Oklahoma's representatives in Congress serve both Oklahoma and the United States.

THINK ABOUT IT

1. What is a democratic republic?
2. What branch of our country's government is led by the President?
3. **FOCUS** What rights and responsibilities do we have as citizens of the United States?
4. **THINKING SKILL** *Compare* and *contrast* our state and national governments.
5. **WRITE** Suppose you want to be elected to the United States Senate. Write a campaign speech telling Oklahomans why they should vote for you.

CHAPTER 10 REVIEW

THINKING ABOUT VOCABULARY

A. Write a sentence for each pair of words below. Include details that give clues to the meaning of the first term in each pair.

1. citizens, elect

2. municipal, mayor

3. county, commissioner

4. bill, veto

5. candidate, United States Congress

B. Number a sheet of paper from 1 to 10. Next to each number write the word or term from those in Part A that best completes the sentence.

1. A _____ is one of the sections into which a state is divided.

2. A _____ is a written idea for a law.

3. A person who runs for office is called a _____.

4. _____ are people who were born in a country or have earned the right to become members of that country.

5. The town or city where you live has a _____ government.

6. One of three leaders of a county government is called a _____.

7. The head of a city government is a _____.

8. In our country, citizens _____ government leaders.

9. The _____ is the legislative branch of our national government.

10. To _____ a bill is to reject it.

THINKING ABOUT FACTS

1. How do the citizens of the United States take part in our local, state, and national governments?

2. What are the responsibilities of a mayor?

3. What is the purpose of the Oklahoma Constitution?

4. What are the three branches of our national and state governments? How does the system of checks and balances apply to them?

5. In which city is the office of our state's governor located? How is the governor chosen and how long does he or she serve?

6. What is the state song of Oklahoma? How did it become the state song?

7. What is a democracy?

8. How many senators are elected by each state to take part in the United States Senate? How many representatives are elected by each state to take part in the United States House of Representatives?

9. Who is the head of the executive branch of the United States government? Name two responsibilities that belong to this person.

10. What will be your right and your responsibility when you turn 18?

THINK AND WRITE

WRITING A PLAN

Suppose a new law is passed that gives more money to your school. Write a plan for the best way your school can use that money.

WRITING AN EXPLANATION

Write an explanation of the three branches of our state government. Describe the responsibilities of each branch.

WRITING AN EDITORIAL

Suppose you are an editor of a newspaper. Write an editorial encouraging people to vote in the next election. Explain why it is an important responsibility for each citizen to vote.

APPLYING STUDY SKILLS

IDENTIFYING FACT AND OPINION

1. What is a fact? What is an opinion?

2. What are some clues you can look for to help you recognize an opinion?

3. Which of the following is an opinion?
   a. All Oklahomans are proud to be citizens of our country.
   b. A mayor is the leader of a city

4. Oklahoma's local governments maintain parks and libraries. Is this a fact or an opinion?

5. Why does a word clue like *I think* often tell you that the speaker is expressing an opinion?

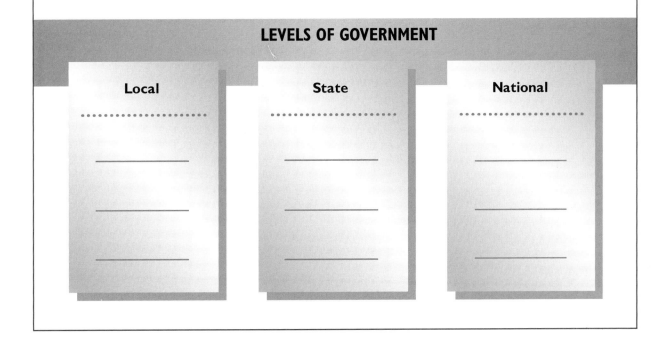

Summing Up the Chapter

Use the following table to organize information from the chapter. Copy the table on a sheet of paper. Then list the people and groups that run each level of government. When you have filled in the table, use it to write a paragraph that answers the question, "What do the local, state, and national governments have in common? How are they different?"

LEVELS OF GOVERNMENT

Local	State	National

Oklahoma and the Future

THINKING ABOUT HISTORY AND CULTURE

In Chapter 11 you will read about how Oklahomans today keep their proud heritage alive. You will also learn about how, by working together, we will shape the world of the future.

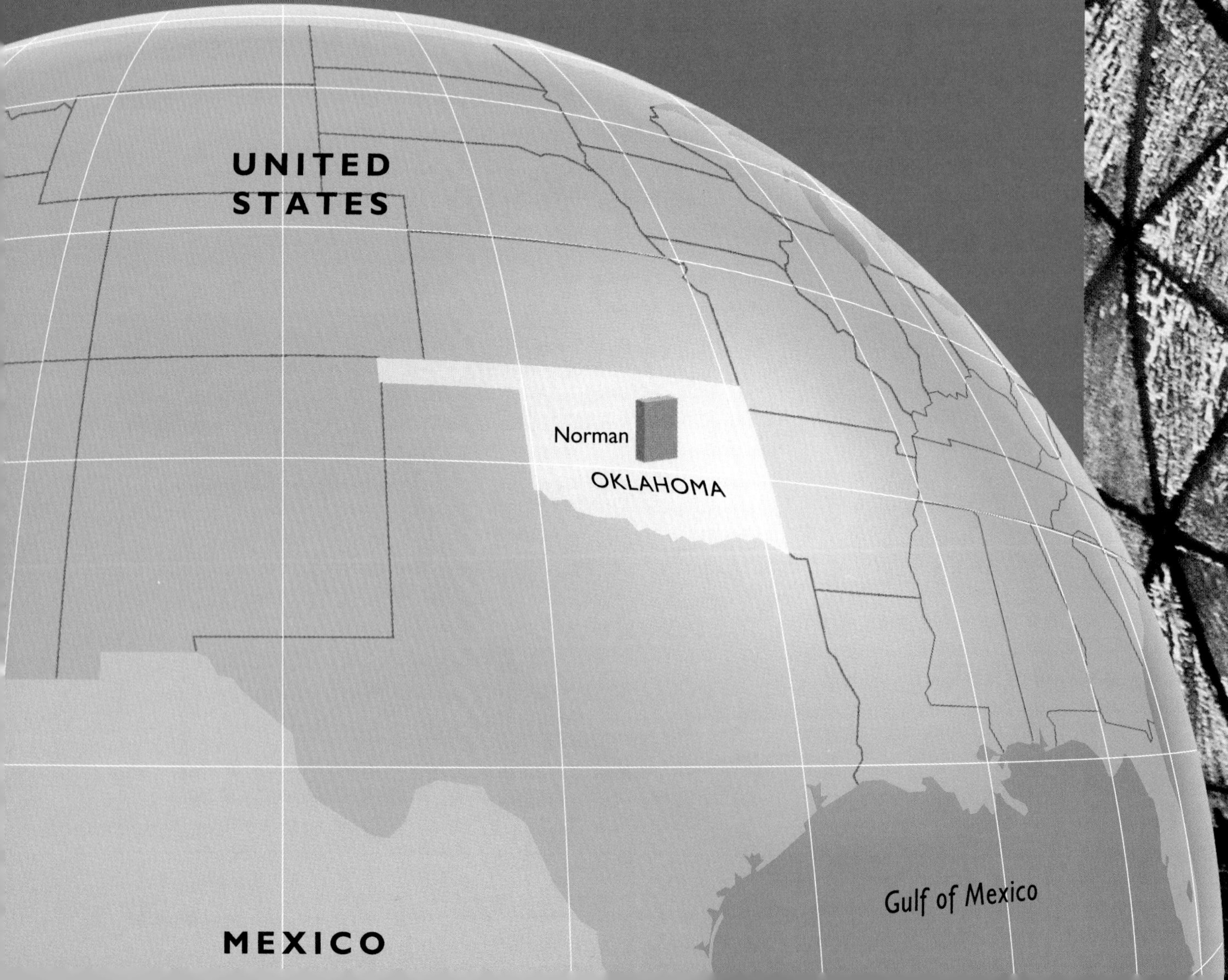

UNITED STATES

Norman

OKLAHOMA

Gulf of Mexico

MEXICO

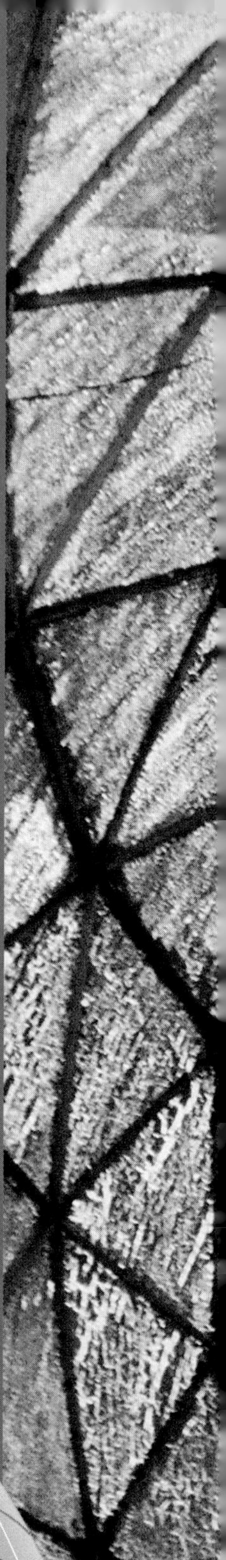

NORMAN

Scientists use radar to help track storms in Oklahoma.

Living Together

Read Aloud

"Living in Oklahoma means meeting people who are different than you. It's exciting . . . . It's what gives our state character."

A newcomer to Oklahoma used these words to describe our state.

Focus Activity

READ TO LEARN

How do the different people of Oklahoma make our state special?

VOCABULARY

- migrant worker
- metropolitan area

PLACES

- Corn
- Enid
- Tulsa
- Guymon

THE BIG PICTURE

Oklahoma is made up of many groups of people. The languages they speak and their beliefs about the world can differ from group to group. This mix of cultures makes our state an interesting place to live.

WHO WE ARE

Over 3 million people live in our state today. Some ethnic groups, like a number Oklahoma's American Indians, have lived here for thousands of years. Other groups have lived here for more than 100 years. They include people whose ancestors came from countries, such as Italy, Germany, Russia, Poland England, and Ireland. The Five Civilized Tribes brought African Americans to Oklahoma in slavery. Later some European American Settlers also brought enslaved African Americans into our state. Oklahoma also has recent immigrants and newcomers from other states.

Today the largest number of immigrants in Oklahoma came from Asia and Latin America. Most of our Asian immigrants are from China, Korea, Japan, Vietnam, and India. Latin American immigrants include Mexicans, Central Americans, South Americans, and people from the Caribbean Islands. Hispanics are the fastest-growing ethnic group in Oklahoma.

Some Oklahomans have no permanent homes. Among this group are the migrant workers. Migrant

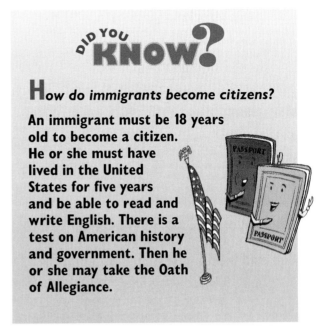

DID YOU KNOW?

How do immigrants become citizens?

An immigrant must be 18 years old to become a citizen. He or she must have lived in the United States for five years and be able to read and write English. There is a test on American history and government. Then he or she may take the Oath of Allegiance.

workers are people who move from place to place to harvest crops as they ripen. Many migrant workers in Oklahoma come from Mexico.

A New Life

Immigrants and migrants come to Oklahoma for many different reasons. Some hope to build new lives. Others are looking for jobs to support themselves and their families.

For most immigrants, it is important to become a United States citizen. Once an immigrant becomes a citizen, he or she can vote. As a citizen he or she can also join the military and run for most government offices.

CELEBRATING OUR HERITAGE

The different ethnic groups in our state speak different languages. They also have different customs, beliefs, and religions. Suppose you were to travel around Oklahoma to learn about these customs. What would you see?

German Feast

Perhaps you will visit the town of Corn in the western central part of our state. If you arrive in March you can see the German Feast and Auction. This is a festival that honors the heritage of Germans in Oklahoma. Here you can see beautiful handmade quilts and wooden toys. There's also plenty to eat. You might even eat a German sausage called a bratwurst (BRAHT werst).

Juneteenth

At the Juneteenth celebration in Enid, crowds enjoy eating chicken and drinking lemonade. Colorful balloons and rides decorate the streets while bands play jazz, gospel, and other types of music. Juneteenth celebrates June 19, 1865, the day when African Americans throughout the Southwest learned that they had been freed from slavery. Oklahomans of all backgrounds look forward to this day as a chance to learn about and enjoy African American culture and heritage.

International Festival

Do you like to learn about people from other countries? If so, in November come to the Children's International Festival in Tulsa. Here you will learn about some of the different cultures of Oklahoma's immigrants. Storytellers will tell you about Latin America. Or you can take a break and enjoy foods from Asian countries.

Where We Live

Oklahomans live in different kinds of communities. Some communities are rural and some are urban, or suburban. Some work on small farms. Others live in towns like Marlow, which has about 4,420 people. The community has many ranchers as well as people who have retired.

Metropolitan Areas

Most Oklahomans live in large cities. Today about 60 percent of all Oklahoman's live in metropolitan areas. A metropolitan area is a large city, or group of cities and suburbs that have grown close together. From the sky they would look like one big city. Tulsa and Oklahoma City are our two largest metropolitan areas. There are more than 1 million people in Oklahoma City's metropolitan area. The area includes towns such as Bethany, Putnam City, Del City, Midwest City, Moore, and Edmond. The Tulsa area has about 780,000 people.

Most of the newcomers to our state today live in or near these areas. Large cities offer many different kinds of jobs and activities. Here's what one recent immigrant had to say about why he liked living near Tulsa:

I love my community. But I also love to get in my car and go downtown to see a concert.

WHY IT MATTERS

Today the Oklahoma way of life is made up of many rich cultures. In the next lesson you will learn about how we all must work to build a bright future for all Oklahomans.

✓✓ Reviewing Facts and Ideas

MAIN IDEAS

- The citizens of Oklahoma belong to many different ethnic groups. It has many American Indians, immigrants from many countries, and migrant workers.
- The different customs and festivals in Oklahoma make our state an interesting place to live.
- Oklahomans live in different types of communities. Tulsa and Oklahoma City are our state's largest metropolitan areas.

THINK ABOUT IT

1. What is a migrant worker?
2. What different countries do Oklahoma's immigrants come from?
3. **FOCUS** How do the different people of Oklahoma make our state special?
4. **THINKING SKILL** How would you *group* the different homelands of Oklahoma's immigrants?
5. **WRITE** Choose one festival mentioned in the lesson text. Write a paragraph about why you would like to attend this festival.

Children have fun at the Czech festival in Yukon (above left). In Boley, African Americans celebrate their heritage at a Black Rodeo.

Reading Circle and Line Graphs

VOCABULARY
graph
circle graph
line graph

WHY THE SKILL MATTERS

In the last lesson you read many facts about immigration. Some told you which countries immigrants came from in the past. Others told what countries immigrants come from today.

It is hard to make a conclusion from a lot of different facts. A graph can help you make conclusions. Graphs are special diagrams that show information in a clear way. By presenting facts in a picture, they tell you a lot with only a handful of words.

USING CIRCLE GRAPHS

Look at the graph on this page. It is a circle graph. This kind of graph can show you how the parts of something make up the whole. Because each part may look like a slice of pie, a circle graph is also called a pie graph.

Read the title of the graph. The circle shows the total number of immigrants who live in the state of Oklahoma today. The "slices" of the graph show the number of people who came from each continent. You can tell that the largest

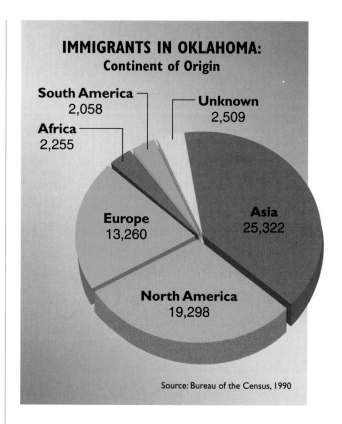

IMMIGRANTS IN OKLAHOMA:
Continent of Origin

South America — 2,058
Africa — 2,255
Unknown 2,509
Europe 13,260
Asia 25,322
North America 19,298

Source: Bureau of the Census, 1990

number of immigrants came from Asia because this is the largest "slice" of the graph.

USING A LINE GRAPH

Unlike a circle graph, a line graph shows you how a piece of information changes with time.

Look at the line graph on page 255. Start by reading the title. The title tells you that this is a graph of immigration to the United States from 1850 to 1990.

Read the labels at the left side of the graph. These give the numbers of immigrants. Then read the dates at the bottom of the graph. They tell you the years these immigrants came.

Trace the line with your finger. Each dot on the line stands for the number of immigrants who came in that year. You can see on the graph that the year when the fewest immigrants came was 1930.

TRYING THE SKILL

Now study the circle graph of immigrants in Oklahoma. What continent has sent the fewest immigrants to Oklahoma? Use the Helping Yourself box for hints.*

Now look at the line graph of immigration to the United States. In what year did the most immigrants arrive? About how many immigrants arrived during that year?**

Helping yourself

- **Circle graphs** show how the parts fit into the whole.
- **Line graphs** show how a piece of information changes over time.
- Study the title, key, and labels.
- Use the **graphs** to compare facts or figures.

REVIEWING THE SKILL

Use the line graph below to answer the following questions.

1. In what years was there a drop in immigration to the United States? What did you do to find out?

2. Between what years did immigration rise most sharply?

3. What kind of graph would you use to show temperatures in your state for the year?

4. How do graphs make it easier for you to understand certain kinds of information?

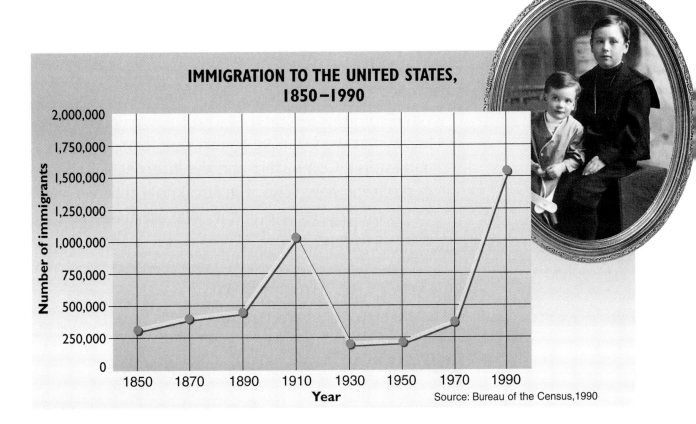

IMMIGRATION TO THE UNITED STATES, 1850–1990

Number of immigrants (y-axis): 0, 250,000, 500,000, 750,000, 1,000,000, 1,250,000, 1,500,000, 1,750,000, 2,000,000

Year (x-axis): 1850, 1870, 1890, 1910, 1930, 1950, 1970, 1990

Source: Bureau of the Census, 1990

* South America **1990; 1,500,000

Where Are We Headed?

Focus Activity

READ TO LEARN

What are some of the problems the United States will face in the twenty-first century?

VOCABULARY

- computer graphics
- website
- endangered species

Read Aloud

". . . We stand on the mountaintop of a new millennium. . . . We should be filled with awe and joy at what lies over the horizon. And we should be filled with absolute determination to make the most of it."

President Bill Clinton spoke these words in January of 2000. He was describing how important it is for all Americans to work hard for future generations.

THE BIG PICTURE

How can Oklahomans make the most of the future? We have reached the mountaintop. But the view from there stretches into the unknown. We know that we will have to use new forms of communication. Computers and the Internet will shape our state in new ways. We also know that we have to protect our environment. Will we make the right decisions?

Microchips allow computers to process information quickly.

A NEW TOMORROW

Technology has always affected people's lives. For example, for thousands of years people used sun and fire for light. But in 1879 a man named Thomas Edison invented a usable light bulb. People's lives were forever changed. Today high technology affects almost every part of your life.

For example, suppose you had pizza for lunch. The cheese and sauce were probably made at a factory that was run by computers. Perhaps the television commercial that advertised the pizza used special images created by computer graphics. Computer graphics are pictures that are made with a computer.

Technology and the Future

In the future, high technology will play an even larger part in our lives. In some areas, it may remove jobs. As more farms and factories use computers, they will need fewer people to work for them. But technology also creates new jobs. This is especially true in fields such as healthcare and software design.

People and businesses use the Internet to get information quickly. For example, people visit websites to get the news, and do research. A website is a location on the Internet that provides information and allows people to communicate with each other on the World Wide Web.

Technology is also changing our classrooms. Read what Dr. John Richards says about technology. How does he think the Internet will affect students and teachers?

MANY VOICES
PRIMARY SOURCE

**Interview with
Dr. John Richards, 1997**

Technology is going to dramatically change classrooms because technology is dramatically changing society. Students are going to have to work in a technologically rich world . . . with technologies we haven't even thought about yet . . . .

Clearly, participation in the internet gives students and teachers immediate access to students and teachers worldwide . . . . This sort of direct contact with other cultures . . . helps to bring people with different backgrounds in contact with each other.

CHALLENGES AHEAD

As technology becomes more and more important to our way of life, it also brings new challenges. You already read that Oklahoma is one of our country's leading oil producers. But oil fields don't last forever. Many wells are pumping oil today. Others have dried up. When oil wells run dry, some owners leave the oil fields as they are. Equipment like pipes gets left behind. Even worse, saltwater produced with the oil leaks into the soil. Soon it begins to kill the surrounding grasses and plants. This land cannot be used to grow crops. It can smell bad, too.

Old oil wells (below) can be dangerous to our environment. Scientists clean the old wells and remove leftover oil (below, right).

Taking Action

In 1993, our State Legislature passed a law that put a small tax on the sale of oil in our state. This money was to be used to clean up the abandoned wells. A special state agency called the Oklahoma Energy Resources Board was formed to clean the oil wells.

Getting to Work

One of the things people do to clean an abandoned well is clear away all the old equipment. This usually takes about a month.

Sometimes scientists use chemicals that will help plants begin to grow. Next, they add new soil and water to the area around the well. In all, it takes about a year to bring the land back to life.

FINDING A SOLUTION

The people of Oklahoma are proud of the good work the Oklahoma Energy Resources Board does. Janice Scroggins of Morrison is one of them. Her father had an abandoned oil well on his farm for over 40 years. She said that one of the things she liked about having the area around the well cleaned up was

> . . . *creating a field where her children could play. . . . We have the most beautiful pasture, where before there was an ugly mess.*

The Oklahoma Energy Resources Board has also had success in educating students about the oil industry. Students learn about the ways in which we must care for our resources.

More Work Ahead

About 1,500 abandoned oil wells have been cleaned up. Even so, there are still hundreds of wells to clean. In time, high technology will help in this task. For instance, new methods of cleaning the polluted soil are being developed. Oil wells are also being drilled that will cause less harm to the environment.

Most important, we can learn from our past mistakes. We can see that it is wrong to destroy land. If we pollute areas, we should restore them or use them as landfill before we abandon them. Before starting any new project, it is important to decide how to recycle the waste. If we use methods that harm the environment, we will only create problems in the future.

An area that was once a polluted oil well is now a grassy field.

HELPING THE ENVIRONMENT

Sometimes it's hard to see that each one of us can help to improve our state. There are many things every person can do to help clean up the environment. One way is to join an organization that works to protect the environment. You can check the Internet for organizations in your community. For example, it may have a group that works to protect endangered species. These are plants and animals that are in danger of disappearing from Earth.

Today, young people across the country have organized environmental projects. Some students hold clean-up days for their local parks or their schools. Others may run a street fair, or a bike ride to raise money for an environmental cause.

Oklahoma's whooping crane and prairie orchid are both endangered.

WHY IT MATTERS

As the influence of technology increases, our lives will continue to change. People must work together to prevent pollution of our soil, air, and water. Only by learning more about the good and bad effects of technology, will we be ready for the challenges of tomorrow.

✓ Reviewing Facts and Ideas

MAIN IDEAS

- High technology is changing the ways Americans live their lives.

- If it is not used properly, technology can affect the environment, causing pollution or other problems.

- Many Oklahomans are working together to clean up the environment and save natural resources. One solution is the use of technology.

THINK ABOUT IT

1. What are endangered species?

2. What kind of information can people find on websites?

3. **FOCUS** What are some of the problems the United States will face in the twenty-first century?

4. **THINKING SKILL** What are some *effects* technology has on our lives today?

5. **WRITE** Write a letter to the president of an oil company in Oklahoma. In it explain why you think it is important to protect the environment.

MAKING A DIFFERENCE

Teaching at the Computer Lab

SALINA, OKLAHOMA—A few years ago, teachers at Wickliffe School set up a computer lab for students to use. "As children came home and started talking about what they were doing in their computer class, the [parents] wanted to know more," said teacher Teresa Knott.

Ms. Knott and her students had an idea. They decided to give a computer class to adults. They called their program, "Helping Hands." The students knew they were meeting a real need when 60 people showed up for the first class. "Not just parents came, but grandparents, aunts, uncles and anybody in the community who was interested came," said one student named Talia Littledave.

In the "Helping Hands" program, students teach adults how to use a computer to write letters and to find information on the Internet. Students also show the adults how to use encyclopedias and other resources on CDs. "Many older people are curious about computers but they are also afraid," said Mrs. Knott. "People shouldn't be afraid of technology just because they don't know anything about it." Many of the families involved have young children. To help these families, the students offer child care while the adults are in class. They put on puppet shows, play cards, and read stories to the young children. "We didn't want people not to come because they couldn't get a babysitter," said Talia. Sometimes the adults ask a question the students can't answer. A computer teacher named Mrs. Strong is on hand to help.

Each student works with no more than two adults. Students like Talia enjoy teaching others. "I like computers and I like learning from people and having them learn from me," she said. "It gives me a good feeling. . . like I've done something important."

. . . it gives me a good feeling . . .

Talia Littledave

CHAPTER 11 REVIEW

THINKING ABOUT VOCABULARY

Number a sheet of paper from 1 to 5. Next to each number, write the letter of the definition that best matches the word.

1. migrant worker
   a. a person who recently moved to this country
   b. a person who stays in one place
   c. a person who lives in two countries
   d. a person who moves from place to place to harvest crops

2. metropolitan area
   a. a large city, or group of cities and suburbs
   b. a farm community
   c. a place far from a city
   d. a migrant worker's home

3. website
   a. a special effect
   b. a software program
   c. a location on the Internet
   d. a type of computer

4. endangered species
   a. plants and animals that are in danger of disappearing from Earth
   b. all of the plants and animals that live on Earth
   c. plants and animals that are dangerous
   d. plants and animals that are no longer found on Earth

5. computer graphics
   a. Internet addresses
   b. parts of a computer
   c. software programs
   d. images that are made with a computer

THINKING ABOUT FACTS

1. About how many people live in Oklahoma?

2. Where do the largest number of immigrants to Oklahoma come from?

3. Why do immigrants come to Oklahoma?

4. Why do many immigrants want to become citizens?

5. Where do many migrant workers in Oklahoma come from?

6. Name three festivals that are celebrated in Oklahoma. Where are these festivals held?

7. Where do most Oklahomans live? Why?

8. Name the two largest metropolitan areas in Oklahoma. About how many people live in these places?

9. Why do some Oklahomans live in communities like Marlow?

10. How does technology influence people's lives?

11. Why do people use the Internet?

12. What is the oil tax used for? Why is it needed?

13. How are old oil wells cleaned?

14. How can people help the environment?

15. How can technology be used to help the environment?

THINK AND WRITE

WRITING A DESCRIPTION
Describe both good and bad ways in which technology affects our lives. Include examples.

WRITING A RESEARCH REPORT
Do some research at the library or on the Internet on an environmental problem in Oklahoma. Note what is being done to solve the problem. Then, write a report about this problem and solution, and share it with the class.

WRITING A LIST
Suppose you are writing a feature about the life of a migrant worker in Oklahoma. Write a list of five questions that you would ask the person. Then write the possible answers he or she might give.

APPLYING STUDY SKILLS

READING CIRCLE AND LINE GRAPHS
Refer to the circle graph of Oklahoma immigrants on page 254 to help you answer the following questions.

1. Describe the difference between a circle graph and a line graph.

2. What is the continent from which the most immigrants have come to Oklahoma?

3. How many Oklahomans have come here from countries in North and South America?

4. What kind of graph would you use to show the amount of rainfall in your community during the last year?

5. How do graphs make some information easier to understand?

Summing Up the Chapter

Use the following spider map to organize information from the chapter. Copy the map on a sheet of paper. Then write at least one piece of information in each blank circle. When you have filled in the map, use it to write a paragraph that answers the question, "How are people in Oklahoma linked with technology and the environment?"

Oklahomans

Technology

Protecting Our Environment

UNIT 4 REVIEW

THINKING ABOUT VOCABULARY

Number a sheet of paper from 1 to 10. Beside each number write **C** if the underlined word is used correctly. If it is not, write the word that would correctly complete the sentence.

1. People who organize and run their own businesses are called <u>investors</u>.

2. Citizens of a city <u>elect</u> their leaders.

3. The <u>judicial branch</u> of government is responsible for carrying out the laws of the state.

4. The legislative branch of our national government is called the <u>United States Congress</u>.

5. The different businesses that sell goods and services to people who travel on vacations is called the <u>mining industry</u>.

6. Cities or towns have a <u>local</u> government.

7. A person who runs for government is called a <u>citizen</u>.

8. A <u>bill</u> is a written idea for a law.

9. A machine that is controlled by a computer is called a <u>website</u>.

10. A large city, or group of cities or suburbs is called a <u>metropolitan area</u>.

THINK AND WRITE

WRITING A RESEARCH REPORT
Choose an ethnic group from Chapter 11, Lesson 1 that you know little about. Do some research about the group. Then write a report and share it with the class.

WRITING A SPEECH
Suppose you are a candidate for the council in your community. Write a speech explaining how you will try to make your town or city a better place to live.

WRITING A PLAN
Suppose a student from another country will be visiting for a week to learn about the government in Oklahoma. Write a plan of activities that will help the student learn about how our local and state governments work.

BUILDING SKILLS

1. **Reading Newspapers** Why is it important to read newspapers?

2. **Reading Newspapers** If you wanted to learn the editor's opinion about an issue, what kind of article would you read?

3. **Reading Circle and Line Graphs** Name the parts of a graph that can help you figure out what it is showing you.

4. **Reading Circle and Line Graphs** Would you use a circle graph or a line graph to show how the population of Oklahoma has changed over the past 100 years? Why?

5. **Reading Circle and Line Graphs** Would you use a circle graph or a line graph to show how you spend your time after school? Why?

YESTERDAY, TODAY &

TOMORROW

Computers have become more important in people's daily lives. They have changed the way people do their jobs, learn, and communicate. Computers are also used to make machines run in ways less harmful to the environment. What new ways do you think computers will be used in the future?

READING ON YOUR OWN

Here are some books you might find at the library to help you learn more.

HOW THE U.S. GOVERNMENT WORKS
by Syl Sobel

Read this book to learn about our country's government and how it works, including the branches of government and how people are elected.

SEEING EARTH FROM SPACE
by Patricia Lauber

Images of Earth from outer space give readers a new perspective.

THEN AND NOW: FARMING
by Katie Roden

This book tells you how farming started and how far it has come.

UNIT 4 REVIEW PROJECT

Make a Government Tree

1. Work in a group to review Chapter 11 and make a list of the different branches of our national, state, and local governments.
2. On a piece of oaktag, create a government tree. Start with the national government. Label each branch, its function, and an example of the types of decisions it makes. Then do the same with the state and local governments.
3. You may use construction paper or draw colored arrows to connect the branches of each type of government.
4. Present your government tree to the class.

REFERENCE SECTION

The Reference Section has many parts,
each with a different type of information.
Use this section to look up people,
places, and events as you study.

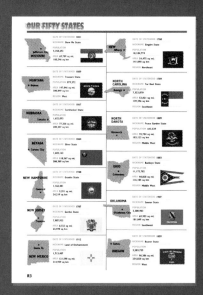

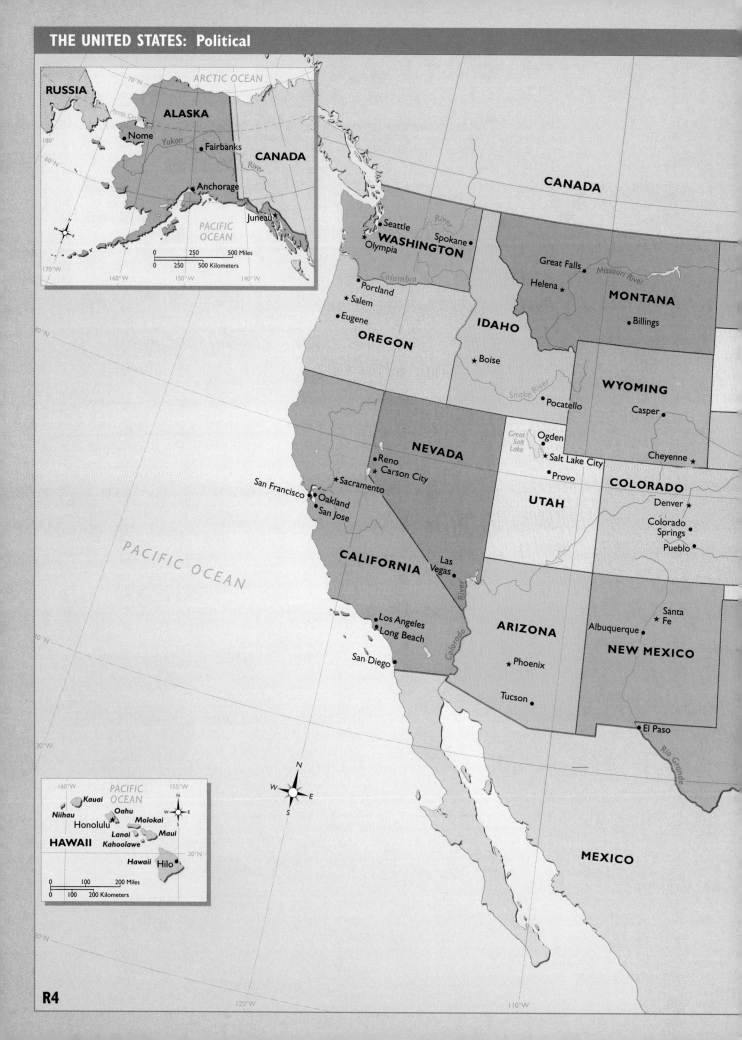

RUSSIA

ALASKA

ARCTIC OCEAN

Nome

Yukon

Fairbanks

CANADA

Anchorage

Juneau ★

PACIFIC OCEAN

0   250   500 Miles
0   250   500 Kilometers

CANADA

Seattle

Spokane

WASHINGTON

Olympia ★

Great Falls

Helena ★

MONTANA

Billings

Portland

★ Salem

Eugene

OREGON

IDAHO

Boise ★

Pocatello

Snake River

WYOMING

Casper

Cheyenne ★

NEVADA

Reno

Carson City ★

Great Salt Lake

Ogden

★ Salt Lake City

Provo

UTAH

COLORADO

Denver ★

San Francisco

Oakland

San Jose

★ Sacramento

Colorado Springs

Pueblo

PACIFIC OCEAN

CALIFORNIA

Las Vegas

Colorado River

Los Angeles

Long Beach

San Diego

ARIZONA

Phoenix ★

Tucson

Albuquerque

Santa Fe ★

NEW MEXICO

El Paso

Rio Grande

MEXICO

PACIFIC OCEAN

Kauai

Niihau

Oahu

Honolulu

Molokai

Lanai

Maui

Kahoolawe

HAWAII

Hawaii

Hilo

0   100   200 Miles
0   100   200 Kilometers

CANADA

NORTH DAKOTA
Grand Forks
★ Bismarck   Fargo

SOUTH DAKOTA
★ Pierre
Sioux Falls

NEBRASKA
Lincoln ★

Duluth

MINNESOTA
Minneapolis • ★ St. Paul

WISCONSIN
Green Bay
Madison • Milwaukee

IOWA
Cedar Rapids   Rockford •
Davenport •
Omaha • ★ Des Moines

Lake Superior

MICHIGAN
Grand Rapids   Lansing ★
Detroit •

Lake Michigan
Lake Huron

Chicago •   Gary •

ILLINOIS
Peoria •
★ Springfield

INDIANA
Fort Wayne •
★ Indianapolis

Toledo •

OHIO
★ Columbus
Wheeling •

Cleveland •
Lake Erie

Lake Ontario

NEW YORK
Buffalo •   Albany ★

MAINE
★ Augusta
Montpelier ★   Portland •
VERMONT   **NEW HAMPSHIRE**
Burlington •   ★ Concord

MASSACHUSETTS
Boston •
Hartford ★   Providence •
CONNECTICUT   **RHODE ISLAND**

PENNSYLVANIA
Pittsburgh •   Harrisburg ★
Newark •   New York •
Trenton ★
NEW JERSEY
Philadelphia •
Baltimore •   Dover ★
DELAWARE
Annapolis ★
Washington, D.C. ⊛   **MARYLAND**

MISSOURI
Kansas City •
Topeka ★   • Kansas City
Jefferson City ★   St. Louis •

KANSAS
• Wichita

Arkansas River

OKLAHOMA
Tulsa •
★ Oklahoma City
Fort Smith •

Red River

TEXAS
Fort Worth •   • Dallas
Shreveport •

Austin ★

San Antonio •

Laredo •   Corpus Christi •

Missouri River
Platte River

ARKANSAS
Little Rock ★

Mississippi River

Evansville •   Louisville •

KENTUCKY
★ Frankfort

WEST VIRGINIA
★ Charleston

VIRGINIA
Richmond ★
Norfolk •

Ohio River

Cincinnati •

Nashville ★   Knoxville •

TENNESSEE
Tennessee River
Memphis •

MISSISSIPPI
Birmingham •
★ Jackson

ALABAMA
★ Montgomery
Columbus •

GEORGIA
★ Atlanta
Charleston •
Savannah •

NORTH CAROLINA
Raleigh •
• Charlotte

SOUTH CAROLINA
★ Columbia

ATLANTIC OCEAN

LOUISIANA
Baton Rouge ★
New Orleans •
Biloxi •   Mobile •

Houston •

Tallahassee ★   Jacksonville •

FLORIDA
Tampa •

Gulf of Mexico

Miami •

THE BAHAMAS

CUBA

| ⊛ National capital | ★ State capital | • Other city |

0   150   300 Miles
0   150   300 Kilometers

50°N   40°N   30°N
100°W   90°W   80°W

70°W

RUSSIA

ARCTIC OCEAN

70°N

BROOKS RANGE

ALASKA

Yukon River

CANADA

ALASKA RANGE

Mt. McKinley
20,320 ft.
(6,194 m)

60°N

Bering Strait

Bering Sea

170°W

160°W   150°W   140°W

0   250   500 Miles
0   250   500 Kilometers

CANADA

Puget Sound

Mt. Rainier
14,410 ft.
(4,391 m)

Mt. St. Helens
8,366 ft.
(2,550 m)

RANGE

COAST RANGES

CASCADE

Columbia   River

Mt. Hood
11,235 ft.
(3,424 m)

COLUMBIA PLATEAU

Snake   River

Missouri   River

Yellowstone River

ROCKY MOUNTAINS

Granite Peak
12,799 ft.
(3,900 m)

TETON RANGE

BLACK HILLS

40°N

130°W

Cape Mendocino

Mt. Shasta
14,162 ft.
(4,316 m)

Sacramento River

Great Salt Lake

GREAT SALT LAKE DESERT

RANGE

WASATCH

Kings Peak
13,528 ft.
(4,123 m)

GREAT PLAINS

COAST

Lake Tahoe

CENTRAL VALLEY

SIERRA NEVADA

GREAT BASIN

San Francisco Bay

San Joaquin River

Mt. Elbert
14,433 ft.
(4,398 m)

Pikes Peak
14,107 ft.
(4,301 m)

PACIFIC OCEAN

RANGES

Mt. Whitney
14,491 ft.
(4,418 m)

Lake Mead

Colorado River

COLORADO PLATEAU

Wheeler Peak
13,065 ft.
(3,982 m)

DEATH VALLEY

MOJAVE DESERT

Humphreys Peak
12,633 ft.
(3,850 m)

Pecos River

30°N

Salton Sea

SONORA DESERT

Gila   River

Guadalupe Peak
8,751 ft.
(2,667 m)

EDWARDS PLATEAU

Rio Grande

160°W   155°W

PACIFIC OCEAN

Kauai

Oahu

Maui

N
W   E
S

HAWAII

Hawaii

20°N

Mauna Kea
13,796 ft.
(4,205 m)

0   100   200 Miles
0   100   200 Kilometers

Gulf of California

MEXICO

120°W

110°W

CANADA

Lake of
the Woods

Lake Superior

GREAT

LAKES

MESABI RANGE

Mississippi

Lake Michigan

Lake Huron

St. Lawrence River

WHITE MTS.

Mt. Washington
6,288 ft.
(1,917 m)

GREEN MTS.

ADIRONDACK
MTS.

Lake Ontario

Cape Cod

CENTRAL PLAINS

River

Platte River

Missouri

River

Wabash

River

Ohio

River

ALLEGHENY
PLATEAU

Hudson River

Susquehanna

River

Long Island

40° N

70° W

APPALACHIAN

MOUNTAINS

Potomac

River

Delaware Bay

Chesapeake Bay

ALLEGHENY MOUNTAINS

Arkansas

INTERIOR

PLAINS

River

OZARK
PLATEAU

OUACHITA
MOUNTAINS

Red

River

Mississippi

River

River

Tennessee

River

River

Mt. Mitchell
6,684 ft.
(2,037 m)

PIEDMONT

Savannah River

ATLANTIC COASTAL PLAIN

Cape Hatteras

ATLANTIC OCEAN

30° N

Brazos

River

Colorado River

River

Alabama

Chattahoochee

GULF COASTAL PLAIN

Mobile Bay

Galveston Bay

Mississippi Delta

Gulf of Mexico

Lake
Okeechobee

Bahama Islands

Florida Keys

Straits of Florida

80° W

N
W   E
S

0   150   300 Miles
0   150   300 Kilometers

90° W

CUBA

R7

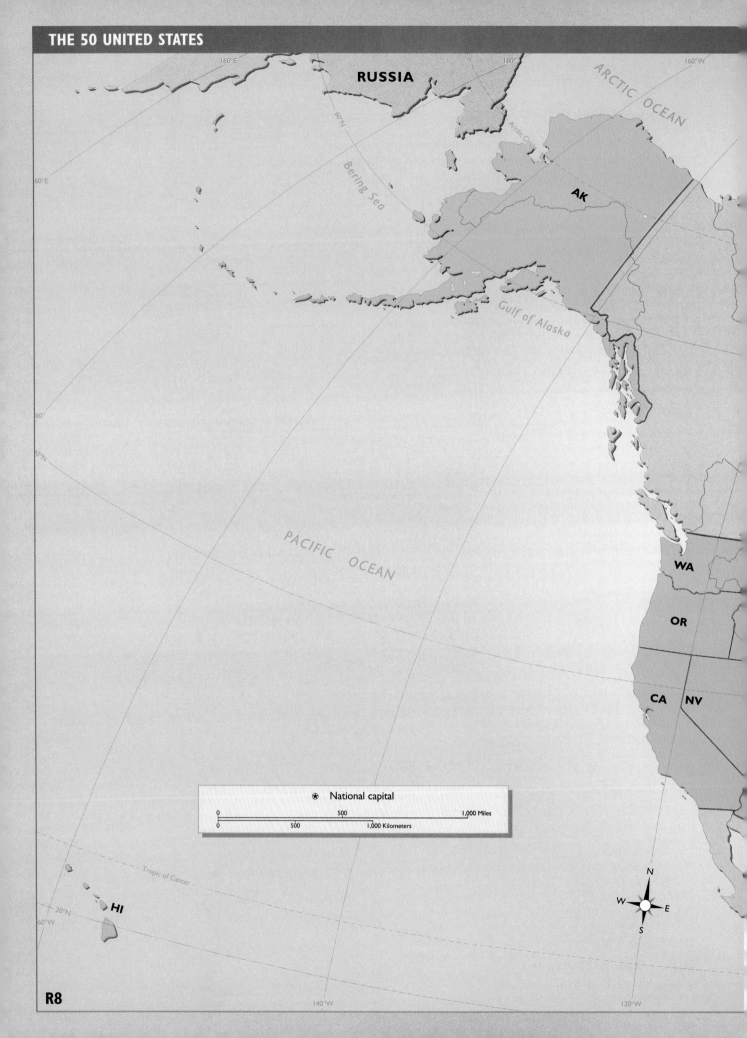

RUSSIA

ARCTIC OCEAN

160°E

180°

160°W

60°N

Arctic Circle

AK

60°E

Bering Sea

Gulf of Alaska

80°

40°N

PACIFIC OCEAN

WA

OR

CA NV

⊛ National capital

0   500   1,000 Miles

0   500   1,000 Kilometers

Tropic of Cancer

20°N

HI

60°W

N

W   E

S

140°W

120°W

Greenland
(DENMARK)

Hudson Bay

CANADA

Great Lakes

MT
ND
MN
MI
WI
MI
ME
VT
NH
NY
MA
CT
RI

ID
SD
WY
NE
IA
IL
IN
OH
PA
NJ

UT
CO
KS
MO
KY
WV
VA
Washington, D.C.
MD — DE

AZ
NM
OK
AR
TN
NC

TX
LA
MS
AL
GA
SC

FL

ATLANTIC OCEAN

Gulf of Mexico

MEXICO

CUBA

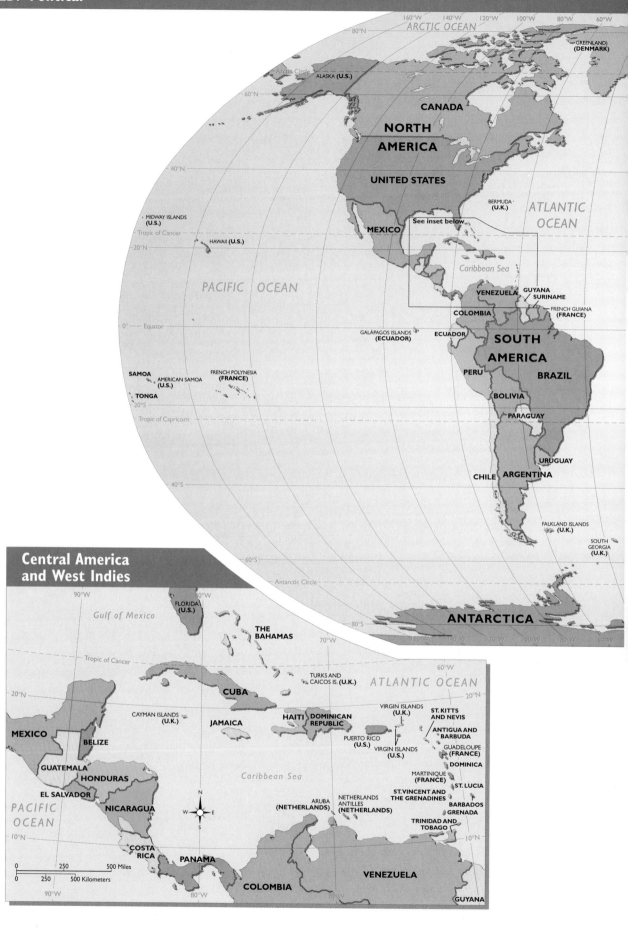

THE WORLD: Political

ARCTIC OCEAN

160°W 140°W 120°W 100°W 80°W 60°W

80°N

GREENLAND)
(DENMARK)

ALASKA (U.S.)

60°N

CANADA

**NORTH
AMERICA**

40°N

UNITED STATES

BERMUDA
(U.S.)

ATLANTIC
OCEAN

MIDWAY ISLANDS
(U.S.)

See inset below

MEXICO

Tropic of Cancer

20°N

HAWAII (U.S.)

Caribbean Sea

VENEZUELA GUYANA
SURINAME

FRENCH GUIANA
(FRANCE)

COLOMBIA

PACIFIC OCEAN

GALÁPAGOS ISLANDS
(ECUADOR)

ECUADOR

**SOUTH
AMERICA**

0° Equator

SAMOA

AMERICAN SAMOA
(U.S.)

FRENCH POLYNESIA
(FRANCE)

PERU

BRAZIL

TONGA

BOLIVIA

20°S

PARAGUAY

Tropic of Capricorn

URUGUAY

40°S

CHILE ARGENTINA

FALKLAND ISLANDS
(U.K.)

SOUTH
GEORGIA
(U.K.)

60°S

Antarctic Circle

80°S

ANTARCTICA

Central America and West Indies

90°W 80°W

FLORIDA
(U.S.)

Gulf of Mexico

THE
BAHAMAS

70°W

Tropic of Cancer

TURKS AND
CAICOS IS. (U.K.)

ATLANTIC OCEAN

60°W

20°N

20°N

CUBA

VIRGIN ISLANDS
(U.K.)

ST. KITTS
AND NEVIS

CAYMAN ISLANDS
(U.K.)

JAMAICA

HAITI

DOMINICAN
REPUBLIC

ANTIGUA AND
BARBUDA

MEXICO

PUERTO RICO
(U.S.)

GUADELOUPE
(FRANCE)

BELIZE

VIRGIN ISLANDS
(U.S.)

DOMINICA

GUATEMALA

MARTINIQUE
(FRANCE)

ST. LUCIA

HONDURAS

Caribbean Sea

ST. VINCENT AND
THE GRENADINES

EL SALVADOR

BARBADOS

PACIFIC
OCEAN

NICARAGUA

N

W E

S

ARUBA
(NETHERLANDS)

NETHERLANDS
ANTILLES
(NETHERLANDS)

GRENADA

TRINIDAD AND
TOBAGO

10°N

10°N

COSTA
RICA

PANAMA

COLOMBIA

VENEZUELA

GUYANA

0 250 500 Miles

0 250 500 Kilometers

90°W 80°W 70°W

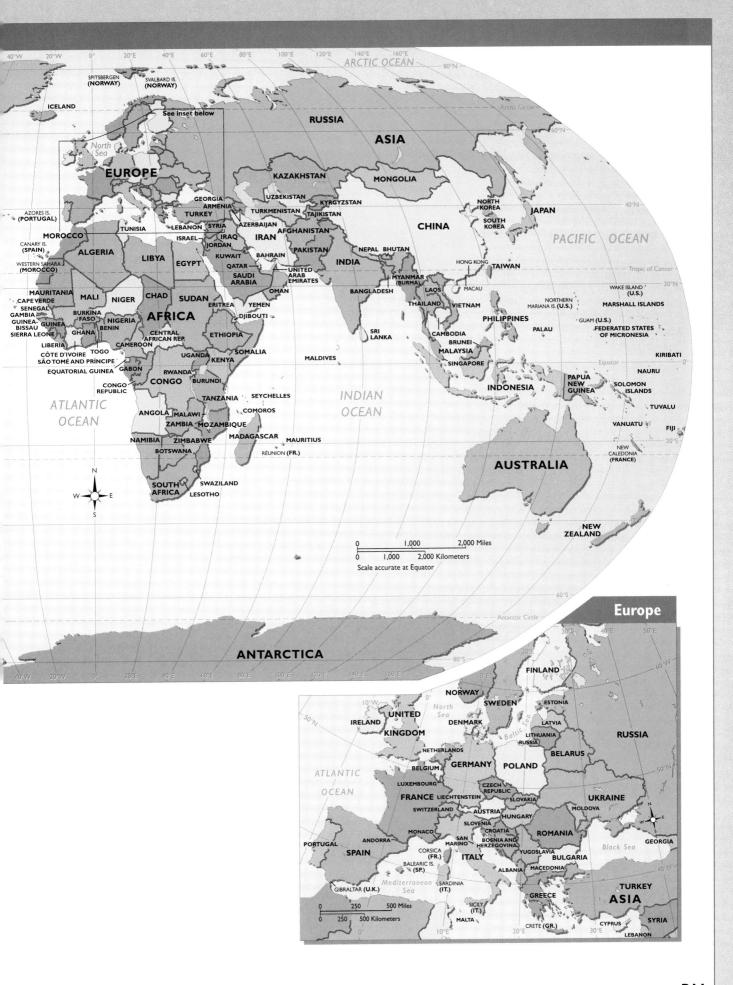

ARCTIC OCEAN

SPITSBERGEN
(NORWAY)

SVALBARD IS.
(NORWAY)

80°N

ICELAND

See inset below

North
Sea

RUSSIA

ASIA

Arctic Circle

60°N

EUROPE

KAZAKHSTAN

MONGOLIA

GEORGIA

ARMENIA

TURKEY

UZBEKISTAN

KYRGYZSTAN

NORTH
KOREA

JAPAN

40°N

AZORES IS.
(PORTUGAL)

TURKMENISTAN

TAJIKISTAN

CHINA

SOUTH
KOREA

PACIFIC OCEAN

MOROCCO

TUNISIA

LEBANON

SYRIA

AZERBAIJAN

AFGHANISTAN

ISRAEL

IRAQ

IRAN

CANARY IS.
(SPAIN)

JORDAN

PAKISTAN

NEPAL BHUTAN

HONG KONG

TAIWAN

Tropic of Cancer

WESTERN SAHARA
(MOROCCO)

ALGERIA

LIBYA

EGYPT

KUWAIT

BAHRAIN

QATAR

INDIA

MACAU

20°N

SAUDI
ARABIA

UNITED
ARAB
EMIRATES

LAOS

WAKE ISLAND
(U.S.)

MAURITANIA

MALI

NIGER

CHAD

SUDAN

OMAN

YEMEN

BANGLADESH

MYANMAR
(BURMA)

THAILAND

VIETNAM

NORTHERN
MARIANA IS. (U.S.)

MARSHALL ISLANDS

CAPE VERDE

ERITREA

SENEGAL

GAMBIA

BURKINA
FASO

NIGERIA

AFRICA

CENTRAL
AFRICAN REP.

DJIBOUTI

PHILIPPINES

GUAM (U.S.)

FEDERATED STATES
OF MICRONESIA

GUINEA-
BISSAU

GUINEA

BENIN

ETHIOPIA

CAMBODIA

PALAU

KIRIBATI

SIERRA LEONE

GHANA

CÔTE D'IVOIRE

TOGO

CAMEROON

UGANDA

SOMALIA

BRUNEI

MALAYSIA

SÃO TOMÉ AND PRÍNCIPE

EQUATORIAL GUINEA

GABON

RWANDA

KENYA

SINGAPORE

Equator

NAURU

LIBERIA

CONGO
REPUBLIC

CONGO

BURUNDI

MALDIVES

INDONESIA

PAPUA
NEW
GUINEA

SOLOMON
ISLANDS

ATLANTIC
OCEAN

ANGOLA

MALAWI

TANZANIA

SEYCHELLES

INDIAN
OCEAN

TUVALU

ZAMBIA

MOZAMBIQUE

COMOROS

VANUATU

FIJI

NAMIBIA

ZIMBABWE

MADAGASCAR

MAURITIUS

NEW
CALEDONIA
(FRANCE)

20°S

BOTSWANA

RÉUNION (FR.)

N

AUSTRALIA

W   E

SOUTH
AFRICA

SWAZILAND

S

LESOTHO

NEW
ZEALAND

SRI
LANKA

0   1,000   2,000 Miles

0   1,000   2,000 Kilometers

Scale accurate at Equator

60°S

Antarctic Circle

ANTARCTICA

80°S

40°W   20°W   0°   20°E   40°E   60°E   80°E   100°E   120°E   140°E   160°E

Europe

FINLAND

NORWAY

SWEDEN

ESTONIA

IRELAND

UNITED
KINGDOM

North
Sea

DENMARK

Baltic
Sea

LATVIA

RUSSIA

LITHUANIA

RUSSIA

BELARUS

NETHERLANDS

GERMANY

POLAND

ATLANTIC
OCEAN

BELGIUM

LUXEMBOURG

CZECH
REPUBLIC

SLOVAKIA

UKRAINE

FRANCE

LIECHTENSTEIN

AUSTRIA

HUNGARY

MOLDOVA

SWITZERLAND

SLOVENIA

MONACO

CROATIA

ROMANIA

GEORGIA

ANDORRA

SAN
MARINO

BOSNIA AND
HERZEGOVINA

PORTUGAL

CORSICA
(FR.)

ITALY

YUGOSLAVIA

BULGARIA

Black Sea

SPAIN

BALEARIC IS.
(SP.)

ALBANIA

MACEDONIA

TURKEY

GIBRALTAR (U.K.)

Mediterranean
Sea

SARDINIA
(IT.)

GREECE

ASIA

SICILY
(IT.)

SYRIA

MALTA

CRETE (GR.)

CYPRUS

LEBANON

0   250   500 Miles

0   250   500 Kilometers

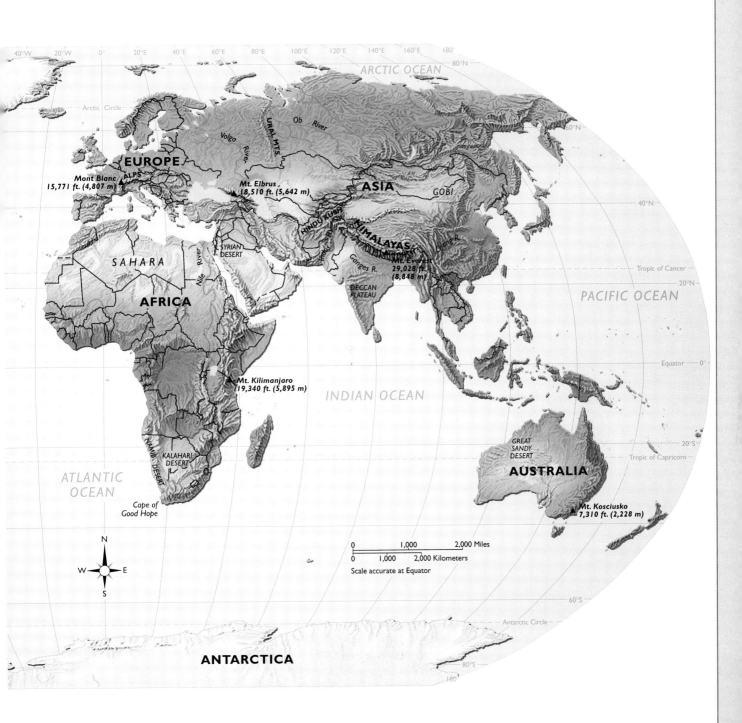

40°W 20°W 0° 20°E 40°E 60°E 80°E 100°E 120°E 140°E 160°E 180°

ARCTIC OCEAN

80°N

Arctic Circle

60°N

Ob   River

URAL MTS.

Volga

River

EUROPE

ALPS

Mont Blanc
15,771 ft. (4,807 m)

Mt. Elbrus
18,510 ft. (5,642 m)

ASIA

GOBI

40°N

HINDU KUSH

HIMALAYAS

SYRIAN
DESERT

Chang R.

Mt. Everest
29,028 ft.
(8,848 m)

Tropic of Cancer

SAHARA

Nile River

Gonges R.

20°N

AFRICA

DECCAN
PLATEAU

PACIFIC OCEAN

Equator 0°

Mt. Kilimanjaro
19,340 ft. (5,895 m)

INDIAN OCEAN

20°S

NAMIB DESERT

KALAHARI
DESERT

GREAT
SANDY
DESERT

Tropic of Capricorn

ATLANTIC
OCEAN

AUSTRALIA

Cape of
Good Hope

Mt. Kosciusko
7,310 ft. (2,228 m)

N
W   E
S

0   1,000   2,000 Miles
0   1,000   2,000 Kilometers
Scale accurate at Equator

60°S

Antarctic Circle

80°S

ANTARCTICA

180°

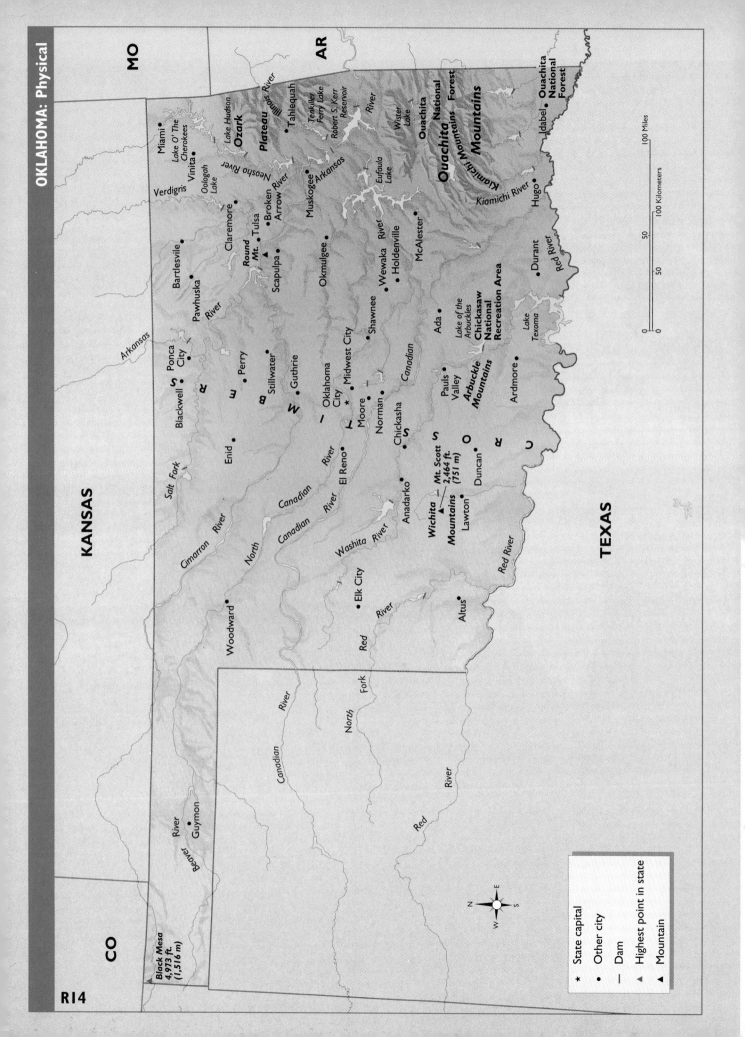

CO

Black Mesa
4,973 ft.
(1,516 m)

KANSAS

MO

AR

Miami
Lake O' The Cherokees
Vinita
Oologah Lake
Verdigris
Bartlesville
Pawhuska
Arkansas River

Neosho River
Illinois River
Tahlequah
Lake Hudson
Ozark Plateau
Tenkiller Ferry Lake
Robert S. Kerr Reservoir
Muskogee
Arkansas River
Wister Lake

Claremore
Round Mt. Tulsa
Sapulpa
Broken Arrow
Okmulgee
Eufaula Lake

Ouachita National Forest
Kiamichi Mountains
Ouachita Mountains
Idabel • **Ouachita National Forest**
Kiamichi River
Hugo

Salt Fork

Ponca City
Blackwell
Perry
Stillwater
Guthrie

Wewaka
River
Holdenville
McAlester

Durant
Red River

B E R
E D

Enid

Cimarron River

North Canadian River

Canadian River
El Reno

Oklahoma City
Midwest City
Moore
Norman
Chickasha
Canadian

Shawnee

Ada
Lake of the Arbuckles
Chickasaw National Recreation Area
Arbuckle Mountains
Pauls Valley

Lake Texoma

Ardmore

S O U R C

Anadarko
Wichita Mountains
Mt. Scott
2,464 ft.
(751 m)
Lawton
Duncan

Washita River

Woodward

Elk City

Red River

North Fork

Red River

Altus

TEXAS

Beaver River
Guymon

Canadian River

North Canadian River

Red River

W-E-N-S

Scale / Legend:
100 Miles
100 Kilometers
50
50

★ State capital
• Other city
| Dam
▲ Highest point in state
▲ Mountain

R14

OKLAHOMA GOVERNORS

OKLAHOMA GOVERNORS SINCE STATEHOOD	TERM
Charles Nathaniel Haskell	1907–1911
Lee Cruce	1911–1915
Robert Lee Williams	1915–1919
James Brooks Ayers Robertson	1919–1923
Jack Callaway Walton	January, 1923– November, 1923
Martin Edwin Trapp	1923–1927
Henry Simpson Johnston	1927–1929
William Judson Holloway	1929–1931
William Henry Murray	1931–1935
Ernest Whitworth Marland	1935–1939
Leon Chase Phillips	1939–1943
Robert Samuel Kerr	1943–1947
Roy Joseph Turner	1947–1951
Johnston Murray	1951–1955
Raymond Dancel Gary	1955–1959
James Howard Edmondson	1959–1963
George Patterson Nigh	January 6, 1963– January 14, 1963
Henry Louis Bellmon	1963–1967
Dewey Follett Bartlett	1967–1971
David Hall	1971–1975
David Lyle Boren	1975–1979
George Patterson Nigh	1979–1987
Henry Louis Bellmon	1987–1991
David Lee Walters	1991–1995
Francis Anthony Keating	1995– Re-elected in 1998

State Capitol Building in Oklahoma City

OUR FIFTY STATES

ALABAMA
★
Montgomery

DATE OF STATEHOOD 1819

NICKNAME Heart of Dixie

POPULATION 4,273,084

AREA 52,423 sq mi;
135,776 sq km

REGION Southeast

★
Hartford
CONNECTICUT

DATE OF STATEHOOD 1788

NICKNAME Constitution State

POPULATION 3,274,238

AREA 5,544 sq mi;
14,359 sq km

REGION Northeast

ALASKA

★
Juneau

DATE OF STATEHOOD 1959

NICKNAME The Last Frontier

POPULATION 607,007

AREA 656,424 sq mi;
1,700,138 sq km

REGION West

★
Dover

DELAWARE

DATE OF STATEHOOD 1787

NICKNAME First State

POPULATION 724,842

AREA 2,489 sq mi;
6,447 sq km

REGION Northeast

DECEMBER 7, 1787

ARIZONA

★
Phoenix

DATE OF STATEHOOD 1912

NICKNAME Grand Canyon State

POPULATION 4,428,088

AREA 114,006 sq mi;
295,276 sq km

REGION Southwest

★
Tallahassee

FLORIDA

DATE OF STATEHOOD 1845

NICKNAME Sunshine State

POPULATION 14,399,985

AREA 65,758 sq mi;
170,313 sq km

REGION Southeast

ARKANSAS
★
Little Rock

DATE OF STATEHOOD 1836

NICKNAME Land of Opportunity

POPULATION 2,509,793

AREA 53,182 sq mi;
137,741 sq km

REGION Southeast

ARKANSAS

★
Atlanta
GEORGIA

DATE OF STATEHOOD 1788

NICKNAME Peach State

POPULATION 7,353,225

AREA 59,441 sq mi;
153,952 sq km

REGION Southeast

CALIFORNIA
★
Sacramento

DATE OF STATEHOOD 1850

NICKNAME Golden State

POPULATION 31,878,234

AREA 163,707 sq mi;
424,001 sq km

REGION West

CALIFORNIA REPUBLIC

HAWAII

★
Honolulu

DATE OF STATEHOOD 1959

NICKNAME The Aloha State

POPULATION 1,183,723

AREA 10,932 sq mi;
28,314 sq km

REGION West

Denver ★

COLORADO

DATE OF STATEHOOD 1876

NICKNAME Centennial State

POPULATION 3,822,676

AREA 104,100 sq mi;
269,619 sq km

REGION West

★ Boise
IDAHO

DATE OF STATEHOOD 1890

NICKNAME Gem State

POPULATION 1,189,251

AREA 83,574 sq mi;
216,457 sq km

REGION West

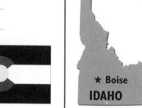

ILLINOIS
★
Springfield

DATE OF STATEHOOD 1818

NICKNAME **The Prairie State**

POPULATION **11,846,544**

AREA **57,918 sq mi; 150,008 sq km**

REGION **Middle West**

MAINE
Augusta
★

DATE OF STATEHOOD 1820

NICKNAME **Pine Tree State**

POPULATION **1,243,316**

AREA **35,387 sq mi; 91,652 sq km**

REGION **Northeast**

INDIANA
★
Indianapolis

DATE OF STATEHOOD 1816

NICKNAME **Hoosier State**

POPULATION **5,840,528**

AREA **36,420 sq mi; 94,328 sq km**

REGION **Middle West**

MARYLAND

Annapolis ★

DATE OF STATEHOOD 1788

NICKNAME **Free State**

POPULATION **5,071,604**

AREA **12,407 sq mi; 32,134 sq km**

REGION **Northeast**

IOWA
★
Des Moines

DATE OF STATEHOOD 1846

NICKNAME **Hawkeye State**

POPULATION **2,851,792**

AREA **56,276 sq mi; 145,755 sq km**

REGION **Middle West**

Boston ★

MASSACHUSETTS

DATE OF STATEHOOD 1788

NICKNAME **Bay State**

POPULATION **6,092,352**

AREA **10,555 sq mi; 27,337 sq km**

REGION **Northeast**

Topeka ★

KANSAS

DATE OF STATEHOOD 1861

NICKNAME **Sunflower State**

POPULATION **2,572,150**

AREA **82,282 sq mi; 213,110 sq km**

REGION **Middle West**

MICHIGAN

★
Lansing

DATE OF STATEHOOD 1837

NICKNAME **Wolverine State**

POPULATION **9,594,350**

AREA **96,810 sq mi; 250,738 sq km**

REGION **Middle West**

KENTUCKY

★
Frankfort

DATE OF STATEHOOD 1792

NICKNAME **Bluegrass State**

POPULATION **3,883,723**

AREA **40,411 sq mi; 104,664 sq km**

REGION **Southeast**

MINNESOTA

St. Paul ★

DATE OF STATEHOOD 1858

NICKNAME **North Star State**

POPULATION **4,657,758**

AREA **86,943 sq mi; 225,182 sq km**

REGION **Middle West**

LOUISIANA

Baton Rouge ★

DATE OF STATEHOOD 1812

NICKNAME **Pelican State**

POPULATION **4,350,579**

AREA **51,843 sq mi; 134,273 sq km**

REGION **Southeast**

MISSISSIPPI

★
Jackson

DATE OF STATEHOOD 1817

NICKNAME **Magnolia State**

POPULATION **2,716,115**

AREA **48,434 sq mi; 125,444 sq km**

REGION **Southeast**

OUR FIFTY STATES

MISSOURI
★ Jefferson City

DATE OF STATEHOOD 1821

NICKNAME Show Me State

POPULATION 5,358,692

AREA 69,709 sq mi; 180,546 sq km

REGION Middle West

MONTANA
★ Helena

DATE OF STATEHOOD 1889

NICKNAME Treasure State

POPULATION 879,372

AREA 147,046 sq mi; 380,849 sq km

REGION West

NEBRASKA
Lincoln ★

DATE OF STATEHOOD 1867

NICKNAME Cornhusker State

POPULATION 1,652,093

AREA 77,358 sq mi; 200,357 sq km

REGION Middle West

NEVADA
★ Carson City

DATE OF STATEHOOD 1864

NICKNAME Silver State

POPULATION 1,603,163

AREA 110,567 sq mi; 286,369 sq km

REGION West

NEW HAMPSHIRE

Concord ★

DATE OF STATEHOOD 1788

NICKNAME Granite State

POPULATION 1,162,481

AREA 9,351 sq mi; 24,219 sq km

REGION Northeast

NEW JERSEY
★
Trenton

DATE OF STATEHOOD 1787

NICKNAME Garden State

POPULATION 7,987,933

AREA 8,722 sq mi; 22,590 sq km

REGION Northeast

★
Santa Fe

NEW MEXICO

DATE OF STATEHOOD 1912

NICKNAME Land of Enchantment

POPULATION 1,713,407

AREA 121,598 sq mi; 314,939 sq km

REGION Southwest

NEW YORK
Albany ★

DATE OF STATEHOOD 1788

NICKNAME Empire State

POPULATION 18,184,774

AREA 54,475 sq mi; 141,090 sq km

REGION Northeast

NORTH CAROLINA

Raleigh ★

DATE OF STATEHOOD 1789

NICKNAME Tar Heel State

POPULATION 7,322,870

AREA 53,821 sq mi; 139,396 sq km

REGION Southeast

NORTH DAKOTA

Bismarck ★

DATE OF STATEHOOD 1889

NICKNAME Peace Garden State

POPULATION 643,539

AREA 70,704 sq mi; 183,123 sq km

REGION Middle West

OHIO
★
Columbus

DATE OF STATEHOOD 1803

NICKNAME Buckeye State

POPULATION 11,172,782

AREA 44,828 sq mi; 116,105 sq km

REGION Middle West

OKLAHOMA

★
Oklahoma City

DATE OF STATEHOOD 1907

NICKNAME Sooner State

POPULATION 3,300,902

AREA 69,903 sq mi; 181,049 sq km

REGION Southwest

★ Salem

OREGON

DATE OF STATEHOOD 1859

NICKNAME Beaver State

POPULATION 3,203,735

AREA 98,386 sq mi; 254,820 sq km

REGION West

PENNSYLVANIA

Harrisburg ★

DATE OF STATEHOOD 1787

NICKNAME Keystone State

POPULATION 12,056,112

AREA 46,058 sq mi; 119,290 sq km

REGION Northeast

VERMONT

★ Montpelier

DATE OF STATEHOOD 1791

NICKNAME Green Mountain State

POPULATION 588,654

AREA 9,615 sq mi; 24,903 sq km

REGION Northeast

RHODE ISLAND

Providence ★

DATE OF STATEHOOD 1790

NICKNAME Ocean State

POPULATION 990,225

AREA 1,545 sq mi; 4,002 sq km

REGION Northeast

VIRGINIA

Richmond ★

DATE OF STATEHOOD 1788

NICKNAME Old Dominion

POPULATION 6,675,451

AREA 42,769 sq mi; 110,772 sq km

REGION Southeast

SOUTH CAROLINA

★

Columbia

DATE OF STATEHOOD 1788

NICKNAME Palmetto State

POPULATION 3,698,746

AREA 32,007 sq mi; 82,898 sq km

REGION Southeast

★ Olympia

WASHINGTON

DATE OF STATEHOOD 1889

NICKNAME Evergreen State

POPULATION 5,532,939

AREA 71,303 sq mi; 184,675 sq km

REGION West

Pierre ★

SOUTH DAKOTA

DATE OF STATEHOOD 1889

NICKNAME Mount Rushmore State

POPULATION 732,405

AREA 77,121 sq mi; 199,743 sq km

REGION Middle West

WEST VIRGINIA

★ Charleston

DATE OF STATEHOOD 1863

NICKNAME Mountain State

POPULATION 1,825,754

AREA 24,231 sq mi; 62,758 sq km

REGION Southeast

TENNESSEE

★Nashville

DATE OF STATEHOOD 1796

NICKNAME Volunteer State

POPULATION 5,319,654

AREA 42,146 sq mi; 109,158 sq km

REGION Southeast

WISCONSIN

Madison ★

DATE OF STATEHOOD 1848

NICKNAME Badger State

POPULATION 5,159,795

AREA 65,503 sq mi; 169,653 sq km

REGION Middle West

TEXAS

Austin ★

DATE OF STATEHOOD 1845

NICKNAME Lone Star State

POPULATION 19,128,261

AREA 268,601 sq mi; 695,677 sq km

REGION Southwest

★

Salt Lake City

UTAH

DATE OF STATEHOOD 1896

NICKNAME Beehive State

POPULATION 2,000,494

AREA 84,904 sq mi; 219,901 sq km

REGION West

WYOMING

Cheyenne ★

DATE OF STATEHOOD 1890

NICKNAME Equality State

POPULATION 481,400

AREA 97,818 sq mi; 253,349 sq km

REGION West

Sources: population—U.S. Bureau of Census; area—U.S. Bureau of Census, 1991; capital—*World Almanac*, 1995.

Dictionary of GEOGRAPHIC TERMS

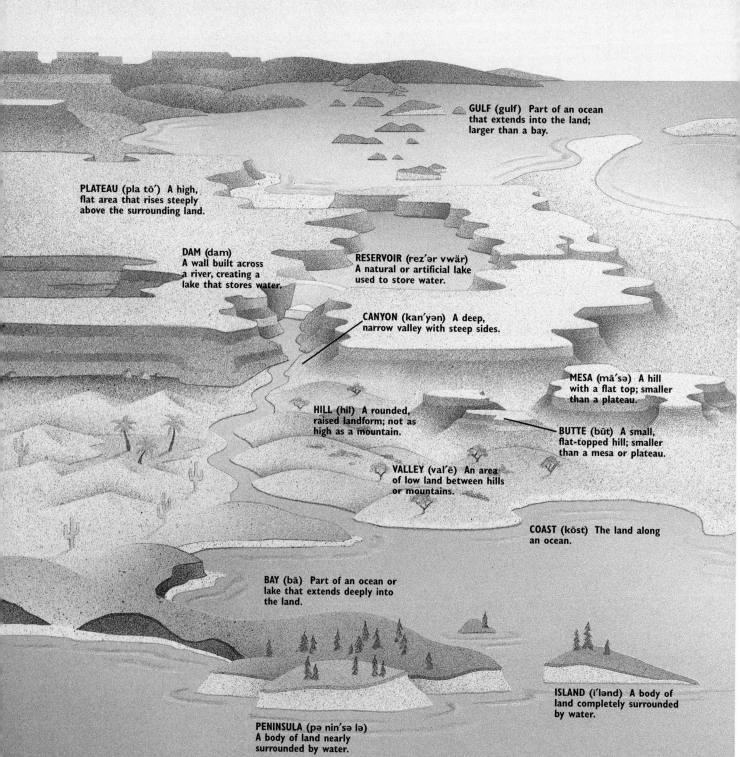

GULF (gulf) Part of an ocean that extends into the land; larger than a bay.

PLATEAU (pla tō′) A high, flat area that rises steeply above the surrounding land.

DAM (dam) A wall built across a river, creating a lake that stores water.

RESERVOIR (rez′ər vwär) A natural or artificial lake used to store water.

CANYON (kan′yən) A deep, narrow valley with steep sides.

MESA (mā′sə) A hill with a flat top; smaller than a plateau.

HILL (hil) A rounded, raised landform; not as high as a mountain.

BUTTE (būt) A small, flat-topped hill; smaller than a mesa or plateau.

VALLEY (val′ē) An area of low land between hills or mountains.

COAST (kōst) The land along an ocean.

BAY (bā) Part of an ocean or lake that extends deeply into the land.

ISLAND (ī′lənd) A body of land completely surrounded by water.

PENINSULA (pə nin′sə lə) A body of land nearly surrounded by water.

VOLCANO (vol kā′nō) An opening in Earth's surface through which hot rock and ash are forced out.

MOUNTAIN (moun′tən) A high landform with steep sides; higher than a hill.

PEAK (pēk) The top of a mountain.

HARBOR (här′bər) A sheltered place along a coast where boats dock safely.

GLACIER (glā′shər) A huge sheet of ice that moves slowly across the land.

CANAL (kə nal′) A channel built to carry water for irrigation or transportation.

LAKE (lāk) A body of water completely surrounded by land.

PORT (pôrt) A place where ships load and unload their goods.

TRIBUTARY (trib′yə ter ē) A smaller river that flows into a larger river.

SOURCE (sôrs) The starting point of a river.

TIMBERLINE (tim′bər lin) A line beyond which trees do not grow.

RIVER BASIN (riv′ər bā′sin) All the land that is drained by a river and its tributaries.

WATERFALL (wô′tər fôl) A flow of water falling vertically.

MOUNTAIN RANGE (moun′tən rānj) A row or chain of mountains.

PLAIN (plān) A large area of nearly flat land.

RIVER (riv′ər) A stream of water that flows across the land and empties into another body of water.

BASIN (bā′sin) A bowl-shaped landform surrounded by higher land.

DELTA (del′tə) Land made of soil left behind as a river drains into a larger body of water.

MOUTH (mouth) The place where a river empties into a larger body of water.

OCEAN (ō′shən) A large body of salt water; oceans cover much of Earth's surface.

Gazetteer

This Gazetteer is a geographical dictionary that will help you to pronounce and locate the places discussed in this book. Latitude and longitude are given for cities and some other places. The page numbers tell you where each place first appears on a map or in the text.

A

Appalachian Mountains (ap ə lā′chā ən moun′tənz) A chain of mountains with rounded peaks that runs through the eastern United States. (m. 13, t. 10).

Arbuckle Mountains (är′ buk əl mount′ ənz) Very old mountains in Lake Country, in south-central Oklahoma. (m. 91, t. 96)

Arkansas River (är′ kən sô riv′ər) A river that flows through Green Country in northeastern Oklahoma on its way to the Mississippi River. (m. 91, t. 93)

B

Beaumont (bō′mänt) City in southeastern Texas, site of early oil boom; 30°N, 94°W. (m. 278, t. 71)

Big Bend National Park (big bend nashiæn æl pärk) National park in western Texas on a bend of the Rio Grande; 29°N, 103°W. (m. 62)

Black Mesa (blak mā′sə) The highest point in Oklahoma, almost 5,000 feet (1,500 m) above sea level; 37°N, 103°W. (m. 87, t. 88)

C

Canadian River (kən ā′dē ən riv′ər) A river that flows east across Oklahoma into Lake Eufaula and the Arkansas River. (m. 87, t. 88)

Chisholm Trail (chiz′əm trāl) A path used for cattle drives from Texas north through central Indian Territory to Kansas. (m. 154, t. 154)

Coastal Plain (kōs′ təl plān) Low plain along the Atlantic Coast from Massachusetts to Texas; sometimes separated into Gulf and Atlantic Coastal plains. (m. 13, t. 9)

Colorado River (kol ə radō riv′ər) A river that flows from the Rocky Mountains to the Pacific Ocean. (m. 62, t. 59)

F

Frontier Country (frun tîr′ kun′trē) Region in central Oklahoma where Oklahoma City is located. (m. 93, t. 95)

G

Grand Canyon (grand kan′yən) Canyon on the Colorado River in northwestern Arizona; 36°N, 112°W. (m. 60, t. 59)

Great Plains Country (grāt plānz kun′trē) Region in southwestern Oklahoma that has our state's best farmland. (m. 93, t. 96)

Green Country (grēn kun′trē) Region in northeastern Oklahoma with prairies and forests. The Ozark Plateau is in its east. (m. 93, t. 93)

Greenwood (grēn wud) A community in Tulsa, built by African Americans during the oil boom of the early 1920s and was all but destroyed by the Tulsa Race Riots. (t. 182)

Gulf of Mexico (gulf əv mek′si kō) A gulf of the Atlantic Ocean bordering five southern states of the United States and into which the Mississippi River flows. (m. G9, t. 70)

pronunciation key

a	at	ī	ice	u	up	th	thin
ā	ape	îr	pierce	ū	use	th	this
ä	far	o	hot	ü	rule	zh	measure
âr	care	ō	old	ù	pull	ə	about, taken,
e	end	ô	fork	ûr	turn		pencil, lemon,
ē	me	oi	oil	hw	white		circus
i	it	ou	out	ng	song		

Guthrie (guth′rē) The capital of Oklahoma Territory and our state's first capital; 36°N, 97°W. (m. 175, t. 177)

H

Honey Springs (hun′ē springz) Site in eastern Oklahoma where a Civil War battle took place in July 1863, after which the Union gained control over Indian Territory; 35°N, 95°W. (t. 148)

Houston (hūs′tən) A port city in southeastern Texas and a major oil-refining center; 30°N, 95°W. (m. 154, t. 73)

I

Idabel (īd′ə bel) A town in southeastern Oklahoma. One of Oklahoma's lowest areas, it is about 350 feet above sea level; 34°N, 95°W. (m. 87, t. 87)

Indian Territory (in′dē ən ter′i tôr ē) The land that is now our state. It was a territory set aside for the relocation of the Five Civilized Tribes from the southeastern part of the United States in the early 1800s. (m. 143, t. 141)

Interior Plains (in tîr′ē ər plānz) The mostly flat land between the Appalachian and Rocky mountains. (m. 12–13, t. 11)

K

Kansas (kan′zəs) A state north of Oklahoma. During the Civil War, Kansas was Oklahoma's nearest Union neighbor. (m. 12–13, t. 22)

Kiamichi Country (kī ə mish′ē kun′trē) Region in southeastern Oklahoma that has many forests and coal deposits. It is named after the Kiamichi Mountains. (m. 93, t. 97)

Kiamichi Mountains (kī ə mish′ē moun′tənz) The tree-covered mountains located in the center of Kiamichi Country, southeastern Oklahoma. (m. 87, t. 97)

L

Lake Country (lāk kun′trē) Region in south-central Oklahoma named for its many lakes. It has a national park. (m. 93, t. 96)

Lake Eufaula (lāk yü′fä lä) Located in east-central Oklahoma, it is one of the largest lakes in the Southwest and the largest lake in Oklahoma; 35°N, 96°W. (m. 87, t. 88)

M

Mexico (mek′si kō) The country directly south of the United States. (t. 52)

Mississippi River (mis ə sip′ē riv′ ər) One of the longest rivers in North America. It flows south from northern Minnesota into the Gulf of Mexico. (m. 12–13, t. 11)

Montgomery (mont gum′ə rē) Capital of the state of Alabama; 33°N, 86°W. (m. 268, t. 194)

Monument Valley (mon′yə ment val′ē) A sandy plain in Arizona and Utah with rock formations carved by erosion; 37°N, 110°W. (m. 62)

O

Oklahoma (ō klə hō′mə) A state in the south-central United States. Oklahoma became the forty-sixth state in 1907. (m. 12–13, t. 7)

Oklahoma City (ō klə hō′mə sit′ ē) Oklahoma's capital and largest city, located in central Frontier Country; 35°N, 97°W. (m. 93, t. 95)

Oklahoma Territory (ō klə hō′mə ter′i tôr ē) A territory in what is today western Oklahoma that was created by Congress in 1890. (m. 174, t. 175)

Oologah (ü lō′gä) Town in Green Country, Oklahoma, where rodeo star and humorist Will Rogers grew up; 36°N, 95°W. (t. 104)

Ozark Plateau (ō′zärk pla tō′) A high, fertile area in Green Country, northeastern Oklahoma. (m. 93, t. 93)

pronunciation key

a at; ā ape; ä far; âr care; e end; ē me; i it; ī ice; îr pierce; o hot; ō old; ô fork; oi oil; ou out; u up; ū use; ü rule, u̇ pull; ûr turn; hw white; ng song; th thin; th this; zh measure; ə about, taken, pencil, lemon, circus

Gazetteer

P

Panhandle (pan′hand əl) The northwestern part of Oklahoma. (m. 87, t. 88)

Pearl Harbor, Hawaii (pûrl här′bər hə wī′ē) United States Navy base near Honolulu, on the island of Oahu, that was bombed by Japanese planes on December 7, 1941; 21°N, 158°W. (m. 268, t. 191)

Prague (prä′ge) Small town east of Oklahoma City in Frontier Country, Oklahoma, where world-famous athlete Jim Thorpe grew up; 35°N, 96°W. (t. 104)

R

Red Carpet Country (red kär′pit kun′trē) Region in northwestern Oklahoma named for its red clay soil. It has many wheat farms and cattle ranches. (m. 93, t. 94)

Red River (red riv′ər) A river that forms Oklahoma's southern border with Texas. (m. 87, t. 96)

Red Rock Canyon (red rok kan′yən) A canyon in central Oklahoma; 37°N, 97°W. (t. 87)

Rio Grande (rē′ō grand) A river that starts in Colorado and flows between Texas and Mexico into the Gulf of Mexico. (m. 62, t. 63)

Rocky Mountains (rokē′ moun′tənz) A high mountain range that stretches from Canada through the western United States into Mexico. (m. 12–13, t. 14)

Round Mountain (round mount′ ən) In northeastern Oklahoma, south of the Arkansas River, the site of a Civil War battle between Opothleyahola's group and Confederate troops; 36°N, 96°W. (t. 147)

S

Shawnee Trail (shô′nē trāl) A cattle trail from southern Texas to Sedalia, Kansas, that went through the eastern part of the Indian Territory. (m. 154, t. 154)

Sonoran Desert (sə nôr′ən dez′ərt) A desert in southern Arizona, southeastern California, and northern Mexico (m. 62, t. 65)

Spiro (spi′rō) Archeological park in eastern Oklahoma where the Spiro Mound is located; 35°N, 95°W. (t. 122)

T

Texas (tek′səs) A state south of Oklahoma, in the Southwest Region of the United States. (m. 12–13, t. 11)

Tinker Air Force Base (tink′ər âr fors bās) U.S. Air Force base opened in Oklahoma City in 1942. (t. 191)

Tulsa (tul′sə) The second-largest city in Oklahoma, located in central Green Country. The city developed around the discovery of oil in the early 1900s and today is home to many oil companies. 36°N, 96°W. (t. 71)

Turner Turnpike (tûrn′ûr tûrn′pīk) The toll highway built by Governor Roy Turner that opened in 1953. It runs from Oklahoma City to Tulsa. (t. 193)

Twin Territories (twin ter′i tôr ēz) The territory created in the 1890s that contained the Oklahoma Territory and Indian Territory. (m. 175, t. 175)

W

Washington, D.C. (wôsh′ing tən dē sē) The capital of the United States of America; 39°N, 77°W. (m. 268, t. 244)

Wichita Mountains (wich′i tô mount′ənz) The rugged peaks found in the center of Great Plains Country in southwestern Oklahoma. (m. 93, t. 96)

pronunciation key

a	at	ī	ice	u	up	th	thin
ā	ape	îr	pierce	ū	use	th	this
ä	far	o	hot	ü	rule	zh	measure
âr	care	ō	old	ù	pull	ə	about, taken,
e	end	ô	fork	ûr	turn		pencil, lemon,
ē	me	oi	oil	hw	white		circus
i	it	ou	out	ng	song		

Biographical Dictionary

The Biographical Dictionary will help you to pronounce and identify the people discussed in this book. The page number tells you where each person first appears in the text.

A

Albert, Carl (al′ bərt), 1908–2000 Member of the United States House of Representatives from 1946–1977. He was Speaker of the House from 1971–1977. (p. 242)

Atkins, Hannah (at′ kinz), 1923– Member of the Oklahoma House of Representatives for 12 years, 1968–1980. (p. 237)

B

Bean, Mark (bēn), mid-1800s Successful farmer and salt maker on the Oklahoma frontier who encouraged others to settle there. (p. 133)

Boudinot, Elias C. (bū dən ō′), 1835–1890 Lawyer who served as Tribal Representative to the Confederate Congress and who believed that lands in Indian Territory should be opened to settlement. (p. 157)

C

Chouteau, Pierre (shü tō′), mid-1800s Builder of one of the early trading posts in Oklahoma. (p. 133)

Clark, William (klärk), 1770–1838 Explorer of the Louisiana Purchase with Meriwether Lewis. (p. 131)

Coronado, Francisco de (kôr ə nä′dō), 1510–1554 Spanish explorer who was the first non-American Indian to visit Oklahoma. (p. 125)

G

Grant, Ulysses S. (grant), 1822–1885 Leader of the Union Army during the Civil War and the 18th President of the United States from 1869 to 1877. (p. 149)

H

Harrison, Benjamin (har′ ə sən), 1833–1901 The 23rd President of the United States He signed the order to open the Unassigned Lands to settlement. (p. 158)

Haskell, Charles (has′ kəl), 1860–1933 First governor of Oklahoma. (p. 176)

Higgins, Pattillo (hig′ ənz, pə til′ ō), 1863–1955 Texas oil driller whose drilling led to the first gusher. (p. 71)

J

Jackson, Andrew (jak′ sən), 1767–1845 Seventh President of the United States, from 1829 to 1837. He signed the Indian Removal Act of 1830. (p. 140)

Jefferson, Thomas (jef′ ər sən), 1743–1826 The 3rd President of the United States from 1801 to 1809. He authorized the Louisiana Purchase of 1803. (p. 126)

K

King, Martin Luther, Jr. (king), 1929–1968 Civil rights leader who worked to gain equal rights for African Americans and others in the 1950s and 1960s. (p. 195)

L

La Salle, Robert (lə′ sal′), 1643–1687 French explorer who traveled down the Mississippi River in 1682 and claimed the land west of the river, including Oklahoma, for France. (p. 126)

Lee, Robert E. (lē), 1807–1870 General who led the Confederate Army in the Civil War. (p. 149)

pronunciation key

a	at	ī	ice	u	up	th	thin
ā	ape	îr	pierce	ū	use	th	this
ä	far	o	hot	ü	rule	zh	measure
âr	care	ō	old	ù	pull	ə	about, taken,
e	end	ô	fork	ûr	turn		pencil, lemon,
ē	me	oi	oil	hw	white		circus
i	it	ou	out	ng	song		

Lewis, Meriwether (lü′ is), 1774–1809 Army officer and scout who explored the Louisiana Purchase with William Clark from 1803 to 1806. (p. 131)

Luper, Clara (lüp′ ər), 1923– African American activist who organized sit-ins in the early days of the Civil Rights movement (p. 194)

M

Murray, "Alfalfa" Bill (mûr′ ē), 1869–1956 Governor of Oklahoma from 1931 to 1935. (p. 189)

O

Opothleyahola (ō poth′ lā yə hō lə), 1798?–1863? Muskogee Creek chief. He tried to keep out of the Civil War but eventually sided with the Union. (p. 147)

P

Page, Sarah (pāj), 1904–? Oklahoman who accused Dick Rowland, an African American, of attacking her. This led to the Tulsa Race Riots in 1921. (p. 183)

Parks, Rosa (pärks), 1913– Civil rights activist who fought to end segregation on buses in Montgomery, Alabama, in 1955. (p. 194)

Payne, David L. (pān), 1836–1884 The leader of the Boomers—a group of people who wanted to push onto the American Indian lands in the Indian Territory. (p. 157)

R

Rice, Larry (rīs), 1953– Member of the Oklahoma House of Representatives and head of a committee on energy, environment and natural resources. (p. 237)

Rogers, Will (räj′ ərz), 1879–1935 World famous humorist, writer, and radio and movie star from Oklahoma. (p. 104)

Roosevelt, Franklin D. (rō′ zə velt), 1882–1945 Thirty-second President of the United States from 1933 to 1945 who created programs to fight the Great Depression and led the country during World War II. (p. 187)

Ross, John (rôs), 1790–1866 Cherokee chief from 1828 to 1866 whose people were forced to march to the Indian Territory in 1838. (p. 142)

Rowland, Dick (rō′ lənd), 1902–? African American accused of attacking Sarah Page, which led to the Tulsa race riots. (p. 183)

S

Sacajawea (sak ə jə wē′ ə) 1787?–1812 Shoshone translator for the Lewis and Clark expedition, 1805–1806. (p. 131)

Sequoyah (sī kwoi′ ə), 1770?–1843 Cherokee who invented a Cherokee alphabet. (p. 144)

Shoulders, Jim (shōl′dərz), 1928– Oklahoman who won 16 world rodeo championships. He is in the Cowboy Hall of Fame. (p. 108)

Sparks, Richard (spärks), 17–? The leader of the first Red River Exploration in the early 1800s. (p. 131)

T

Tallchief, Maria (tôl′ chēf), 1925– World-famous ballerina of American Indian heritage. (p. 109)

Thorpe, Jim (thôrp), 1888–1953 Athlete from Oklahoma who won two gold medals in track and field at the 1912 Olympics. (p. 104)

Turner, Roy (tûr′ nər), 1894–1973 Governor of Oklahoma from 1947 to 1951 responsible for building the turnpike between Oklahoma City and Tulsa. (p. 193)

W

Wilkinson, James (wil′ kən sən), 1757–1825 An army officer who explored Northeast Oklahoma. (p. 131)

Wilson, Charles Banks (wil′ sən), 1918– Oklahoma painter whose murals in the State Capitol building show over 400 years of Oklahoma's history. (p. 110)

pronunciation key

a at; ā ape; ä far; âr care; e end; ē me; i it; ī ice; îr pierce; o hot; ō old; ô fork; oi oil; ou out; u up; ū use; ü rule; u̇ pull; ûr turn; hw white; ng song; th thin; th this; zh measure; ə about, taken, pencil, lemon, circus

Glossary

This Glossary will help you to pronounce and understand the meanings of the vocabulary in this book. The page number at the end of the definition tells where the word first appears.

A

adaptation (ad əp tā′ shən) Changes made by a species of plant or animal over time in order to survive in its environment. (p. 65)

adobe (ə dō′ bē) Sun-baked bricks used as a building material, most commonly in the Southwest. (p. 125)

Allies (al′ īz) Countries that fought against the Axis Powers in World War II, including the United States, Britain, France, the Soviet Union, and China. (p. 191)

ancestor (an səs tər) A person in your family, starting with your parents, who was born before you. (p. 36)

aquifer (ak′ wə fər) A layer of rock or gravel that traps water underground. (p. 67)

artifact (är′ tə fakt) An object left behind by people who lived long ago. (p. 120)

assembly line (ə sem′ blē līn) A line of workers and machines working together to make a product. (p. 212)

Axis Powers (ak′ sis pou′ ərz) Countries that fought the Allies in World War II, including Germany, Italy, and Japan. (p. 191)

B

basin (bā′ sin) A low, bowl-shaped landform surrounded by higher land. (p. 9)

bill (bil) A written idea for a law. (p. 236)

Boomer (bü′ mər) A farmer who wanted to enter the Indian Territory illegally and take American Indian land. (p. 157)

boom town (büm toun) Communities that grow rapidly. (p. 181)

butte (būt) A flat-topped hill. (p. 58)

C

candidate (kan′ di dāt) A person who seeks or is put forward by others for an office or honor. (p. 243)

canyon (kan′ yən) A deep, narrow valley with steep sides. (p. 59)

cattle drive (kat′ əl drīv) A journey in which cowboys herded cattle north to railroad depots in the late 1800s. (p. 153)

checks and balances (cheks and bal′ ən səz) The system in which the power of each branch of government is balanced by the powers of other branches. (p. 235)

citizens (sit′ ə zənz) People who are born in a country or who have earned the right to become a member of that country by law. (p. 228)

city council (sit′ ē koun′ səl) An elected body that makes laws for a city. (p. 230)

civil rights (siv′ əl rīts) The rights of people to be treated equally under the law. (p. 194)

Civil Rights Act of 1964 (siv′ əl rīts akt) A law that made it illegal for businesses to discriminate against anyone because of their race, sex, or religion. (p. 194)

Civil War (siv′ əl wôr) The war in the United States between the Union states of the North and the Confederate states of the South, 1861–1865. (p. 146)

claim (klām) Land settled by a homesteader under the Homestead Act. (p. 157)

climate (klī′ mit) The pattern of weather of a certain place over many years. (p. 20)

coast (kōst) The land next to an ocean. (p. 9)

combine (kom′ bīn) A large machine used to harvest crops. (p. 218)

commissioner (kə mish′ ə nər) A person in charge of a department of government. (p. 231)

computer graphics (kəm pūt′ ər graf′ iks) Pictures and drawings that a computer makes. (p. 257)

Confederacy (kən fed′ ər ə sē) The government formed by the 11 Southern states that seceded from the United States, 1860–1865. (p. 147)

conservation (kon sər vā′ shən) The careful use of a natural resource. (p. 25)

constitution (kon sti tü′ tən) A plan of government which explains the parts of the government and outlines the most important laws. (p. 143)

county (koun′ tē) One of the sections into which a state or country is divided. (p. 231)

pronunciation key

a	at	ī	ice	u	up	th	thin
ā	ape	îr	pierce	ū	use	th	this
ä	far	o	hot	ü	rule	zh	measure
âr	care	ō	old	u̇	pull	ə	about, taken,
e	end	ô	fork	ûr	turn		pencil, lemon,
ē	me	oi	oil	hw	white		circus
i	it	ou	out	ng	song		

cow town (kou toun) A town at the end of a cattle drive. (p. 154)

crude oil (krüd oil) Petroleum that comes out of the ground. (p. 74)

culture (kul′ chər) The way of life shared by a group of people, including language, beliefs, customs, governments, and arts. (p. 34)

Curtis Act (kûrt′ is akt) A law that said that American Indians had to live by the laws of the United States and had to become citizens in order to own land. (p. 176)

custom (kus′ təm) The special way a group of people does something. (p. 35)

D

demand (di′ mand) Demand is the amount of an item that people are willing to buy. (p. 207)

democracy (di mok′ rə sē) A system of government in which the power to rule comes from the people. (p. 243)

democratic republic (dem ə krat′ ik ri pub′ lik) A government in which citizens elect representatives to make decisions for them. (p. 243)

desert (dez′ ərt) A dry area that gets less than 10 inches of rain each year. (p. 14)

discrimination (di skrim′ ə nā shən) An unfair difference in the treatment of people. (p. 182)

drought (drout) A long period with very little rain. (p. 167)

dry farming (drī fär′ ming) Methods of growing crops by using only rain water. (p. 67)

dugout (dug′ out) A shelter built into the side of a hill. (p. 165)

Dust Bowl (dust bôl) An area of the Great Plains with droughts and dust storms in the 1930s. (p. 66)

E

economy (i kon′ ə mē) The way a country or other place uses or produces natural resources, goods, and services. (p. 44)

elect (i lekt′) To choose by voting. (p. 229)

Enabling Act (i nā′ bəl ing akt) A law that called for joining the Twin Territories into the state of Oklahoma. (p. 177)

endangered species (en dān′ jərd spē′ shēz) Wild animals or plants that are close to becoming extinct. (p. 260)

entrepreneur (än trə prə′ nər) A person who forms and runs a business. (p. 204)

environment (en vi′ rən mənt) The surroundings in which people, plants, and animals live. (p. 15)

erosion (ir ō zhən) The action of water, wind, or ice in wearing away soil and rock. (p. 59)

ethnic group (eth′ nik grüp) A group of people whose ancestors are from the same country or area. (p. 37)

executive (eg zek′ yə tiv) The branch of government that carries out laws. (p. 235)

expedition (eks pə di sh′ ən) A journey of exploration. (p. 125)

explorer (eks plôr′ ər) A person who travels to unknown places. (p. 124)

F

Five Civilized Tribes (fīv siv ′ə līz′ ed trībz) Name used for the Choctaw, Cherokee, Muskogee Creek, Chickasaw, and Seminole, the American Indian tribes who lived in the Southeastern United States. (p. 141)

food processing (füd pros′ es ing) The industry that turns crops and livestock into food products. (p. 217)

fossil fuel (fos′ əl fū ′əl) A fuel formed from the remains of prehistoric plants and animals. Coal and petroleum are fossil fuels. (p. 180)

free enterprise (frē en′ tər prīz) The economic system that allows people to own and run their own businesses. (p. 44)

frontier (frun tîr′) Land at the edge of an area where people have settled. (p. 95)

fuel (fū ′əl) A substance used to produce energy. (p. 27)

G

geography (jē og′rə fē) The study of Earth and the way people, plants, and animals live on and use it. (p. 8)

Great Depression (grāt di presh′ ən) A time during the 1930s when many people lost their jobs and businesses failed. (p. 187)

gusher (gush′ ər) A well that sprays large amounts of oil into the air without being pumped. (p. 181)

H

heritage (her′ i tij) The history and traditions that a group of people share. (p. 37)

high-tech (hī tek) The use of computers and other electronics to meet people's needs. (p. 211)

history (his′ tə rē) The story of what happened in the past. (p. 52)

Homestead Act (Hōm′ sted akt) A law passed in 1862 that gave settlers 160 acres (64 ha) of land if they would live and work it for five years. (p. 157)

I

immigrant (im′ i grənt) A person who comes to a new country to live. (p. 36)

industry (in′ də strē) All the businesses that make one kind of goods or provide one kind of service. (p. 211)

interdependent (in tər di pen′ dənt) Relying on one another to meet needs and wants. (p. 48)

investor (in ves′ tər) Someone who puts money into a business and expects a share of the profit. (p. 46)

J

judicial (jü dish′ əl) The branch of government that makes sure laws are obeyed. (p. 237)

L

labor (lā′ bər) The strength, skills, and talents of people who make products or provide services. (p. 207)

landform (land′ fôrm) Any of the shapes that make up Earth's surface. (p. 9)

Land Run (land run) A race for land by settlers hoping to stake a claim in what is today Oklahoma. (p. 159)

legacy (leg′ ə sē) A tradition that is handed down from one generation to the next and is a valued part of people's lives today. (p. 16)

legislative (lej′ is lā tiv) The branch of government that makes laws. (p. 236)

livestock (liv′ stok) Animals kept on a farm such as cattle, hogs, and chickens. (p. 219)

Louisiana Purchase (lü ē zē an′ ə pûr′chəs) The land bought by the United States from France in 1803 that nearly doubled the size of the country. (p. 127)

M

mammoth (mam′ əth) A kind of large elephant with long, curving tusks and shaggy, brown hair. The last mammoths died about 10,000 years ago. (p. 121)

manufacturing (man yə fak′ chər ing) Making large amounts of goods in factories. (p. 46)

mayor (mā′ ər) The person who is the official head of a city or town government. (p. 230)

mesa (mā′ sä) A flat landform that rises steeply above the surrounding land. (p. 58)

mesquite (mes kēt′) A small thorny tree with long roots that dig deep to find water. (p. 94)

metropolitan area (met rə pol′ i tən âr′ ē ə) An area including a city or cities and suburbs. (p. 253)

migrant worker (mi′ grənt wûr′ kər) Worker who moves from place to place to harvest different crops as they ripen. (p. 251)

mineral (min′ ər əl) A nonrenewable natural resource that is found in the earth. (p. 27)

mining (mi′ ning) The business of digging valuable resources out of the earth. (p. 213)

Mound Builders (mound bil′ dərz) Early American Indians whose extensive earthworks are found from the Great Lakes down the Mississippi Valley to the Gulf of Mexico. (p. 122)

municipal (mū nis′ ə pəl) Having to do with the government and affairs of a city or town. (p. 229)

N

natural resource (nach′ ər əl rē′ sôrs) Something found in the environment that people use. (p. 24)

New Deal (nū′ dēl) Government programs started by President Franklin D. Roosevelt in the 1930s to aid businesses, farms, and the unemployed to recover from the Great Depression. (p. 187)

nonrenewable resource (non ri nü′ ə bəl rē′ sôrs) A natural resource that is limited in supply and cannot be replaced, such as a fuel or mineral. (p. 27)

O

Organic Act (ôr gan′ ik akt) A law ordering a government to be formed for the Oklahoma Territory. (p. 175)

P

petrochemical (pet rō kem′ i kəl) Any substance made from petroleum, including paint, plastics, cloth, insulation, fertilizers, and pesticides. (p. 73)

petroleum (pə trō′ lē əm) A fuel, commonly called oil, that formed underground from dead plants. (p. 70)

plain (plān) A large area of flat or nearly flat land. (p. 9)

plateau (pla tō′) A high, flat area that rises steeply above the surrounding land. (p. 9)

political party (pə lit′ i kəl pär′ tē) A group of citizens who share similar ideas about government. (p. 243)

pollution (pə lü′ shən) Any substance, such as a chemical, that makes air, water, or soil dirty. (p. 26)

population (pop yə lā′ shən) The number of people who live in a place or area. (p. 103)

poultry (pōl′ trē) Chickens, turkeys, geese, and other birds raised for their eggs or meat. (p. 219)

prairie (prâr′ ē) Flat or gently rolling land thickly covered with grasses and wildflowers. (p. 103)

precipitation (pri sip i tā′ shən) The moisture that falls to the ground. (p. 21)

profit (prof′ it) The money a business earns after it pays for tools, salaries, and other costs. (p. 45)

R

raw materials (rä mə tîr′ ē əlz) The untreated or natural resources a business uses to make a finished product. (p. 207)

recycle (rē sī′ kəl) To use something again instead of discarding it. (p. 25)

Red Earth (red′ ûrth) A celebration of American Indian culture held in Oklahoma City. (p. 107)

refinery (ri fī′ nə rē) A factory where crude oil is cleaned, separated into parts, and treated to make petroleum products. (p. 72)

region (rē′ jən) An area with common features that set it apart from other areas. (p. 51)

renewable resource (ri nü′ ə bəl rē′ sôrs) A natural resource that can be replaced or regrown for later use, such as a forest. (p. 26)

robot (rō′ bot) A machine run by computers. (p. 212)

S

segregation (seg ri gā′ shən) The practice of setting one group apart from another by law. (p. 194)

service (sûr′ vis) A job people do to help others, rather than to make things. (p. 44)

settlement (set′ əl mənt) A place on the frontier where people live. (p. 133)

slavery (slā′ və rē) The practice of making one person the property of another. (p. 36)

sod house (sod hous) A shelter built on the prairie, made of bricks of sod. (p. 166)

software (sôft′ wâr) Programs that tell a computer what to do. (p. 211)

Sooner (sü′ nər) A person who entered the Unassigned Lands ahead of the Land Run in order to claim the best land. (p. 159)

stampede (stam pēd′) A sudden, wild running of a frightened herd of animals. (p. 154)

States' Rights (stāts rīts) The belief that each state should be allowed to make its own decisions about issues affecting it. (p. 146)

stocks (stoks) Shares or parts of ownership in a company. (p. 187)

suburb (sub′ ûrb) A community outside of but near a larger city. (p. 192)

supply (sə plī′) Supply is the amount of an item a business is willing to make. (p. 207)

T

tax (taks) Money people pay to the government so that it can perform public services. (p. 229)

teepee (tē′ pē) A cone-shaped dwelling made of animal skins and poles used by Plains Indians. (p. 134)

temperature (tem′ per ə chər) A measurement of how hot or cold something is. Often air temperature is used to describe weather or climate. (p. 21)

tourism (tür′ i zəm) An industry that sells goods and services to people who travel on vacations. (p. 214)

trading post (trād′ ing pōst) A place on the frontier where people could get goods they needed in exchange for crops they had grown or things they had made. (p. 126)

treaty (trē′ tē) An agreement among nations. (p. 141)

Trail of Tears (trāl uv tîrz) The forced movement of Cherokee and other American Indians to what is now Oklahoma in the 1830s. (p. 142)

transportation (trans pər tā shən) The moving of goods or people from one place to another. (p. 48)

turnpike (tûrn′ pik) A highway with more than two lanes and no intersections or stoplights. Turnpikes are used for fast travel between cities. (p. 193)

U

Unassigned Lands (un ə sīnd′ landz) The land In Indian Territory on which no one lived. (p. 157)

Union (yōōn′ yən) The states that stayed loyal to the U.S. government in the Civil War, 1860–1865. (p. 147)

United States Congress (kon′ gris) The legislative branch of the United States government, which makes national laws. (p. 244)

urban (ûr′ bən) Of or like a city. (p. 192)

V

veto (vē′ tō) The power of a president, governor, or another official to reject a bill passed by a legislature. (p. 236)

W

website (web′ sīt) A location on the Internet that provides information and allows people to communicate with other people on the World Wide Web. (p. 257)

windmill (wind′ mil) A machine that uses the wind to provide mechanical power by turning vanes or sails at the top of a tower. (p. 167)

index

This Index lists many topics that appear in the book, along with the pages on which they are found. Page numbers after an *m* refer you to a map. Page numbers after a *p* indicate photographs, artwork, or charts.

CREDITS

Cover: McGraw-Hill School Division

Maps: MapQuest

Chapter Opener Globes: Greg Wakabayashi

Charts and Graphs: Eliot Bergman: pp 25, 41, 72, 212

Illustrations: A-R Editions Inc.: pp 238; Hal Brooks: pp 23, 52, 73, 251; Joe Forte: pp 118, 119, 138, 139, 162, 163, 238-239; Rosanne Kakos-Main: pp 50; Hima Pamoedjo: pp 12-13; Joel Synder: pp 148; Wayne Vincent: pp 74; Nina Wallace: pp 236; Jerry Zimmerman: pp 94;

Photography Credits: All photographs are by the McGraw-Hill School Division (MMSD) except as noted below.

H15: l. Visual Horizons/FPG International; t.r. John Terence Turner/FPG International; b.r. Tony Freeman/PhotoEdit. i: MMSD. iii: t. UPI/Bettman (LS/Tom Salyer); b. Carrie Goeringer. iv: t. Hulton-Duetsch Collection/Corbis; b. John Elk III. v: t. Inga Spence/Visuals Unlimited; b. Oklahoma Department of Commerce. G2: t. Nathan Benn/Woodfin Camp and Assoc; b. Gary Braasch. G2-3: Elizabeth Wolf. G3: r. David Alan Harvey; t.l. Robert Brennan/PhotoEdit; b.l. Chris Cross/Uniphoto. G6: Monica Stevenson for MMSD. **Chapter 1** 2: t. Jim Argo; m. Roberto Soncin Gerometta/Photo 20-20; b. Brian Parker/Tom Stack and Assoc. 3: Carrie Goeringer. 7: t. Ivor Shap/Image Bank; t.m. Ray Ooms/Masterfile; b.m. John W. Varden/ Superstock; b. Mark Kelley/Stock Boston. 8: t. Steve Proehl/Image Bank; b. Manfred Gottschalk/Tom Stack Assoc. 9: James Marcus. 10: t. James Marcus; b. Jeff Greenberg/ PhotoEdit. 11: t. Grant Heilman; b. Uniphoto. 14: b.r. James Marcus; b.l. Toyohiro Yamada/FPG International; t.r. Jim Steinberg/Photo Researchers. 15: James Marcus. 16: Pat Canova/Silver Image. 17: t. Ansel Adams Publishing Rights Trust; b. Thomas Cole/Albany Institute of Art. 20: t. Julie Habel/Westlight; b. Bengt Hedberg/Panoramic Images. 22: t. Jim Simmen/Tony Stone Images; b. Tony Freeman/PhotoEdit. 24: Mark Lewis/Liaison International. 26: r. Chuck O'Rear/Woodfin Camp; t.l. Paul R. Kennedy/Liaison International; b.l. David Young-Wolff/ PhotoEdit. 27: b.r Tony Freeman/PhotoEdit; b.l. L.D. Gordon/The Image Bank; t. Richard Haynes for MMSD. 28: t. Unified Sewerage Agency of Washington Country. 28-29: b. Jim Levin for MMSD. **Chapter 2** 33: B.Kulik/Photri. 34: UPI/Bettman (LS/Tom Salyer). 35: l. David J. Maenza/Image Bank; r. Peter Gridley/FPG. 36: all frames by Scott Harvey for MMSD, t.l. Courtesy Amelia Cervantes; b.l. Bettman Archive; t.r. Jane Ito/courtesy of Nihonmatsu Family; b.r. courtesy Ruth Donaldson Gessner; t.m. courtesy Melissa Knight. 38: b.l. Charles Burnham; b.r. Lawrence Migdale. 39: Granger Collection 1939 Carl Van Vechten. 40: Dallas and John Heaton/Westlight. 41: r. Kunio Owaki/The Stock Market; l. Statue of Liberty Museum/National Parks Department of the Interior. 42: t. Jim Argo; b. Jeff Nass/The Stock Market. 44: t. Jim Levin for MMSD; b. Burke/Food Pix/Picture Quest. 45: l. Jim McHugh/Outline; b.r. Jim Levin for MMSD. 4647: Jim McHugh/Outline. 48: l. Visual Horizons/FPG International; t.r. John Terence Turner/FPG International; b.r. Tony Freeman/PhotoEdit. 49: Jim Levin for MMSD. 50: John Elk III. 52: Anestis Diakopoulos/Stock Boston. 53: Bob Daemmrich/Stock Boston. 55: t. Larry West/Bruce Coleman; b.r. L.A. Frances/The Stock Market. **Chapter 3** 57: b. Inga Spence/Tom Stack & Associates; t.m. John Elk III; b.m. Henry Georgi/Comstock; t. George H.H. Huey. 58: t. Katherine S. Thomas/Bruce Coleman; b. Jeff Greenberg/Photo Edit. 59: Richard Kolar/Earth Scenes. 60: t. insert Wiley/Wales/Profiles West; t.l. Tim Brown/ Profiles West; b.r. Francis Westfield for MMSD. 62: Robert Landau/Westlight. 63: b. David Muench/Tony Stone Images; t. Lowell Georgia/Photo Researcher, Inc.; m. Paul Chesley/Tony Stone Images. 64: t. Adstock; b. John Shaw/Panoramic Images. 65: Frank Rapp. 66: Brown Brothers. 68: Jim Cumming/FPG International. 69: b. courtesy of Russ Schlittenhart; t. The Nature Conservancy; m. courtesy Donal Hutchinson. 70: t. Bill Ross/Tony Stone Images; b. John Boykin/Photo Edit. 71: Gladys City Boomtown Museum. 75: Joseph Sohm/Tony Stone Images. 76: b.r. Bob Wallace/Stock Boston; t. Shawn Henry/SABA. 79: MMSD. 81: Robert Milazzo for MMSD. **Chapter 4** 82: t.r., b. Fred W. Marvel/Oklahoma Tourism; t.l. Hulton-DuetschCollection/Corbis. 83: John Elk III. 85: b., t.m. David G. Fitzgerald; b.m., t. Jim Argo. 86: b. John Elk III; t. Inga Spence/Visuals Unlimited. 88: b. John Lund/Tony Stone Images; t. Jim Argo. 90: Carrie Goeringer. 92: t. Georg Gerster/Photo Researchers, Inc.; b. John Elk III. 94: Richard Smith. 95: Fred W. Marvel/Oklahoma Tourism. 96: b., l. inset, r. inset John Elk III. 97: Joe McDonald/Visuals Unlimited. **Chapter 5** 100: t. Bob Daemmrich/Stock • Boston/ Picture Quest; m. SuperStock; b. Andy Sacks/Tony Stone Images. 101: t.l. David Young-Wolff/Photo Edit; m.l., b.l. SuperStock; t.r. A. Ramey/Photo Edit; m.r. Michael Newman/Photo Edit/Picture Quest; b.r. Dave Rosenberg/Tony Stone Images. 102: b. Stephen Dunn/Allsport USA; t. David Stoecklein/The Stock Market. 104: l. SuperStock; r. Topical Press Agency/ Hulton Getty Picture Library. 105: t. People Disc/Hulton Getty Picture Library; b. Will Rogers Memorial Museum Claremore Oklahoma. 106: b.r John Elk III; t., b.l. Jim Argo. 107: b. John Elk III; t. Bonnie Kamin/Photo Edit. 108: b.l. Paul B. Southerland/The Daily Oklahoman; b.r. Jim Argo; 109: t. Hulton-Duetsch Collection/Corbis; b. Jerry Laizure/Associated Press AP. 110: David G. Fitzgerald. 111: Courtesy, Riley Pagett. 115: Monica Stevenson for MMSD. **Chapter 6** 116: t. John Annerino/Gamma Liaison; m. Culver Pictures; b. W. A. Todd Jr./The Picture Cube. 117: Carrie Goeringer. 120: t. inset, b. Pictures of Record; t. John Elk III. 121: r. A. J. Copley/Visuals Unlimited; l. John Elk III. 122: inset Archives & Manuscripts Division of the Oklahoma Historical Society; t. Oklahoma Musuem of Natural History. 124: b. Stock Montage; t. David G. Fitzgerald. 126: inset, b. North Wind Pictures. 130: b. SuperStock; t. The Granger Collection. 132: b. SuperStock; t. John Elk III. 133: t. Archives & Manuscripts Division of the Oklahoma Historical Society; b. Bob Bozarth/Cherokee Heritage Center Tahlequah, OK. 134: Western History Collections, University of Oklahoma Libraries. **Chapter 7** 140: t. Western History Collections, University of Oklahoma Libraries; b. Bob Bozarth. 141: l., m., r. Archives & Manuscripts Division of the Oklahoma Historical Society. 142: The Granger Collection. 144: l. Smithsonian Institution; r. Fred W. Marvel/Oklahoma Tourism. 145: t.l. John Elk III; b.l. The Granger Collection; r. Lawrence Migdale. 146: t. The Granger Collection; b. Carrie Goeringer. 147: t. The Granger Collection; b. Carrie Goeringer. 148: David J. Elcher/Welltraveled Images. 149: Nawrocki Stock Photo. 150: l. Lowell Georgia/Corbis; r. David Stover/Stock South/PictureQuest. 151: t., b. Archives & Manuscripts Division of the Oklahoma Historical Society; m. The Newberry Library/Stock Montage. 152: t. SuperStock; b. Bettman Archives. 153: Sam C. Pierson, Jr. 154: Buffalo Bill Historical Center. 156: b. Culver Pictures; t. The Granger Collection. 157: r. Culver Pictures; l. J. R. Toland. 158: The Granger Collection. **Chapter 8** 164: t. Visuals Unlimited; b. Western History Collections, University of Oklahoma Libraries. 165: Culver Pictures. 166: Archives & Manuscripts Division of the Oklahoma Historical Society. 167: b. Photodisc; inset Culver Pictures. 168: t. Bob Bozarth; b. Western History Collections, University of Oklahoma Libraries. 169: t. Art Resource; b. Kim Sayer/Corbis. 174: t., b. Archives & Manuscripts Division of the Oklahoma Historical Society. 176: t.l. David G. Fitzgerald; b. Archives & Manuscripts Division of the Oklahoma Historical Society; t.r. Bob Bozarth. 178: Archives & Manuscripts Division of the Oklahoma Historical Society. 179: t., m. Archives & Manuscripts Division of the Oklahoma Historical Society; b. University Archives, John Vaughan Library Northeastern State University Tahlequah, Oklahoma. 180: t. Phillips Petroleum Company; b. Western History Collections, University of Oklahoma Libraries. 182: Western History Collections, University of Oklahoma Libraries. 183: Western History Collections, University of Oklahoma Libraries. 184: t. The Daily Oklahoman; inset Western History Collections, University of Oklahoma Libraries; b. Paul Waffle/Conoco Visual Communications. 185: t.l., t.r. Phillips Petroleum Company; b. Siede Preis/Photodisc. 186: t., b. Culver Pictures. 187: Associated Press FDR Library. 188: b., l. inset Western History Collections, University of Oklahoma Libraries; r. inset Visuals Unlimited. 189: Archives & Manuscripts Division of the Oklahoma Historical Society. 190: t. Courtesy of the 45th Infantry Division Museum of Oklahoma City; b. US Army Photo/Hulton Getty Picture Library. 191: Women's Archives at OSU, Oklahoma State University Library, Stillwater, OK. 192: Lake County Museum/Corbis. 194: The Granger Collection. 195: Steve Sisney/The Daily Oklahoman. 199: Greg Miller. **Chapter 9** 200: b. inset Oklahoma Department of Commerce; b. R. E. Lindsey/Lindsey Enterprises Inc.; t. Jim Argo. 201: r. Fred W. Marvel/Oklahoma Tourism; l. John Elk III. 203: t. David Halpern/Photo Researchers, Inc.; t.m. Herman J. Kokojan/Black Star/Picture Quest; b.m. John Elk III; b. Jim Argo. 204: b. Bob Daemmrich/Stock • Boston; t. Photodisc. 205: m. John Elk III; l. Don Smetzer/Tony Stone Images; r. The Stock Market. 206: Jim Argo. 207: The Stock Market. 208: t. inset Kate Denny/PhotoEdit; m. inset Jim Argo; b. inset Chad Slattery/Tony Stone Images; b. Myrleen Ferguson/PhotoEdit. 209: Michael Newman/PhotoEdit. 210: t. Jim Argo; b. Jim Pickerell/Stock Connection/Picture Quest; b. inset Vladimir Pcholkin/FPG International. 211: Bob Daemmrich/Stock • Boston/Picture Quest. 213: b. John Elk III/Stock • Boston; inset SuperStock. 214: Elena Rooraid/PhotoEdit. 215: r. Jeff Zaruba/The Stock Market; l. Jeff Greenberg/PhotoEdit. 216: b. Jim Argo; t. Michael Rosenfield/Tony Stone Images. 218: Inga Spence/Visuals Unlimited. 219: Jim Argo. 220: l. Mike Brooks; r. Hank Morgan/Rainbow. 221: SuperStock. **Chapter 10** 227: inset Jim Beckel/The Daily Oklahoman; b. SuperStock. 228: t. Jerry Laizure/Associated Press AP; b. Alan R. Moller/Tony Stone Images. 229: b. Carrie Goeringer; t. Cheri Soliday/Sac and Fox Nation. 232: J. Pat Carter/Associated Press AP. 233: Courtesy, Stephanie Sims. 234: b. Jim Argo; t. MMSD . 237: b. inset Jim Argo/The Daily Oklahoman; t. inset Courtesy, Larry Rice; b. Jim Corwin/Tony Stone Images. 240: t. Stuart Ostler; b. Courtesy, Hardy Summers. 241: Betty McElderry. 242: b. G. Vidakovic/Visuals Unlimited; t. Carrie Goeringer; m. Frank W. Marvel/Oklahoma Tourism. 243: b. inset Greg Gibson/Associated Press AP; t. Karin Cooper/Gamma Liaison. 245: Charles Tasnadi/Associated Press AP. **Chapter 11** 249: Jim Argo. 250: t. John Annerino/Gamma Liaison; b. inset Fred W. Marvel/Oklahoma Tourism; b. Jim Millay/Panoramic Images. 252: t. Fred W. Marvel/Oklahoma Tourism; b., b. inset Chip Coleman. 256: t., t. inset NASA; b. M Stock/Stock Connection/Picture Quest. 257: Richard T.Nowitz/Corbis. 258: l. R. E. Lindsey/Lindsey Enterprises Inc.; r. Tod Bryant/Oklahoma Energy Resource Board. 259: Tod Bryant/Oklahoma Energy Resource Board. 260: r. Richard Hamilton Smith/Corbis; l. C. C. Lockwood/Animals Animals. 261: Courtesy, Talia Littledave. 265: Learning Design Associates. R3: SuperStock. R15: SuperStock.

Acknowledgments continued:

p. 65 excerpt from **The Desert Is Theirs** by Byrd Baylor. Copyright © 1975 by Byrd Baylor. Used by permission of Simon and Schuster.

p. 92 quote by George Sibley from **Oklahoma: A History of Five Centuries** by Arrell Morgan Gibson. Copyright © 1980 by the University of Oklahoma Press.

p. 106 excerpt; p. 110 excerpt from **"There is a circle..."** by Charles Red Corn. Copyright © by Charles Red Corn.

p. 120 excerpt; p. 124 excerpt; p. 125 quote by Francisco de Coronado from **The History of Oklahoma** by Arrell Morgan Gibson. Copyright © 1954, 1964 by University of Oklahoma Press.

p. 124 excerpt from **Oklahoma: A History of the Sooner State** by Edwin McReynolds. Copyright © 1954, 1964 by University of Oklahoma Press.

p. 130 excerpt from **A Journal of Travels into Arkansas** by Thomas Nuttall. Copyright © 1980 by University of Oklahoma Press.

p. 140 quote by John Ross; p. 216 excerpt from **Oklahoma Our Home** by Daisy Moore Duvall and Palmer H. Boeger. Copyright © 1985 by Daisy Moore Duval. Used by permission of J. Samuel Publishers.

p. 152 lyrics from **"Doney Gal,"** collected, adapted, and arranged by John A. Lomax and Alan Lomax. Copyright © 1938, 1966 by Ludlow Music Inc.

p. 156 excerpt; p. 164 excerpt from **Oklahoma: The Story of Its Past and Present** by Edwin C. McReynolds, Alice Marriott, and Estelle Faulconer. Copyright © 1961, 1967, 1971, 1975 by University of Oklahoma Press.

p. 166 excerpt from **Pioneer Woman: Voices from the Kansas Frontier** by Joanna L. Stratton. Copyright © 1981 by Joanna L. Stratton. Used by permission of Simon & Schuster.

p. 179 quote by Charles B. Ames from **Oklahoma: A History of the State and Its People** v. 2 by Joseph B. Thoburn and Muriel H. Wright. Copyright © 1929 by Lewis Historical Publishing Company, Inc.

p. 193 quote by Harold A. Todd. Copyright © 2000 by Harold A. Todd c/o Oklahoma Historical Society.

p. 210 quote by a GM assembly plant worker. Copyright © 1988 by General Motors Corporation.

p. 222 excerpt from "**Bellmon Touting Alternative Crops"** by Michael McNutt from November 17, 1988 issue of *The Daily Oklahoman*. Copyright © 1988 by The Oklahoma Publishing Company.

p. 237 quote by Oklahoma State Representative Larry Rice. Copyright © 2000 by Larry Rice.

pp. 238–239 from **Oklahoma!** Music, lyrics, and arrangement by Oscar Hammerstein and Richard Rodgers. Copyright © 1943 by Williamson Music, Inc.

p. 240 quote by Oklahoma Chief Justice Hardy Summers. Copyright © 2000 by Hardy Summers.

p. 253 quote by Julian Yoo from interview with Dan Elish. Copyright © 2000 by Julian Yoo.

The Princeton Review
— Handbook of —
Test-Taking Strategies

READ QUESTIONS CAREFULLY

The most common mistake students make when they take a test is to answer the questions too quickly. Rushing through a test causes careless mistakes. Don't rush. Read each question carefully. Make sure you understand the question BEFORE you try to answer it.

Use the map to answer questions 1 through 3.

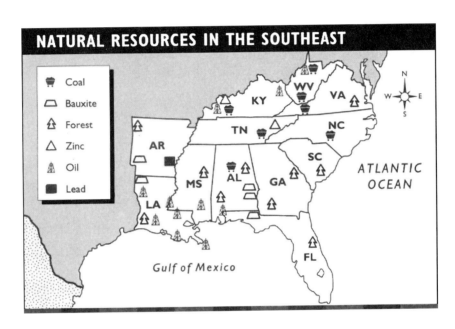

NATURAL RESOURCES IN THE SOUTHEAST

Coal
Bauxite
Forest
Zinc
Oil
Lead

1 In which state is oil an important natural resource?

  A Georgia   **C** Louisiana
  B North Carolina **D** Tennessee

2 South Carolina's natural resources include

  F bauxite   **H** coal
  G zinc   **J** forest

3 In which state would a lead miner be most likely to find a job?

  A Arkansas   **C** Florida
  B West Virginia **D** Alabama

Remember: Do not write in your textbook.

TIME LINES

Historical information is sometimes presented in the form of a time line. A time line shows events in the order in which they happened. Time lines are usually read from left to right, like a sentence. If the time line is drawn vertically, it is usually read from top to bottom.

If you read carefully, you should do very well on time line questions.

Look at the time line below. Then answer questions 1 and 2.

Groups Arrive in Hawaii, 500–1900

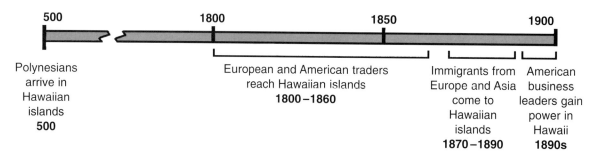

1   Which group was the first to reach the Hawaiian islands?

A   Europeans   C   Asians

B   Americans   D   Polynesians

2   Which of the following most likely occurred in 1845?

F   Traders from Europe and America came to the Hawaiian islands.

G   The first Polynesians arrived in the Hawaiian islands.

H   American business leaders gained power in Hawaii.

J   Asian immigrants came to the Hawaiian islands.

Remember: Do not write in your textbook.

LOOK AT THE DETAILS BEFORE YOU START

Some test questions contain lots of details. These questions may use:

- charts
- graphs
- flow charts

- time lines
- word webs
- maps

Before you try to answer questions like these, take a few moments to study the information that the charts, graphs, maps, or other visuals contain. The questions will be much easier to answer, because you will know exactly where to look for information!

Study the bar graph. Then do questions 1 and 2.

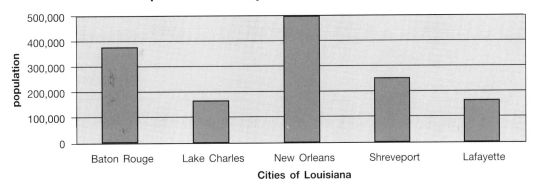

Population of Major Louisiana Cities, 1990

1 In 1990, which Louisiana city had a population of about 380,000?

A Lake Charles
B New Orleans
C Shreveport
D Baton Rouge

2 In 1990, which two Louisiana cities had approximately the same population?

F Baton Rouge and New Orleans
G Lake Charles and Lafayette
H Shreveport and Baton Rouge
J New Orleans and Lake Charles

Remember: Do not write in your textbook.

DIFFERENT TYPES OF GRAPHS

Different types of graphs are used to present numerical information. A **line graph** shows how something changes over time. A line graph might be used to show how the population of the United States has grown over the years. A **bar graph** compares amounts. A bar graph might show the population of different United States cities. A **circle graph** shows how a whole is divided into smaller parts. For example, a circle graph might show how the government divides its budget to pay for roads, education, and other services.

Sometimes you will see a set of questions accompanied by more than one graph. Each question will contain clues to tell you which graph you should read to find the answer. Take the extra time to make sure you are looking at the correct graph. This will help you avoid careless mistakes.

Use the graphs below to answer questions 1 and 2.

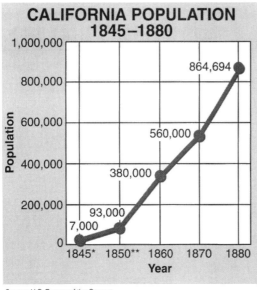

Source: U.S. Bureau of the Census

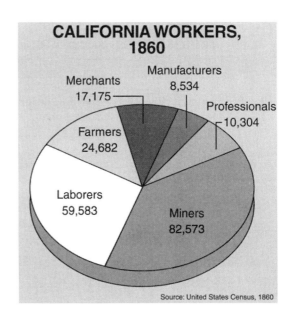

Source: United States Census, 1860

1 In what year did the population of California reach 380,000?

- **A** 1840
- **B** 1850
- **C** 1860
- **D** 1870

2 How many people were working as professionals in California in 1860?

- **F** 10,304
- **G** 17,175
- **H** 59,583
- **J** 82,573

Remember: Do not write in your textbook.

PROCESS OF ELIMINATION

Sometimes when you read a test question, you will not know the answer right away. If you don't know the answer, don't give up. You may be able to find the correct answer another way.

On a multiple-choice test, you can look at the answer choices. One of the answers will be the best answer. The others will be wrong, or not as good. Look at the choices and see if there are any that you know are definitely wrong. If there are, you can ELIMINATE, or ignore, those answers.

Sometimes you will be able to eliminate all of the answers except one. When that happens, it means that you have found the best answer by the PROCESS OF ELIMINATION.

Try using the process of elimination to answer this question:

1   The largest city in South Dakota is

    A   Los Angeles
    B   Dallas
    C   Sioux Falls
    D   Mexico City

Were you able to eliminate any *wrong* answers? How many?

Now try using the process of elimination to answer this question:

2   The section of the United States Constitution that protects the freedom of Americans is called the

    F   Declaration of Independence
    G   Bill of Rights
    H   Civil War
    J   Star Spangled Banner

OUTSIDE KNOWLEDGE

Many questions on multiple-choice tests ask you to look at a map, a chart, a graph, or a drawing. Then you are asked to choose the correct answer based on what you see. On these questions, the information you need to answer the question will be in the map, chart, graph, or drawing.

Sometimes, however, multiple-choice tests will ask you to remember a fact that you learned in social studies class. You won't be able to find the correct answer on a map, chart, graph, or drawing; the correct answer will be in your memory. We call these OUTSIDE KNOWLEDGE questions.

If you are sure you know the answer to an OUTSIDE KNOWLEDGE question, choose the correct answer. It's that simple! When you're NOT sure what the correct answer is, use the PROCESS OF ELIMINATION to answer the question.

1 Which of these books would probably provide the most information about the life of Martin Luther King, Jr.?

    A   an atlas

    B   an encyclopedia

    C   a novel about the South during the Civil War

    D   a collection of poetry

2 Which of the following statements about the southern portion of the United States is true?

    F   The South does not have many farms.

    G   The South is home to the largest cities in the United States.

    H   The South is the most mountainous region in the United States.

    J   The South has a warmer climate than the northern United States.

            Remember: Do not write in your textbook.

FLOW CHARTS

A flow chart shows the sequence of steps used to complete an activity. It shows the steps in the order they happen. A flow chart usually uses arrows to show which step happens next.

The first thing to do when you look at a flow chart is to see if it has a title. The title will tell you what the flow chart is about. The next thing you should do is find the arrows. The arrows tell you the order in which to read the chart.

Read flow charts carefully. Don't just look at the illustrations. Make sure to read any text beneath the illustrations.

Study the flow chart. Then do questions 1 and 2.

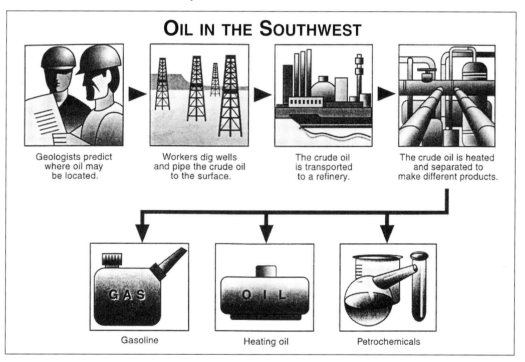

OIL IN THE SOUTHWEST

Geologists predict where oil may be located.

Workers dig wells and pipe the crude oil to the surface.

The crude oil is transported to a refinery.

The crude oil is heated and separated to make different products.

Gasoline

Heating oil

Petrochemicals

1 Which of these questions is answered by the flow chart?

A What are some of the products that can be made from crude oil?

B How much does it cost to produce heating oil?

C Where in the United States is the most crude oil found?

D How many automobiles are there in the United States?

2 The crude oil is probably transported to the oil refinery in

F automobiles

G large ships

H helicopters

J tractors

Remember: Do not write in your textbook.

MAPS

The ability to read and understand maps is an important skill in social studies. Many of the multiple-choice tests you take will require you to read a map.

Look carefully at all the parts of a map. Maps contain a lot of information. Whenever you see a map, you should ask yourself questions like these:

- What does the title of the map tell you?
- Where is the map key?
- What symbols are on the map key? What do they stand for?
- Where is the compass rose?
- What does the compass rose tell you?
- Is there a map scale?

Use the map of Pennsylvania to answer questions 1 and 2.

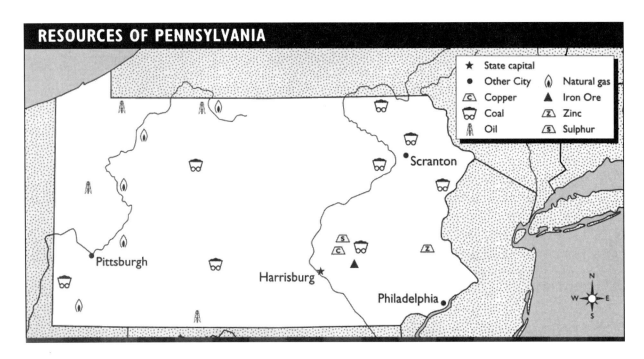

RESOURCES OF PENNSYLVANIA

1 Which natural resource is found only in the western part of Pennsylvania?

   A zinc

   B natural gas

   C coal

   D iron ore

2 Which of these people would be most likely to find a job near Scranton?

   F a driller of oil wells

   G a coal miner

   H a miner of iron ore

   J a zinc miner

                      Remember: Do not write in your textbook.

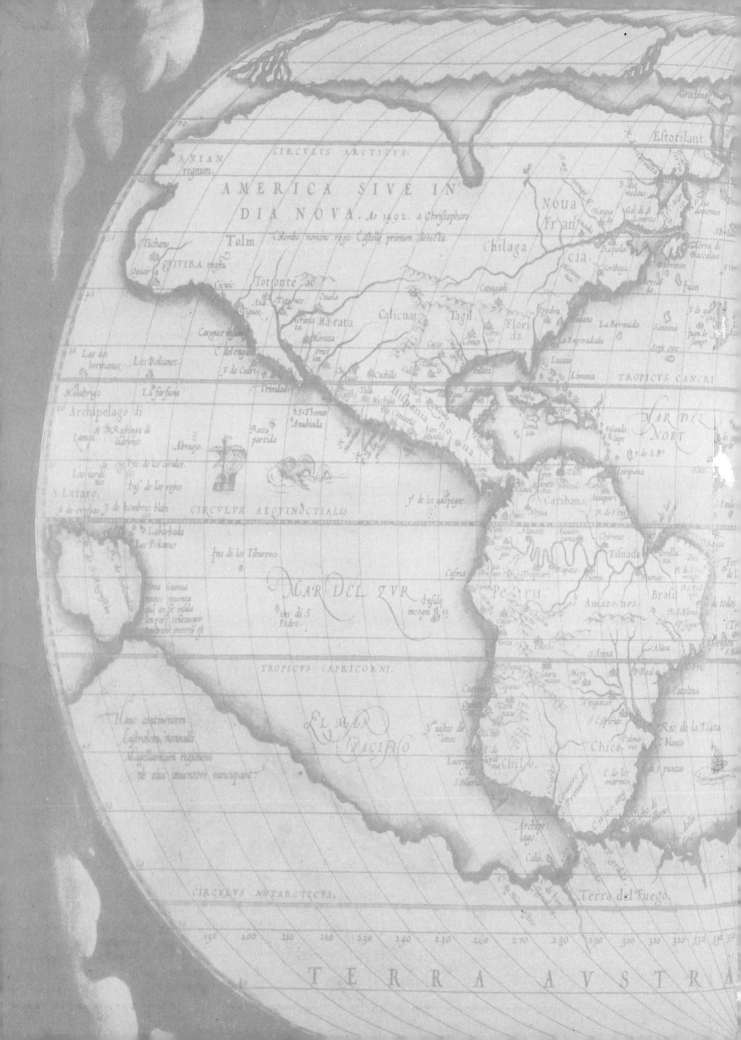